WILD
LEGEND

YOUNGBLOOD

SEORAS WALLACE

Iˢᵗ EDITION

Published in 2019 by Wolf and Wildcat Publishing

ISBN Paperback: 978-1-9999170-4-3
Ebook: 978-1-9999170-5-0

A CIP catalogue copy of this book can be found
in the British Library.

Published with the help of Indie Authors World
www.indieauthorsworld.com

IndieAuthors
World

www.facebook.com/InDiScotland

Wolf & Wildcat publishing
+44(0)7766 584 360
www.wolfandwildcat.com
www.facebook.com/Wallace.Legend
Clan Wallace PO Box 1305 Glasgow G51 4UB Scotland

Dedicate to the memory of a great clansman…
RIP Ronnie *the Moray* Murray

Acknowledgements

Big thank you for the writing support from
my hard working family and friends

About the Author: Seoras Wallace

After a career in the film industry spanning over thirty years, in such films as Highlander, Gladiator, Rob Roy, Braveheart, Saving Private Ryan and many more. In 1997 following a serious horse riding accident, Seoras turned his valuable experience to becoming an author, and parallel to his professional life. Seoras has also served as acting chief executive of the Wallace Clan Trust for Scotland.

"An experience like no other," said Seoras, "One of the constants in my vocation has been the revelation of private or secretive documents and accounts from many unusual sources that gave me a wholly different perspective of William Wallace, that shaped him as a man who became a nations Iconic patriot and world hero in the eyes and hearts of many. At first I used to think that the information I witnessed was too incredible to be true, but when certain parts of that narrative repeated from different sources, another story from the academic norm began to emerge. Growing up in a remote west coast village, that was extremely patriotic and nationalist, I was taught from the clan elders at an early age the family legend of Wallace, but that too did not match the publicly available narrative. On my many travels around the world, especially after the release and success of the film Braveheart, people would often say upon hearing my account, "You should write a book about the Wallace." "I have always replied that no one would ever believe it, but following my accident, I decided to leave the family legacy as a fact based fictional narrative for my family and future generations, almost as a historical bloodline diary. The epic account I have written about the Life and Legend of William Wallace has been an inspiration and brought to me a newfound love for the man, the people and the country he fought for. Many who have been test reading the epic series as it developed, have a constant response that stands out more than any other comment, "Seoras, I've researched what you've written, and it's true…" My reply has always been… "Naw… it's just fiction!"

THE SUMMER WALKERS

The Wallace Clan host a late summer gathering in Glen Afton, with many kith and kin arriving from all corners of Scotland. Revellers travel from the western Isles, Glasgow, Dundee, Aberdeen, Galloway and the disputed border territories with England to join in the lá bainise Fèis, the wedding day festival of Stephen ua H'Alpine to Katriona Graham. Even wee Maw had made it down to meet her granddaughter once more.

At the end of the gathering, Wee John, Ròsinn and Stephen return to Ireland as auld Stephen had fallen gravely ill. William and Alain resume the end-summer hunt in the great Wolf and Wildcat Forests of Ettrick and Galloway, with the bond between them growing ever stronger, sharing not only a great friendship, but also a mutual satisfaction in their newfound relationship as father and son. As summer turns to fall, time passes slowly for William upon his return to the black Craig fastness; he spends his time honing his trapper crafts and frequently stalks the monarch stag with the stealth of a heather spider trapping a fly. William knows he is born to be free and hunt as his ancestors have done before him. He is now fulfilling his dream of emulating his father's skills as a lead huntsman and master archer.

His father Alain, introduces William to many of the Ceàrdannan, the travelling folk, and learns from them a curious form of Galloway Gaelic, the *'Beurla-reagaird'* He grew a fondness of the Ceàrdannan, the so-called; *Summer walkers*. These travelling communities have no settled land of their own, preferring a life moving throughout the realm following the seasons, a proud nomadic people who move from place to place freely. These unique and gifted travellers are also affectionately called 'Tinklers' due to the noise of their constant hammering of metals on tin or silver, while making or mending fine objects and utensils.

Wherever the Proud Ceàrdannan temporarily settle, they mend pots, pans, plates and refresh horse harness and tack amongst their many gifted skills, providing sustenance and valuable assistance on Clan territories and estates all over Scotland, enhancing the lives of the 'settled people. Their accepted social standing is to bring news, music, crafts and infuse happiness to the settled caretakers of each Clan community and noble estate. The Ceàrdannan are highly regarded and respected as valuable contributory community and truly understand what nurture and love of nature really means, with their common held belief the land belongs to all.

One particular Clan of Ceàrdannan William hunts with, is the Clann na ua Bruan, (Children of the Bear) a Scots-Irish family from the ancient Kingdoms of Galloway in Scotland and Antrim in Ireland, known as the *Dál Riatans*. William romances a beautiful young Ceàrdannan princess, Affric, daughter of Marchal ua Bruan, chief of the Ceàrdannan, keeper of the Wolf and wildcat forest deerhounds and master huntsman for *'Queen'* Devorguilla of Galloway, mother to Lord John Baliol, the future king of Scotland. William has also become firm friends with Affric's brother, Coinach ua Bruan, whose personal craft is in the construction of hunter cross and short bows. Coinach would often join William on the seasonal hunt. Alain, William and Coinach go out in one last late season hunt to trap and supply fresh wild game and meat for all the priories and churches of the region, including an ancient tradition, whereby, all the trappers would include a catch surplus of vitals for the Bruin poor houses of each community, in that none may ever go hungry.

Winter is almost upon them when Alain and William make their way back to Glen Afton in order to larder and settle in for the winter, when news comes that will change William's destiny forever.

The Lanarch Tavern

Arriving back in Glen Afton from the last hunt of the year, Alain, William and Coinach are met unexpectedly by Malcolm, Mharaidh and Leckie mòr. After a brief welcome, Alain enquires with concern in his voice. "I can see by your faces that something is badly amiss. What ails you all?" He pauses a moment, then, with a sense of urgency, he enquires, "Malcolm, it's no' wee Maw is it?"

"Naw Alain," replies Malcolm, "but its sad news that I bring to you in regards to our Aicé Yolande." Alain enquires, "What's with her regard?" With heavy heart, Malcolm continues, "On saint Catherine's day in Clackmannan priory, the magnates eagerly awaited the birth of the heir to the throne of Scotland, as yie know, but when the child was born, it was a boy sure enough, but sadly, he was dead."

Alain sinks into his chair at the feasting table, for none could tell him of what pain grief could be. His personal friendship with Yolande is extremely close through her frequent visits to Glen Afton with the late King Alexander. After a moments thought, Alain enquires, "How fairs Yolande?"

Leckie replies, "She's otherwise o' good health considering her plight, but her mind is so distraught and she cannae be consoled, not with the loss of her child and then compounded with mourning the terrible loss of Alexander too. The tragedy of bearing a dead child has her grief beyond all ken, and there isn't anything anyone can do to comfort her." Alain shakes his head mournfully, "My heart is liltin' sore for Yolande and I lament for the young Queen's state of mind and her loss, especially with so much tragedy coming into her life these past few months. Has she spoken to you Malcolm? I know she trusts you more than any other from the court of Alexander."

"Aye," replies Malcolm, "We've talked often, and about many things, but she's made a particular decision that will have an affect on us all. Yolande has rejected the Regency and insists upon returning to France."

"Yie cannae faze her for that," says Alain "Yolande has sure suffered an affliction of such terrible tragedies of a late Malcolm. Who could fault her for wishing to be returning to her homeland to be with her own family." William moves quietly to a seat in the corner of the hall to listen intently to the information that so concerns them all. Leckie produces a roll of velum parchment from a bag and lays it contemptuously upon the table.

"This is a posted writ we found being distributed abroad in all the towns and villages by the Franciscan Friars of Carlisle Alain. They're surreptitiously posting it about Scotland and all of England too. It's something you should read."

Picking up the writ, Alain enquires, "What is it?" Leckie replies, "It's a publication of falsehoods called the Lanercoste Chronicle… read it." Bemused, Alain exclaims, "What the fuck's an English chronicle got to do with anything up here in Scotland?"

Malcolm replies, "It's a scribed account of current affairs and supposed truths produced for consumption by all the Noble families and ecclesiastical hierarchy of England. I reckon someone has brought them north to Scotland with much malice in their heart to destroy the reputation of

Yolande and to do our Aicé and Royal house much ill and melancholy. What eludes us is the purpose behind this scurrilous shite." Looking at the parchment, Alain screws up his eyes. After a moment, he holds it high in the air, but he is exasperated, he spoke angrily, "I cannae be reading this shit without the great glass in my hand."

Reaching out, Mharaidh takes the parchment from Alain. "Here, I'll read it for you." Mharaidh begins reading the chronicle; suddenly, she drops it to the table as she clasps her hands to her mouth. Alain is bewildered by her actions. "What does it say?" Mharaidh replies, "I'm sorry Alain, I'll read this for you, but for the first part that I did read, my heart sank." Picking up the chronicle from the table, Mharaidh clears her throat then begins to read aloud the content...

"The Scottish nobility wax lewd with no shame, by example of their Queen through her wealth and deliverance by her despotic rule. Giving way to wantonness, the Scotch do violate each other's wives or seduce each other's daughters. And by such common practice, the vile congregation of heathens frequently replenish bishop Wishart's purse with silver by way of repentance. By repeating this offence, they are almost continually upon his roll of ignoble character. The Lady Yolande, widow to King Alexander, who God in his vengeance struck down and did so smite upon that of his children just punishment for his sins of lewdness and bestial fornications'. Yolande is resorting to wretched feminine crafts by deceiving all to think her to be with child. Her scheme is to cause the feeble-minded Scotch to postpone their decision to regard another regent, that she might more readily attract popularity to herself. But just as a woman's cunning turns out wretchedly in the end, so she disquieted the land with her pretences from the day of the King's death till the feast of purification. Nor would she admit respectable matrons to examine her condition in order that

she might return ignominy upon those from whom she had received reverence and honour. The wretched whore of Babylon determines to deceive the Scotch by foisting upon herself the dead child of another. It is also true she has caused a pure font to be made of white marble in her own image, yet she dawns the garb of a lascivious whore while frequenting bawdy places in Edinburgh, inclined to lustfulness wanton lewdness..."

Mharaidh pauses for a moment, shaking her head in disbelief. "I cannot read this diatribe, it is beyond the ken of decent people. How can they write such awful lies?"

"Please Mharaidh, continue," urges Alain. "You must tell me of all that is in this chronicle." Mharaidh reluctantly continues to read from the English chronicle...

"*The whore Yolande has contrived to have the dead son of a play-actor brought to her bed so that he might pass the child as her own. When as many as have collected to dance by licence in honour of so important an accoutrement had come to where the aforesaid lady was staying at the time. She had brought to her bed prior prepared, a wrap containing a dead boy child actor. By the grace of God, her scheming was soon detected and revealed by the sagacity of William of Buchan, much to the confusion of all present and to all those willing to trust her who heard of it afterwards. Thus, did she Yolande, who was first attracted to Scotland from over the sea by famishing greed and the prospect of wealth and lechery, was united to Alexander in a salacious ribald union and false marriage. Through the revelations of her many deceptions, shame and in haste, she must now depart from that realm, regarded commonly as a shameful and deceitful whore of vantage.*"

Mharaidh concludes in a trembling voice, "*All that I have said is so much about the fidelity and the evil pestilence of the whore Yolande... ...Walter of Hemingbrough, Lanercoste Chronicler.*"

Mharaidh's hands shake. She leans on her arms, placing her hands over her eyes to try and wipe away what she has read. For a moment no one speaks; they just look at each other with incredulity and total disbelief upon hearing the full text of the chronicle. Alain is outraged. "What the fuck… do people really believe these lies? And for what purpose are they broadcast?"

"Some choose to believe it Alain," says Leckie, "and many are displaying a need to believe this shite, and for what purpose… I believe its part of a plan to cause strife and division in our realm during this interregnum, that much I do believe." Malcolm speaks, "There are those who will interpret this as God's word Alain, and they will no doubt plan to use it as a pretext to foster their own salacious ambitions. It would appear that the Church of England also rejects Yolande's claim to the throne of Scotland and they actually condone the chronicle. This is no coincidence, nor is it a solitary diatribe. We saw in the skreevin in another chronicle from Lanercoste that expressed similar vulgarities set to place shame upon the memory of Alexander." Alain slams his fists down upon the table.

"I don't believe it, there must be something we can do to refute this venomous bile."

"There's nothing we can do," says Malcolm, "it's already out there. Yolande is aware of this falsehood and now sets her heart upon a return to France and all has now been arranged." Alain looks at Malcolm and enquires, "When does she intend to be leaving?" Malcolm replies, "Immediately, she cannot be thwarted, nor her zeal quenched to be returning to France." Alain enquires, "What will happen in the Realm without Yolande?" Malcolm replies, "By the oath of Roxburgh, it's to be Alexander's granddaughter Margaret, the princess of Norway who will be offered the throne. The oath confirms that upon his death, if his eldest daughter Margaret has children by King Eric of Norway, it is she or her children who shall succeed the throne according to the oath in Scots law and custom." Leckie is uncharacteristically concerned, "Alain, there are many worrying signs. We're seeing ill will and malignancy stirring fast within the realm. We know that some of the Norman Earls and Barons will not accept the Maid as their Queen, for they have said as much. Nor will they suffer a female child to rule over them, no matter who guides her during her minority."

"What?" Exclaims Alain. "That's no' possible, this cannot be. If Maid Margaret is the legitimate heir to the throne, then to contest her right is unthinkable… it's treason? Who are these treacherous bastards who would dare challenge our ancient laws of the Aicé ascendency and assent of the Guardians?" Leckie scowls, "Old Robert le Brix would be one, he and his sons Robert and Richard. Also Patrick de Dunbar and Walter Stewart, the Earl of Menteith, old friends to us all. But now…"

"This is a fuckin' madness to reject the Maid." exclaims Alain. Leckie continues, "De Brix fervently believes the crown and honours should be his and there are many nobles abroad who support him." Malcolm states firmly, "Aye but there are many more powerful men, imminent churchmen, senior nobility, the Breitheamh Rígh who will never support him, or any other usurper, especially the Garda Ban Rígh, they are pledged upon blood oath to do nothing to diminish the realm's independence, nor allow any to bring harm to the dignity of the royal household or our beloved Aicé."

"That's true," says Leckie, "and these loyal nobles, they'll do everything possible to have our rightful Aicé the Maid of Norway on the throne, though we have tae mind too that De Brix was the acting regent during Alexander's minority, he was also a signatory at the convention of Scone." Malcolm spits the words out. "Aye, he was also among those who swore an oath to Alexander nigh on fifteen years ago in Rosbroch castle, advancing the succession of any female successor to Alexander as the heir upon his death." Becoming incensed, Alain demands, "How the feck can de Brix spurn his own sacred oath to our late King? To do so brings a curse upon his very name and family, and should Yolande or the maid for whatever reason fail to ascend, then it falls to Lady Devorguilla by right to ascend."

Shaking his head almost in despair, Malcolm says "It's inviting a civil war if we don't get a firm grip o' this madness, and do it right now. Only recently the Guardians held a council at Clackmannan where all men of note were called to be in attendance. The Earl of Carrick, Robert Brus and his father, De Brix of Annandale, arrived with an armed squadron supported by many nobles, all foresworn and bonded to support him. Old Brix is intent on making his claim to the throne and ready to fight any and all who would oppose him."

"This cannot be …" exclaims Alain. "The council of the Guardians is a sacred gathering… to bring weapons let alone a small army into its sanctuary is punishable by death."

"Aye, if we had a King," says Leckie. "But we don't have a King. De Brix and his allies caught everyone off guard and it took some clever negotiating to avert a bloody outcome."

Taking a long deep breath, Alain sits back with his hands behind his head as Leckie continues, "I think the Lords Comyn and Douglas would have risen to the insult and given their lives freely to slay de Brix and his sons there and then if it hadn't been for Malcolm here, Bishop Wishart and Duns Scotus. They used their friendship with the great chief Colin Campbell and the Stewarts of Menteith and Dundonald who had arrived with de Brix, otherwise who knows what may have transpired." Malcolm speaks, "If the Comyn Douglas and Baliols throw together as claimants and de Brix still insists on enforcing his claim supported by his bonded allies, then Scotland will surely fall to a bloody civil war, or at the very least the entire west coast and border marches will soon be under flame and bloody sword." Alain exclaims, "This is too much to be considering that Scotland may fall to blood feuding and civil war. What has spurred the house of Brus to such an evil adventure as this? Surely there is a greater game at play here?"

For a moment there is a morbid silence, then Leckie replies, "Immediately after the death of our bonnie Alexander, apparently de Brus, at the behest of his father who had just arrived from England, held a meeting at his castle in Turnberry. Many nobles gathered there to witness the Brus making this scurrilous claim. They then established a 'Pact' to support de Brix and reject Margaret of Norway. This treasonous Pact is a formidable and an intimidating force Alain, as de Brix and his allies well know. De Brix has also called upon support from Ireland, the Isles and his estates in England... his English levies are flocking to his Pact banners as we speak." Alain enquires, "What are these fuckin' nobles thinking?" Leckie says, "It was very nearly a battle with de Brix when he arrived at Clackmannan with se' many armed men. Comyn and Douglas immediately sent for their retinues who were camped near Airth." Alain continues. "How did you manage to persuade them not to take up arms?"

Malcolm replies, "Myself, Malcolm, Wishart, Scotus, Bisset and bishop Fraser intervened, explaining in no uncertain terms what many of us knew would be the outcome if Brix didn't take heed." Leckie says, "If it hadn't been for the presence of Malcolm's Garda Ban Rígh and other Céile Aicé attending in full strength, Brix may not have been stopped. He was told emphatically, and those of his pact, that they would not see another morn break if Brix continued with his claim that day. Malcolm here stressed the Garda ban Rígh were one thousand strong and with Baliol's contingent from northern England and the Comyns and Douglas men camped so close, the outcome would certainly not favour auld Brix, nor his pact." Despairingly, Alain says, "I fear this may be a hothead bloody business that could destroy Scotland, especially if we do not hold firm." Malcolm agrees, "Aye Alain, the Guardians of the realm will need to be at their sharpest wit if this is not to slip into a disastrous war." Alain enquires, "What happens to the future of the Garda bahn Rígh if the Queen's heart is now set on returning to France?" Malcolm holds his hands in the air. "To be disbanded for fucks sake, by order of the Guardians, at least until we are called upon to serve our next Queen."

"This is a feckin madness," exclaims Alain. "To disband such a dedicated force as the Garda bahn Rígh, what are the Guardians thinkin' we need them more than ever now…"

"That's the way of it," sighs Malcolm, "Our last duty is to escort Yolande to Dreux and deliver her safely to her family in good and fair heart." Alain enquires, "Who will be in attendance with you on the journey?" Malcolm replies, "Many of the magnates, and some imminent Bishops are going too who will then travel on to Rome." Alain laughs sardonically… "It's a pity you couldn't leave those pious feckers in France and bring back Yolande instead." The unexpected moment of humour eases the solemnity of the meeting, then Malcolm continues. "I think Bishop Fraser of Saint Andrews is going, and there's also a delegation of religious and diplomatic representatives leaving with Duns Scotus and young Baldred Bisset to be travelling on to Paris."

Alain enquires, "Are you travelling through England with them?" Malcolm replies, "Naw brother, we'll all be departing from the port of Berwick. The Hansa marshals and Flanders Knights fleet will escort the Queen's royal ship to France. Arrangements are being made as we speak, so I reckon we shall be leaving these shores within days." Alain shakes his head. "These are worrying times. If there are magnates and chiefs who don't accept the Maid as Queen, what state does this leave our Kingdom? How many will choose to stand with our bloodline heir and how many will rebel?"

"This we cannot say," replies Leckie. "De Brix caught everyone by surprise when he made his move. But we think he has played his hand too early. He identified to us there will be a power struggle of such a weighty proportion, that these impatient earls will surely bring the whole realm to a bloody war, and who is there to stop them?"

Malcolm replies, "Wishart could, and the Bishops. No matter how reckless these nobles may be to try and seize the crown, they cannot assert any Royal authority without the blessing of the church, nor that of the Pontiff of Rome. These nobles may vie for position and shout loudest about their claim, and they may also have their charters of lineage in place, but without God's blessing and the balm of the Holy Chrism, they'll never succeed, and most likely not survive." Leckie says, "There is already talk from Bishop Fraser and many others to be asking the King of England to intervene and adjudicate. We should pray dearly that this play does not come to be, for Longshanks is certainly no fool. But his realm is near bankrupt where ours thrives, he will not miss this opportunity to make mischief."

Malcolm says, "We're aware of what Longshanks has done to bring slaughter to the Jewry in England in order to amass their wealth and assets as his own. And also what he has done in Cymru and Erinn is much the same in his desperate search for wealth and resources. Longshanks by these very examples and his imperial nature will stop at nothing to be filling his treasury coffers, and if he sees that Scotland is divided…"

"Aye," interrupts Leckie, "This English King who has committed regicide previously when he had murdered Llewellyn ap Gruffydd, the last blood prince of Wales. Then he sent Llewellyn's head to London and crowned it with ivy, mocking his memory as a King of Outlaws. I heard that Longshanks then installed his own people in that land as masters of the Welsh, and laughingly he calls this usurpers council the Parliament of the People. What he's really doing is sucking the life blood from that realm and enslaving its youth for his army."

Malcolm nods his head in agreement; "It's only been two years since the sovereignty of the Welsh was ended by the English imposing upon the Cymrans the Statute of Rhuddlan. Now Longshanks Barons and his Sheriffs levy a severe taxation upon the Welsh and is using the sons of Cymru bought for English gold to hunt and slaughter their own brothers and fathers, whom Longshanks decreed as rebels and outlaws. The only Cymran freemen left alive are now living beyond God's protection in the mountains of that fair country. Mark my words ma friends, it will happen here too if Longshanks is invited to adjudicate here."

Leckie says, "Aye, it's well known that Longshanks has subjected Wales to brutal and punitive English rule. I hear he's built a series of strategic castles and towns throughout that country too then he settled them with the sons of English nobles and Barons. All the native Welsh must now pull their forelock s and beards on bended knee or are subject to immediate execution if they don't. And would yie believe that the English are doing this with Welsh monies extorted through local taxation, supposedly for the protection of the Welsh?"

"It's the same in Ireland." says Alain, "Auld Stephen told me just a few months back that Longshanks' claim to Ireland was granted in legacy by an English pope many years ago, and that Longshanks has been planting his Barons sons there ever since. Thankfully though, Ireland is a much greater landmass to that of Wales and Longshanks' planter English Lords are not finding it se' easy over there." Alain reflects, "I sure hope wee John and Ròsinn will be all right over there in Connaught. I've heard that there is an on going war with the clans in the north-west of Ireland against the Normans and their brutal rule."

"That's right enough," says Leckie. "But there are also Normans knights fighting with the Irish against Longshanks too, and now there are Irish fighting with the fuckin' English against their own people, all settling black blood feuds. What outcome of peace that will ever bring to Ireland I cannot see in our lifetime." Malcolm is deeply concerned, "If the uprisings in Ireland and Wales are anything to be seen as an example of English intervention, then it's paramount that we stay independent and we continue to be separate and free of the English crown its church's evil tentacles."

"Fuck..." exclaims Alain, "if we show any sign of weakness, I cannot see someone as intelligent and ruthless as Longshanks not taking a vantage. We all know he's still rankled over Alexander not paying homage to him after he married Edwards' sister. "

"Worse than that," says Malcolm, "If this goes to a claim of thrones, then Longshanks has royal Scots blood in him too, thin as it is may be, it's not impossible that he may claim the throne as magnate supreme of these Islands." Alain enquires,

"How is it possible that Longshanks could have a claim to the throne of Scotland?" Malcolm replies, "Edward could make his claim to the Scots throne as a descendant of Malcolm III."

"Longshanks with Scots blood?" exclaims Alain.

"Aye," says, Malcolm, "I know this to be true. As the Commander o' the Garda ban Rígh, I know well the lineage of our Queens. King Malcolm's daughter, Edith, married Henry I of England. They had a daughter called Adelaide, mother of Edward's great-grandfather. That's the basis for any claim Longshanks could make." Leckie says, "What's also worrying me about this possible invitation is that Longshanks has many friends up here with land in both realms, nobles would benefit greatly if he were to arbitrate. Look at de Brix, he fought on the crusades with Longshanks and helped put down the English Barons rebellion led by Simone de Montforte, Longshanks' own godfather. When Longshanks subdued him, he had de Montforte hacked to pieces on the field by de Brix' own men... Scots levies."

"That's right," says Malcolm. "Auld Brix, Brus or whatever the fuck he's calling himself, helped Longshanks with the subjugation of Flanders and Gascony, then he fought for the English King with his Irish and Welsh campaigns. That's when Longshanks appointed Brix to be the first Lord Chief Justice of the royal bench of England as a reward for a lifetime in support of the Plantagenet cause."

Alain ponders, "There'll be a bloody reckoning in this country if we don't get this right." Suddenly a lone voice booms from the corner of the hall. "Ach, if those fine but awfy misguided English souls wander over the border, then it's into the sea we will be drivin' them, just like we did with the Romans, Norse, Jutes and Saxonach long before them." Everyone turns to see who has interrupted the conversation. Mharaidh enquires "Wee Graham... what are you doing here?" He replies politely, "Vittals, ma'am." Standing to attention, wee Graham holds a large wooden platter with flagons of craitur upon it, made with wee Maw's special recipe honeydew whisky. Beside him on the table, are other flagons filled with the best of the Loch Fyne wine. Wee Graham continues, "All fresh from our bonnie shabeen Ma'am." Everyone laughs as wee Graham's welcome interruption has broken the solemn conversation.

Still laughing, Alain says, "I don't think if Longshanks brings his army over the border it's the sea we would be driving them into." Wee Graham replies, "Och aye sur, of course we would. For that way they would never come back, just like we did to the feckin Norse." A relieved Mharaidh says, "Graham, I don't think I've been so glad to see you, these men have been worrying me to death with their talk of war." Wee Graham replies with a stoic expression, "I know what yie mean Ma'am." Malcolm exclaims haughtily, "Excuse me?" while glaring at wee Graham. But Alain's wee bodyguard instantly replies, "Yer excused sur."

As quickly as he had appeared, wee Graham slams one flagon down on the table, turns and leaves the room with one full flagon of the golden nectar still on the platter. Leckie notices William sitting quietly. "Would you be wanting a wee nip o' the craitur too William? C'mon over here and have a seat and a nip beside me." Alain smiles then waves him to come over and attend. He says, "I'm sorry son, I forgot you were still sittin' listenin' to all this banter."

William is surprised, the great feared and un-feck-in-friendly Leckie mòr is inviting him to sit and drink in his company? This is a first. He walks over and joins the company at the table. Leckie grins as he pours William a wee nip o' craitur. "And don't be telling anyone yie have been having a drink wie me young Wallace, for I have ma reputation to think about." Leckie slaps William on the back, knocking the breath out of his body. Alain enquires "And where are yie going from here Malcolm?" Placing his goblet thoughtfully on the table, Malcolm replies. "In the morn, I'll be going to meet Sir Hugh Braidfuite up at saint Kentigerns in Lanark. We're meeting there with the Flemish guard then over tae Berwick to catch the boats for the journey to France." Alain enquires, "What about you Leckie?" Leckie replies, "Ach, I'll be going back to ma smithy up in Carlibar. Ma son thinks he can smithy, but yie know what boys are like nowadays, they're more interested in hammerin' into the bonnie lassies than hammerin' into a fine brand forge iron." Leckie suddenly splutters out his craitur. "Sorry Lady Mharaidh, I just plain forgot ma place… It's been a long day, I hope you forgive ma wee indiscretion."

"You're forgiven," says Mharaidh smiling. "I've heard far worse on many occasion between Alain, Auld Tam and wee Graham."

Everyone laughs and begins to relax as auld Jean and Katriona brings some more vittals and refreshments. "Well, Malcolm," says Alain, "I'm going to Lanark early in the morrow too with filled wagons of the end-seasons hunt catch, then I'm bringing back the last o' the winter provisions for Glen Afton." Malcolm smiles, "That's fine, we can make the journey together then." William, who has been listening to the conversation, enquires, "Is it all right if I go to Lanark with you too Dá?" Mharaidh looks at William, his cheeks flush at her inquisitive glance. She enquires, "Someone you're looking to meet, William?"

"Naw… naw," mumbles William. "It's just that I have no' been to Lanark for such a long time, I just thought it would be good to be seeing a busy wee town on a market day, just for a change of scenery. And maybe meet up with some of the folks I've no' seen in awhile." Later that night in his Obhainn, William lies in his crib thinking the Maid Marion may be there...

Early next day, the carts and teams of horses of the Wallace clan enter the Westport gatehouse of the royal burgh of Lanark, where every street vennal and square is alive and bustling with throngs of people selling, trading and bartering goods. William and Alain are unhooking the game catch from their packhorses and carts when a female voice calls out... "Co'nas a tá tú Ualaicé mac Álainn?" A voice that William instantly recognises, he turns on his heels to met by the dual grins of his woodland sweetheart and her brother.

"Affric, Coinach..." exclaims William. "How are yie both doin? Ach it's great seeing yie both here this day." Coinach replies with a broad grin, "We're keeping just fine Wallace, glad yie could make it to the fair." William grins, "Aye, me too." He gazes and smiles at the black haired, olive skinned, petite little beauty sitting and swinging her bare legs from the back of a bow-wagon. William roars "How are yie bonnie Affric?" He puts his hands affectionately around her slender waist and lifts her from the wagon. Holding her close, they look into each other's eyes; then they embrace passionately. "Great to see you here Wallace," beams Affric. "Now I'll be having a real man this night instead of these townies who don't know what the loving of a good woman is all about, even if they do have to pay for it."

"Affric," exclaims William in a chastising tone of voice as he gently lowers her to the ground. "So how is trade in the Lanark fair for yiez this fine day?"

"No' bad Wallace," replies Affric. "Trade could be better though, mind you it's only early morn." With a wry smile, she winks and begins pulling her cottee loose, revealing her pert breasts to tease him. William laughs, "You'd better no' let the Priests catch you showing me your breasts or they'll be chastising yie with a thick leather tawse, and then what will yie do?"

"Ach, fuck them," replies Affric while playing with William's long hair. "They're me best customers anyway. They don't pay much, but at least they wash, well most o' them do…" William laughs, "You're on fine form this morn, darlin."

Affric smiles and tugs his beard. "It'll make the day a lot more bearable for me now that you're here, me fine big handsome Wallace." Coinach calls out. "Wallace, d'yie fancy coming for a look at the smithy market? They've some sound forge metals worth a look at and I've fine clutches of arrows and quarrels I'd like to be tradin." Affric flicks her long black hair behind her head. "Right you fellas, be going the now, for yiez are keeping all of these handsome wee red faced Christian fellas away from my warm sanctuary in the bow-wagon." Affric giggles, "And then what would me and my bonnie sisters o' lovin' passion do for any fun without siller' gain?" William smiles and begins to walk away, when Affric calls out… "Wallace, you come back here and be giving me a lovin' squeeze afore yie go."

William laughs and walks back to his sometime forest lover. He throws his arms around Affric, lifts her up and kisses her on the forehead then he says to her, "Yer a true we Scots wildcat me bonnie darlin." He places her back onto the step of her bow-wagon where she leans over the edge of the wagon towards him and clasps him by the shoulders to give him a gentle loving embrace. She pauses and looks lovingly into his eyes then they kiss passionately. Coinach calls out, 'C'mon Wallace…" Affric playfully slaps him on the shoulder. "Right, big fella, git goin' and I'll be seeing you later."

Looking into his eyes, Affric sits back in the bow-wagon. "And you Wallace, being an Ettin from the loins of Ben an

Donnar… or maybe even Fion MacCumhail (Fin McCool). Do yie think you could find the time to give me some real lovin' later this night?" Affric quickly grips William by his ears and gives his head a little shake, then without any warning, she reaches down and grabs hold of his prized possessions. "Ha Wallace, see, you're still a giant in more ways than one me fine big handsome fella." Affric laughs impishly at William's perplexed expression. Coinach sighs, "Will yie be puttin' the man down, Affric?"

William and Affric smile at each other, the magical connection between them is there for all to see, for they are living legends by their bawdy associations. They both know they could never be lovers by Christian blessings, but they know that their bacchanalian friendship would only ever end when one or both found their Anam Chara (Soul mates) from their own 'clan'. William and Coinach walk away from the wagon of Affric's eternal pleasures toward their own wagons to unload them, when Affric calls out once more… "Wallace, will yie be comin' tae the Fionn's eve Fèis o' the Sabbat on the Yule?" He calls back, "Will you be making your potent ale and magical mushroom Craitur?" Affric replies, "Aye of course, that I will big fella, will you be comin' then?"

"I'll think about it," replies William as he walks back to his father's wagons with Coinach. Affric calls back to him "What d'yie mean yie will think about it ya big feckr? It's not like you to be missing a fine Fèis. Aha, is it a bonnie Scot's bluebell that has your heart's attention set on William Wallace?"

"It might be," replies William with a grin. Affric laughs and smiles till her attention is taken by two monks desperately vying for her favours without drawing any unwanted attention to themselves. As the two friends walk away, Coinach laughs, "Aye Wallace, and who is this that's captured the heart o' the Fèis stallion?" William grins, "Surely you cannae mean me?"

They both laugh and joke as they unload the wagons, when Coinach notices something unusual. "Wallace, would you be seein' what I'm seein'?" William enquires as he pulls at the last deer carcass from a packhorse. "What are yie talking about?" Coinach points, then he exclaims, "Would yie be lookin' at those bonnie Knights ridin' up the hill towards the Town fair on those great big feckn horses?" Twenty Knights ride two abreast up the high road toward Saint Kentigerns church on magnificent destriers dressed in the finest of armour with the most unusually emblazoned surcoats. Not anything local people would recognise.

Flying boldly from their lances, are the pennants of Flanders and Capetian flags of France. Alain, standing nearby talking with Malcolm and Leckie, also notices the Knights riding towards them. Leckie says, "There's Sir Guy de Dampierre comin' now, and that's his son, Robert of Béthune. Those other fellas' are the Capetian guard." Alain is surprised, "What's Sir Guy doing here? I thought the Flemmards were at odds with the Capetians." Malcolm replies, "They're here to meet us Alain, it's political expediency that we all travel together, for Yolande's sake and safety. We didn't have time enough to tell you yesterday. C'mon we must be greeting them." As the Knights close with the group, Malcolm, Alain and Leckie welcome them. The Prince dismounts and they all warmly embrace upon meeting each other. William watches these fine knights of France and Flanders greet his father.

A few moments later, Alain walks back to William and Coinach. "William, when you've unloaded the wagons, take the spare salted game to the Bruin house for me, I'll meet yie later this eve down at the Lanarch inn." William enquires, "Early eve or late eve?"

"No' too late, son." says Alain. "We'll stay here in Lanark this night and be heading to Glen Afton early in the morn."

William enquires curiously, "Who are those fellas Dá? I've never seen armour like that before, nor the coats o' arms on their flags and surcoats." Looking over at the Knights in admiration, Alain replies, "They're Flemish and Breton Knights, son." Alain points to one in particular. "Do yie see that Knight with the gold band on his helm, gold surcoats and the Black lion on his shield and tabard? He's the Lion of Flanders, Robert Béthune. The man beside him is William of Crèvecoeur. The older man is Guy de Dampierre the Count of Flanders; he's the granduncle to Queen Yolande. The others two beside them are old friends of mine, sir Gerard van Damme and Adolf of Niewland. They've come from Berwick to join with your Uncle Malcolm to ensure the safe return of Queen Yolande to her home in Dreux."

William exclaims, "Feck, that's amazing looking armour Dá." Alain smiles. "Aye, son, the Flemmards and Capetian Knights can look very dandy at a hop. Mind you, when we were in Flanders, they says the same thing about our armour and coats. The powerful looking knights in strange but magnificent armour impress William.

"Why are they here Dá? I mean, how do you know them?" Alain replies, "They've come from the wool traders guild in Flanders and Berwick. The Flemmards and Scots supply most of Christendom with the finest of wool and the Flemish traders have built a great trading stockade in Berwick called the Red Hall, that's where I first met them. The French are blockading and banning the Flemmards trading in wool in order that the French may take over their realm. The Flemish also have an embassy in Berwick as they're being persecuted by the French, now the Flemmards and Capetians are forming their own alliance's with Scotland and many other independent realms." William says, "They sure wear their armour well Dá, don't they?" Alain looks at William, "Aye, they do look braw right enough son. Anyway, you had better be going about our business and see to the hunt stock. And mind you be collectin' the vittals for Glen Afton." William replies, "Right yie are Dá. I'll be seein' yie later then?"

Putting his hand on William's shoulder, Alain looks at his son with a father's proud smile. "And don't you be getting into trouble with the Tinkler lassies for I have heard all about the antics of you and the bonnie young Affric." William smiles upon hearing his father's comment. He says, "It'll be too late for me to stop now Dá if you've heard the Bothie gossip already." Alain laughs then he walks over to join Malcolm who's waiting with the Capetian and Flemish Knights. William turns to Coinach. "C'moan, lets be finished here, then we can take the rest of the vittals on up to the bruin house."

"What's your rush?" enquires Coinach as they unload the last of the stock and game from the wagons. "You'll see," replies William. "Aha…" sighs Coinach. "Now I get it. It's the Maid Marion, isn't it? Yie've got that lusty glint in yer eye Wallace. I can see it by the look in yer face too." Coinach laughs. "Mind you. I have to admit though, she is the bonniest lass in Lanark… for a townie." Coinach looks at William, then he enquires, "Surely such a bonnie and cultured lassie as Marion is bred to be, will no' be wanting a big rough country lump like you?" William smiles, "I sure feckin hope she does." Coinach laughs again upon seeing the nervous expression on William's face. Soon, all the heavy end of fall catch has finally been unloaded when William asks Coinach to drive the wagon to the bruin house with the surplus, while he rides his horse on ahead and making good speed riding to the Bruin house,

William jumps off his horse and fast paces towards the Bruin door before his horse has stopped its canter. Arriving at the door, he's met by two old biddies. Breathless, William enquires, "Is the Maid Marion here?"

"Naw, she is no' here the day son," replies one auld biddy as she hands food and salt to a poor family of the town. The other old biddy continues, "Her wee brother master Brian is here though, he's unloading the winter salt wagons. He's round the back o' the hoose if yie want to speak with him." William, though he's disappointed hearing this news is not entirely losing hope of seeing Maid Marion. He rushes round to the back of the Bruin house and meets with young Brian Braidfuite. "Wallace," exclaims Brian, "what are you doin' here? Though it's good to be seeing you." William replies, "We've brought the last of the fall and excess game for the Bruin hoose. Coinach is following behind with a cartload from the Wolf and Wildcat hunters and we've got many warm-fragged skins for yie."

"Aye William," replies Brian, "I'll be thanking you and your hunters for the making of the gifts. It's always welcome sustenance for the poor the auld and the needy o' this town. The vittals that you and the other hunters bring to us are a valuable for sure."

William looks to see if Marion is about, but he doesn't see her. He tentatively enquires, "Is your sister hereabouts or nearby?" Brian enquires, "Who do yie mean Wallace, Brannah?" William looks at Brian. "Naw, I mean Marion." Brian laughs. "Naw, she's no' here. Haven't you heard?" William enquires with concern in his voice. "Heard what? There's nothing ailing her is there?" Brian replies, "Naw naw… she's fine, but Marion and Brannah are away to join Yolande as her ladies-in-waiting for her trip to France. She'll be nearing Berwick with the Queen by now and likely preparing to depart for France." "You are jestin' with me wee man?" says William sounding very disappointed.

Brian replies, "Naw Wallace, she's gone, like ah said, she left yesterday."

"Fuck," exclaims William. Feeling totally deflated he looks at Brian. "How long will she be away?"

"For good I think." William exclaims, "For good?"

"Aye, I think so," says Brian. "She's off to France for good as her place is now with Yolande, and that's a lifetime position, well until she is wedded." Brian notices the demoralised expression on William's face… "Do you want me to pass on a message when I write to her?"

"Naw, its fine," says William. "No wait, will you tell her I came up to be seeing her and if she is of a mind, she can be writing to me from France and if it pleases her to do so, that would be fine too, even if it's just to let me know she's safe and well over there."

Brian stops working for a moment, looking at William curiously, he laughs, "Ah ha, Wallace, you have a wee soft spot for her then?"

"Naw, naw…" replies William, trying not to appear eager. "I just liked her company when we met earlier this year, that's all. We had such good blether together and I just thought I would say hello and pass on my regards to her." Brian sighs, "Ach, a that's such a pity," William thinks that is a curious thing for Brian to say. He enquires, "What d'yie mean by that?" Brian replies, "Marion told Brannah and I that she had a soft spot for you, but that's life I suppose." William feels even worse now. Not only had he missed seeing Marion by a day, but he also felt he was telling her little brother he's not romantically interested, but in reality, he is more than interested. He thinks, 'What a dilemma…' Brian looks at William, "Are you all right there Wallace? Yie look as if you might have the fall melancholy upon you." William thinks a moment. "Naw it's no' that Brian. But I was just thinking, when you write to Marion, will you definitely tell her that I was asking after her." Suddenly, he remembers something that seems appropriate to say. "And will you tell her I smell much better now."

"What?" exclaims Brian looking curiously up and down William's large frame.

"Ach, nuthin', replies William. "It's just a wee joke that might put a smile on her bonnie face." Brian laughs to himself at the emotional clumsiness of William and his failing attempts to hide his real passions for his sister Marion, "Aye, I'll tell her for yie." He looks William straight in the eye and enquires with a grin. "And shall I be telling her that you've a soft spot for her too?" William looks down at the wee fellow. Though Brian is young and of gentle demeanour, he carries a kindness in his face that melts William's resistance to be manly over his romantic notions for Marion. William eventually replies... "Aye, tell her I've a soft spot for her too." Brian laughs, "I'll be doing as you ask Wallace, I know she'll be glad to hear it."

At that moment, Coinach arrives with the wagon carrying salted vittals for the bruin house; sitting beside him on the wagon is the priest in training, John Blair. "Haw, Wallace, what's happenin'?" Shouts Blair as he jumps from the wagon to greet his childhood friend. William replies, "Blair? My it's great to be seeing you again, wee priesty me boy. Wait, I thought you were supposed to be away to France?"

"Naw," replies Blair. "The priests and monks at Paisley priory caught me coming out of the fish-wives Bothie the morning after we last met, and one of the bonnie wee lassies said later I might be the father of her child. Ach It caused a bit of a stushie (Commotion) and the priests eventually had to pay off the old maw to shut her up. And for me to repay the priests they made me stay behind and clean out the cludgie (Toilet) passages of the priory for the rest of the year as punishment for my indiscretions." William enquires, "So what are yie doing now?"

"Cleaning out cludgies o' the priory Wallace… did I no' just tell yie that?" Coinach, Brian and Blair laugh as William scowls. "Naw Blair ya wee feckr, I mean what are you doing here in Lanark?" Blair replies, "I've been given grace for putting such a fine polish on the cludgie skids that I've been granted the opportunity to be leaving with the delegation going to Rome. I'm also going to Cluny in France with Yolande's entourage." William sighs, "Feck Blair, I wish I was going with yie. It seems everyone in Scotland is going to feckin France except me." Blair grins, "I don't think that will be possible, you should have stayed at the ecclesiastical training for that to happen."

Coinach calls out, "Haw you, Wallace, will yie be helping me with this wagon or are you going to romance wee priests all day?" Blair laughs at Coinach's remark and slaps William on the back. He says, "I need tae be going now anyway. It's likely I'll be away for a few years, so I reckon it'll be a long time afore we meet again, mo chara…"

"Blair, can yie wait a moment?" says William. "When you see Maid Marion, will you put in a good word for me? Will you say to her that I was asking after her?"

"That I will," replies Blair. "But from what I hear about you and the bonnie Tinkler lassies, yie'll be needin' a very good word from me to be persuading Marion that you really are that good." William groans, "Awe naw Blair, tell me she doesn't know what goes on in the woodland Fèis?" Blair, Coinach and young Brian all laugh out loudly. "Are yie se' loose about the head Wallace?" enquires Blair. "Yiez are both the talk o' the cloisters with your excesses o' fornication in the lusty passions o' the heathen ways, ahm so feckn jealous." Blair continues. "Everybody knows about it."

"Awe naw," exclaims William, "I'm done for. And it sounds even worse when yie say it like that. I'm surely no' going to find favour with Marion and her affections now."

"We'll see," replies Blair. "I'll be passing on your regrets to her anyways." William scowls at Blair. "Feckin regards I said."

They all laugh as William continues. "I'll be thanking yie Blair for your considerations. So you mind and be safe on your journey, and keep yourself sharp wits about yie wee fella. Don't get caught with those French fish-wives, for I've heard it so that the French cludgies are very ripe with the heat o' the sun, and the aroma can stick to yie worse than any dog shit or pitch oil." Blair smiles then says, "Cannae be worse than the smell of some o' those priests cludgies in Paisley." William laughs, "Aye right enough Blair…" The companions bid Blair a fond farewell, then William and Coinach secure the empty wagon and also bid farewell to Brian.

Coinach jumps up onto the wagon, William mounts his horse and they slowly meander towards the Lanark taverns. Coinach looks at William as they slowly drive the horses and wagon toward the centre of town. He thinks he will try to cheer up his miserable looking friend. "Well Wallace, is it the Fionn's eve Fèis for yie after all?" William replies, "It looks like it." Coinach replies with a devilish smile. "We cannae be complaining at all Wallace. Look on the bright side, yie could be a giant double o' Blair there and having to hide your lusts and passions away instead o' enjoying them openly in such fine company as us like-minded heathens." William replies with an indignant tone in his voice. "I'm no' a feckin heathen."

"Och aye Wallace, that's right, your no' a heathen," says Coinach sarcastically. "We live in the heath, work from the heath, sleep on the heath and enjoy everything the heath gives to our lives. We even feed and get medicinals' from the heath, but yer right, we're no heathens."

Still smiling and poking fun at William's lovelorn demeanour, Coinach cracks the leathers of his reigns as he drives his wagon beside William's horse toward the Lanarch tavern. William appears very down in the mouth, thinking that his reputation has most likely thwarted his love interest with Marion before he can explain his feelings for her. Coinach, seeing his big friends demeanour, thinks to lighten his spirits. "C'mon, ya miserable big heathen feckr, I'll race yie to the tavern, first there gets the ale in." William looks at Coinach then replies. "You'll be too slow driving that lumberin' cart." Coinach grins, "Exactly…"

It takes a moment for William to realise what Coinach said, then a smile broadens across his face. The two friends continue their journey down through the bustling Lanark town, with William's thoughts of Marion still to the fore. Ever since he first laid eyes on her tall slender beauty, he always has her at the back of his mind and feels butterflies in his stomach when he thinks of her. She has given him hope. He thinks to himself, 'Maybe one day…'

Later that evening, William and Coinach walk into the noisy packed Lanarch tavern to see the Tinkler girls wearing naught but loose flighty skirts swirling around naked legs. With bosoms bare, the Ceàrdannan girls dance like legendary banshee warriors to wild Scots music, much to the pleasure of the taverns clientele. William notices Affric, she too is bare breasted and pushing her way through the crowd, bringing flagons of ale and wine to her friends sitting round a large barrel. William and Coinach go over where he planks his miserable frame on a seat. When Affric sees the sadness in his face she sits herself on his knee, slamming four jugs of ale on the table, she says, "Awe ma bonnie Ettin, was your wee bluebell after letting yie down?" She puts her arm round William's neck and strokes back his long tousled hair from his face. Pouting her lips, she says, "Awe ma poor sad Wallace, isn't love of the heart an awful affliction of the mind?"

William looks deeply into the beautiful almond eyes of Affric; she is truly a beauty of the Wolf and Wildcat Forest Ceàrdannan. Petite, elfin-like features, with long raven-black silken hair and tresses mixed with posy flowers flowing down her slender back. He senses her hair and air of her body, so sweetly scented from the woodland fire-smoke, her perfumes created from wild worts, plants and flowers. This pixie woodland princess also has a wild smouldering look in her eyes and a sensual smile of alluring charm that can bewitch all men, causing their hearts to melt, especially when she wants something from them.

"Ach, William, you and me both..." sighs Affric while looking to her erstwhile lover." Do we not have our hearts elsewhere, yet often we fight the chill of a lonely night together so heart-felt with the passions of unbridled love. Are we cursed or blessed big fella?" Affric snuggles her bare breasts into his chest and neck as she clings on to him. As Affric playfully nibbles his ear, he replies, "I don't know... Feck, am no' sure."

Alain, Sean Ceàrr, auld Tam and wee Graham come through the tavern door, on seeing William and Coinach, they make their way over to where they're sitting. Wee Graham shouts over the noise. "Alain, you and Sean go and sit over there with William, me and Tam here will get the craitur in." Affric lifts two jugs of ale and passes them to Alain and Sean, then she says, "That's the last you will be seeing of those two till the morn then Alain, so you might as well have these." Alain laughs, "You're right there bonnie Affric." William smiles, "Aye Dá, wee Graham is done for now," then he enquires, "Did everything go well for you this day?"

"Aye, it was fine son, your uncle Malcolm and Leckie

had to leave though with much haste, for word came the Norwegians have sent a delegation to Scotland and may arrive in Edinburgh as early as this night." William enquires, "Why are the Norwegians coming here?"

Slaking his thirst with the ale, Alain replies. "They want to be settling Maid Margaret's arrival and to finalise the arrangements for her coronation. King Eric of Norway wants this affair settled quickly." William sighs, "Ach well, I won't be seeing Uncle Malcolm before he leaves for France?" Alain replies. "I reckon no' son, he left with the Flemmards and Capetians for Berwick a wee while ago." William enquires, "Are we leaving for the Glen Afton soon, for it's getting late and it'll be too dark to be travelling on the road on a moonless night." Alain replies, "Naw, we'll leave early in the morn." Alain looks at Coinach then enquires, "What about you young Coinach ua Bruan. What are your plans?" Coinach replies, "Me and the lassies will be travelling back the morn headin' for the Corserine, and If it's all right by you Alain, we'll journey with your train as far as the Black Craig, for we heard all the lower southern roads are no' longer passable?" Alain smiles, "Aye, that'll be fine Coinach, your company will be welcome as always."

"That's grand," says Coinach. "If you be needing any help in the morn getting your wagons driven, my sister Affric here and all the other lassies are fair dab hands with the whips and horse leathers." Alain replies, faking a temperate frown that gives way to a smile… "Aye, Coinach, I have heard as much elsewhere."

Surprised at his father's bawdy reply, William laughs out loud at the banter between his father and Coinach. Then he thinks of Marion and wonders if he might ever see her again. Suddenly he feels a warm tongue running sensually up the edge of his ear. He turns his head and there, smiling at him, is bonnie Affric. "Yie gave me a start there Affric." Looking bemused and curious, Affric enquires, "What d'yie mean Wallace?" William smiles, "I though that was big Sean Ceàrrs' tongue." They both laugh as Affric resumes her tongue teasing, close enough that he can sense her hot breath on his neck. She slowly brushes her lips across his cheek till he can feel her gentle breath in his ear. She whispers, "Will you be joining me in the bow-wagon this night then my handsome William Wallace? I'll even lay down the blessed Dinoghaidé's pelt for our pleasures…"

"You would lay down Dinoghaidé's pelt for me darlin'?"

Later that night, William and Affric sit in the back well of the bow-wagon, she has lit several small clay cooking ovens to keep them warm during this freezing night. William gazes at the beautiful Affric, looking into her smouldering eyes that defy him to dismiss her charm.

"How could I resist such a beautiful fae o' nature as you wee Darlin, and for you to lay out for us the magical brat of Dinoghaidé too?" He pulls her close till she presses her tiny nose against his. Their lips meet and they kiss deeply with a passion, then she slowly and tantalisingly begins to undress. Affric picks up a white winter wolf-skin brat and wraps it around her shoulders to keep warm her naked body. William lies down on a makeshift crib as Affric moves sensually toward him, not stopping till she is straddling over his head, then she lowers herself and sits astride him. William reaches underneath the wolf-skins, gently caressing her breasts. She giggles then places one knee on the crib and swings her leg over his head. William closes his eyes and the sweet scent of Affric's womanhood fills his senses with lust and passion. He moves his hands gently up each silken smooth side of her body, then lifts her till she is helplessly poised above him, as he lowers her down, she begins to caress his manhood with her hot breath and warm lips… William is distracted when he hears unusual noises outside the bow-wagon … "Affric… can yie hear folk outside?" Lost in her own sensual delights, Affric's focus pays no heed to William's enquiry.

Suddenly the back flap is flung open and wee Graham calls out, "Wallace, yie had better come quick, the Sherriff o' Lanark is looking for yer Dá…" William enquires, "What does he want?" Wee Graham replies, "Ah dunno, but it sounds mighty serious. C'mon, get yer kit on and get out here, there might be trouble…" Affric groans and pulls the covers over her head as William quickly throws on his Léine, grabs his sword and clambers out of the wagon to follow wee Graham. They soon approach a campfire, where the Sherriff of Lanark is talking with Alain with an extremely animated and agitated expression. William approaches his father… "What's going on Dá?" Alain turns and sees his son. "William, this is sir Andrew de Levingston, the Sherriff o' Lanark…"

William smiles wryly, "Aye Dá, we've met… on occasion…" De Levingston acknowledges William then continues talking with Alain. "It's vital that you get back to Glen Afton by first light Alain and make ready, should any further information come to me, I'll send outriders to keep you appraised of any developments." Alain replies, "I'll make sure we'll be gone from Lanark by first light."

De Levingston and his men bid farewell, quickly mount their horses and ride towards Lanark Castle. William enquires, "What's happening Dá?" Alain replies, "Nobody quite knows son, there are reports coming to the Sherriff o' Lanark that English mercenaries have crossed over the border, led by auld Lord Brix of Whittle, he was the Lord chief Justice in the English law courts and a close hand with the English King so that makes it doubly worryin'… there's also reports that Irish soldiers are coming up from the Solway under the command of the Red Earl of Ulster. William enquires, "What are they all doin' in Scotland?" Alain pulls on his beard, then he replies, "Rumours have it they're here intent on attacking all o' Lord Baliols, estates…"

"Is Scotland at war with the English or Irish Dá?"

"Naw son, I cannae see that happenin' especially no' the Irish, but it could mean that we are on the brink of a bloody civil war, for Lord Brix is firmly laying his claim to the throne of Scotland on behalf of his son, the earl of Carrick…" William ponders…"De Brix… isn't he the grandfather o' young Robert Bruce…?"

Martial Glory

anark is smothered with a thick hoar frost and low freezing mist as William and the Wolf and Wildcat hunters rise before dawn and prepare for their journey home to Glen Afton. The wind-chill and freezing tempera- ture has frozen the wagon wheels firmly to the ice packed earth as Scotland approaches the winter celebrations the Ceàrdannan, country and woodland people all call Látha an Dreoilín, the day of the Wren and '*Hagmonaidh*.' The Glen Afton and ua Bruan travellers scuttle about in the freezing misty morning, wrapped heavily in thick Brat's and mantles to keep themselves warm. The last task to perform is to release the wagon wheels from the grip of frozen ice before they can leave the old royal burgh of Lanarch. After pouring hot water taken from the morning vittal cauldrons left simmering on the night fires onto the frozen earth-locked cartwheels, some of the wagons still remain ice welded to the ground. Men and women alike begin urinating on the wheels to thaw then release them, much to William's amusement.

After much boisterous joking and peeing, all wagon wheels are finally released from their icy trap. William and his father tether their horses to the back of their wagon and move off. Sean Ceàrr, auld Tam and wee Graham follow in their wagons with their packhorses tied behind as the little wagon train moves off toward Lanark Westport. Coinach, Affric and the girls follow at the tail end of the train in their bow-wagons, all fully loaded with provisions. For safety, Alain decides to take the high road to Glen Afton. It will be longer in time and distance, but much safer, for many of the southern fords would be impassable due to snowfall, early winter spey, overflowing rivers and the vast flood plains now covering the summer drove roads. Alain drives the lead wagon with William by his side as they pass through the west-port gates, leaving behind the sleepy burgh of Royal Lanark.

A crisp early morning sun rises to greet the wagon train as they trundle alongside the meandering Abhàinn a' Chluaidh (Waters of the Clyde). William is curious about the meeting with the foreign Knights rendezvous he saw with his father and Uncle Malcolm, he enquires, "What happened yesterday at the meeting in Saint Kentigerns?" Alain looks up, almost forgetting William is sitting beside him, such are the thoughts that concern him. "It was a long and difficult day for your Uncle Malcolm son, he's in a very precarious position." William enquires, "So why's that then Dá?"

"Well, your Uncle Malcolm will soon be the former commander of the Garda ban Rígh once Yolande is safely back in France, but upon his return, he must first arrange and be prepared to protect young Margaret on her arrival upon these shores from Norway, whenever that may be." Alain looks at the sky and shakes his head. "Though I reckon at this time of year, it will be near impossible for her to make any attempt at a safe voyage across the great sea, not at least until the early spring at least." William enquires. "How does that put Uncle Malcolm in a difficult position?" Alain replies, "It's not just the arrangements that's difficult for him, it's also that many of the Norman nobles here are objecting to her becoming regent or Queen because she's doesn't reside in Scotland. They also say she's too young, well, that's their excuse anyway, because some o' them are already vying for power and looking to claim the throne for themselves, the bigger problem is that the Garda ban Rígh have been ordered to stand down and that may cause serious problems."

"Aye," sighs William. "Is that what the strife was all about with Levingston earlier this mornin?" Alain replies, "Aye, partly so, it's mainly the Normans though, they are a fickle bunch without a strong king to keep them in check." William says, "I remember that's what Stephen said to me months ago, that the Normans would start fighting over here amongst themselves with us havin' no King, just as they had done in Ireland."

Cracking the reigns on the oxen, Alain glances at William. He's proud to speak with his son of a man's concerns, and yet it could have easily been so different.

"Aye William, I'm afraid young Stephen could be right. It's those o' Norman blood that's fermenting this discontent by quoting that shite we heard from the Lanercost Chronicles, and these same Normans are using their marriage into Scots families as justification for their parasitic claims." Alain pauses a moment as though pondering over some deep secret, then he glances at William. "Your Uncle Malcolm has a duty to protect the life of the young Aicé Maid Margaret Canmore, regardless of any Norman antics son, he's pledged by honour and bound by previous oath-making to King Alexander. Both your uncle and I were called as witness many years ago down in Roxburgh to a signing by the nobles to the *Charter of Succession*." William enquires, "Is it not so that both a male or female heir can to rise to the throne of Scotland?" Alain replies, "Aye, right enough, but auld Brix and Baliol have already pleaded their case through tanistry and primogeniture, claiming they're from a female of royal descent, this makes them both the credible competitors for the throne should anything happen to the Maid." Alain sighs, "When Alexander's daughter Margaret married King Eric of Norway, there was a treaty signed at Rosbroch about fifteen years ago. Alexander's eldest son David had already passed away, leaving our Ard Rígh with only one legitimate son, consequently the treaty included a provision for any children of Queen Margaret and King Eric of Norway to succeed Alexander upon his death."

"So Dá," says William, "Now that the Aicé Yolande won't produce an heir, is that why the Maid of Norway is to be our Queen?"

"That's right," replies Alain. "It's Yolande's children that should ascend the throne according to our laws and customs. But that'll no longer happen now that she's lost Alexander's child. But Alexander was prepared for this possible event and included these oath bound provisions in the Rosbroch treaty, which in itself is a lengthy complex charter setting out the detail determining the succession of the throne from both primogeniture or proximity for his heirs." William is confused. "Dá, if that was the Ard Ríghs' wishes, and all the nobles signed and gave oath to uphold his honour, what's gone wrong?"

Alain searches for an answer. "I don't know son. The treaty was signed by all Scots nobles of merit, and sworn under oath before God in the presence of our most imminent clerics. But now these same fuckin' Normans think they may break their oath as though their word to a King is but an unwelcome inconvenience." William exclaims, "Ahm sickened upon hearing this misuse of the sacred pledge by these nobles Dá, I believe an oath must always be upheld. How can you live by oath then break your oath? How is that possible?"

"Yie cannae son, not if you and others live by the complete faith in your word as being your bond, be you Cruathnie

Céile Aicé or Christian. After Alexander's first son died, the Ard Rígh sought to protect his lineage and throne by an amicable treaty of the magnates and nobles, which was subsequently agreed upon. Now those same feckin nobles are causing this realm great alarm with their vying for power."

"How can they object Dá? That doesn't seem right. Especially after a blood oath?"

"They feckin object all right, but it's a worthless gesture so long as the Maid lives and is crowned princess regent at Scone Palace." William half laughs, "It would seem that a blood oath with a Norman is worth about as much as a pile o' shit." Both Alain and William laugh, then William enquires, "Could these nobles really put their own man on the throne?" Alain ponders over the question. "Naw it's no' possible, not without starting and then winning a civil war. The Maid has inalienable rights protected by ancient laws to succeed to the throne. That's our hereditary custom going back to the first Aicé."

"It seems to be a very convoluted business Dá. Why is it that Alexander set out such a complex issue in the first place?"

Alain shakes his head. "When the Ard Rígh lost his first wife and then his eldest son David, he had to think of the survival of the royal lineage, in the event that he lost his last surviving son, young Alexander." William smiles, "I remember him. We became good friends after us meeting when I was at Dun Ceann Orran with Uncle Malcolm. Alexander óg was the first close friend I ever knew that died, if he hadn't died, then I reckon all this strife wouldn't be happening." William reflects on his friendship with the young prince, "I still miss him."

"It was a sad business right enough son," says Alain. "If he'd survived, our late Ard Rígh had arranged his marriage to the daughter of Guy de Dampierre, the count of Flanders, that was the fella you saw yesterday." William exclaims, "Ah, is that who that was?" Though it really didn't mean anything to him. "Aye son, the Lion of Flanders is pretty much an important person of standing on the continent, and a good friend to Scotland."

"Yie reckon Dá? I met a Flanders Knight about the same age as me at the Lanarch tavern. We had a great laugh and got on well, his name is Bouden de Vos. He told me he was staying at the Red Hall in Berwick and explained much about European customs and about some trader federation called the Varjag Hansa. Maybe some day I might visit Flanders."

"Aye," says Alain. "Alexander saw much in the mainland continent that brought great benefits to Scotland, and it's made our wee realm very prosperous, but the Maid of Norway will surely face a serious and turbulent time whenever she sits her wee arse upon the throne."

William knowingly quips, "The Normans don't recognise women as equal to any man or even to have a viable in wit do they Dá?" Alain laughs, "It's a lot worse than that for a woman In Norman society son, women are seen and judged only for good breeding or useful for trade in marriage contracts… that's about it. And the women in England don't have any of the same rights as they do here in Scotland; unfortunately it's the same in most Christian kingdoms, and that's what's upsetting the Normans in Scotland. Our matriarchal preference recognises the rights of the Maid or any female to rise to the throne as a child. But because she's female, the Normans cannot abide that thought."

"Feck Dá, it's a lot different up here right enough. Can yie just imagine?" Alain laughs, "We'd better no' be telling wee Maw, Mharaidh, Affric or any of our women that kinda stuff or we'd be getting the blame and a tongue roastin' tae boot." William laughs, "I couldn't see any o' our women accepting that state of affairs neither. I can't even be understanding that sort of notion Dá, can yie imagine wee Maw, Mharaidh or even Affric being told to keep their mouths shut or told that they've less rights than a Norman hunting hound."

As the wagon train trundles onwards, William is still dogged by thoughts of his friend the young prince, he says "Feck, if only young Alexander had survived his malaise Dá, and he fair loved a feisty woman."

"You were good friends then?" enquires Alain.

"Aye, I liked him a lot. With me, wee John and him getting fight training from auld Leckie. I knew I had a friend for life in prince Alexander. I just couldn't believe it the way he died, he was as fit as I am. I just don't understand what happened?"

"Aye son, it was awfy strange the malady that took him. He was a fine and strong young fella, certainly off his father's back and following well in the footsteps o' the King. But it was upon the Princes death that the Àrd Rígh realised the vulnerability of the house of Canmore. That's when he sought to secure Margret of Norway's right to the throne if it fell to her."

"So what did the Alexander do?"

"Alexander gathered all of Scotland's Earls, Magnates, Barons and Chiefs at Roxburgh, including the great Gaelic Chiefs, Sander of Argyll, Aonghas Mòr of Islay, Alan MacRuari of Garmoran, the Gallóglaigh Chiefs o' Galloway Roderick MacKie, Hamish MacSween, and Sean MacDhuibhshíthe. They collectively made a bonded oath securing the Maid's succession to the throne. Even Robert de Brix signed the oath, agreeing that Maid Margret's claim would be forever inviolable by both Scots and Breitheamh law. He pledged to support her hereditary right to the throne in the event of Alexander's death." William ponders. "Was that before Alexander married Yolande?" Alain nods, "Aye son, it was. But now she's lost their child too and heading back to her home in France. That leaves Margret the Maid as sole heir and regent in all but coronation."

"So what's the problem with the nobles?"

"I don't know," replies Alain. "Other than being power hungry bastards and having a fermenting hatred of any woman with balls, I reckon if those treasonous bastards get their way, they'll surely drag this realm down if someone doesn't take control of them." William enquires, "Who has that much power?"

"The church," replies Alain. "The nobles cannot move without church support and I know Wishart and his ecclesiastical council will never allow them to subvert the Maid's accession."

"Is that because Wishart is Ceil Aicé Àrd Rígh o' the Tuatha Dé Cruinne-cè?" Alain is surprised to hear William so accurately describe Wishart's role within this ancient fraternity. "You've been taught well about our ancient faith?" William smiles, "Aye, wee Maw, Leckie, Wishart, Uncle Malcolm…" Alain too smiles and places his hand on William's shoulder, "So you're my brother in faith then?" William grins at this gesture from his father.

"Dá, this is sure some strange time to be livin' isn't it? I've never felt before the way I do now. It's like the world was cheery bright yesterday and everything was set in on summerbreeze sunbaked stone, but when Alexander's house started dying off one way or the other, then our Artur himself, the feelin' in the realm has become very strange. It's like something's going to happen… but nobody seems to know what that something is."

Alain looks at William, then he says, "I grew up great friends with King Alexander when he came down to reside in Glen Afton as a young prince, a bit like yourself son, it was there we both learned all about the hunt together, and you're right, it's a strange feeling since his death, and that of his late wife and children too. But things will sort themselves out, you'll see. It's just a time when we don't have any royal leadership and everyone is just a wee bit frightened and uncertain as to what will happen next." William exclaims, "After that fella de Brix riding a fully-armed force to the Clackmannan parliament with his son the Earl of Carrick, that didn't seem to do the realm any favours." Alain smiles upon hearing William's observation… "Don't be worrying so William, once folk get used to the Guardians running things and wee Margaret comes over from Norway, everything will settle back down again." William enquires, "Are any o' these problems got anything to do with all those English soldiers being gathered at the border earlier on this year?"

"Ah don't know son," says Alain with a frown, "but it sure looks like it now though. Nobody is quite sure what they are doing here, nor what the Irish levies o' de Burgh are doing here too just sitting about camped at Carrick. But somebody is causing great bloodshed in auld Galloway…" William enquires, "That's been near on six months they have all been waiting, surely they wouldn't wait that long to attack us would they?"

"Son, ah'v known of armies to sit for years waitin for their orders to move. The lords o' these poor fella's don't see their men as actual men, those lords think that they are great kinda huntsmen who are controlling a pack o' wild animals' and they treat ther' men brutally as their property, to do with what they will." William sighs, "It's been some year Dá?" Alain cracks the leathers of the reigns once more, "Aye son, it's been some year right enough." The little wagon train moves steadily forward through the hills of the Wolf and Wildcat Forest, stopping occasionally for rest. It was at one of these stops near a crossroads that they rested awhile and made a fire to cook some hot vittals. William looks to the sky and sees it's turning dark with sheet black clouds looming. "Snow's comin' Dá." Alain looks up. "Aye, it'll be falling soon by the look of it." Sensing something else in the air, William quickly turns around and scans along the horizon. Suddenly, on the road from Lanark on which they had travelled, he can see appearing hundreds of cavalry, riding at speed towards their impromptu camp. Everyone in the train is now watching. William notices a group riding a little ahead of the main column. It isn't long before large cavalry units arrive in and around the camp.

The lead group of horsemen halt and dismount beside Alain and quickly gather round the small cooking fire where Alain greets them. William can see it is his father's friends, The Comyn, Leckie mòr, Sir William Sinclair, Sir Bryce Blair, Sir John de Soulis and Sir James Douglas. Curiously, William notices that Bishop Wishart is dressed in full fighting armour under his religious mantle. He watches silently and in amazement as hundreds of mounted soldiers begin arriving all around their small camp. It takes a long time till the great column finally stops and the men are all dismounted. William has never seen so many fully armed riders as this, not even when the magnates arrived at Ach na Feàrna months before. Then he sees his testy auld fight master Leckie mòr ordering the soldiers to make cooking fires and take rest. Comyn and Wishart approach Alain and they bid each other warm greetings. William sits beside the fire as his father and friend's meet to converse.

Sir Bryce, with a grim countenance speaks first. "Alain, we must present you with these seals, for it is with this authority we implore you to consider what we urgently require of you." Leckie mòr, the tough little hammerer to the late King, joins them. William studies the stature of this stocky man who has had such an affect on his formative years. Although small by comparison to himself, Leckie's tough features had shown he'd never backed down from any fight, with his short thickset broken nose and ruddy features. His arms and chest twice near thrice that of a normal man, so obviously muscle-bound, honed and developed by a lifetime as a master hammerer on the late King's forge. Leckie says. "Wishart and Comyn here have both been appointed Guardians of the realm Alain."

They hand Alain their personal seals of the Guardianship of Scotland. On the front side of these seals are affixed and embossed the arms of Scotland, a rampant lion and testament *'The seal of Scotland appointed for the Governance of the Kingdom.'* On the nether side is the raised mark of a resting cross with the testament *'Saint Andrew be the leader of the Patriots.'*

Leckie says, "I vouch for the authenticity of these seals Alain, and I know you have never faulted the integrity of any of these men."

Alain nods in agreement as Leckie continues. "Alain, you must be getting back to Glen Afton and muster all the hunters, trackers and men-at-arms of the Wolf and Wildcat Gallóglaigh." Alain enquires "What is the cause?"

Wishart replies. "It's De Brix the Lord of Annandale, and his son Robert Brus, Earl of Carrick, they've raised a flag of rebellion in Turnberry. They've conscripted levies and have standing troops to form an army called the 'Pact'. Their objective appears to be the seizing of the throne of Scotland for De Brixs' son the earl. The Pact forces have already moved to attack all o' John Baliol's castles and Keeps' in Galloway. We've also heard that de Brix plans to siege and take into his possession all of the royal and strategic castles on the border Marches too. It's been made known to us that the Pact army have already killed and slaughtered many who de Brix thinks will stand in his way."

"De Brix the auld fool," exclaims Alain. "He'll take this country to a full and bloody civil war if he's not done so already." Bryce speaks. "If all we have heard is true, our good friend here the Comyn will be forced through these circumstance's to rally with his kinsman Baliol, they are both honour bound by blood and oath to attack de Brix in defence of their people and property, and this will surely bring all in Scotland to war through Clan, family loyalties and blood oaths to the late King." Alain enquires, "Does De Brix really plan to seize the Crown?" Bryce replies. "Aye, its fairly certain that's his intention, if it's not for himself, then most definitely it is for his sons' benefit the Earl of Carrick. It's very grim prospects indeed Alain, there are many adventurers from Brixs' homelands in England who've also joined his cause, and there are more forces that are arriving near here from Ireland with de Burgh, the Red Earl of Ulster." Leckie speaks, "De Brixs' English mercenaries are known to be brutalising the remote communities of Galloway and Nithsdale."

Wishart speaks. "Alain, De Brix has made a sworn pact with a sizable group of Lords and Chiefs, we've also heard that he is gaining some support from many English and Norman Irish Barons, all set against the Maid of Norway being the legitimate Queen of Scotland."

A despondent Leckie says, "Some of this treasonous pact are amongst the most powerful magnates and Norman Scottish Barons." Alain enquires, "How has this come about? And who else is supporting him?" Leckie replies, "We don't know yet exactly who all is called to arms with de Brix and his Pact. What we do know is that at least four powerful English Barons are in attendance, including Henry de Percy, Sir Thomas de Clare, his brother, Gilbert the Earl of Gloucester and Richard de Burgh the paladin Earl of Ulster." Alain grips his beard thoughtfully. "Is this an invasion of our realm from England and Ireland to support de Brix?"

"No," replies Leckie. "But it's certainly a Norman dynastic attack on the Crown of Scotland from Lords of those lands." Wishart says, "The de Clare's are nephews to Brixs' wife and naturally anxious to support Brixs' claim to the throne." Alain enquires, "Who else would dare such a treasonous play?" Wishart replies. "James Stewart, the High Steward, Walter Stewart the Earl of Menteith and of course, Brixs' son Robert Brus, the Earl of Carrick and his brother, Sir Bernard Brus of York." Alain is perplexed. "If these Lords and Barons have raised a Flag of war, then the strength they may bring to bear upon any battlefield is formidable." Leckie says, "Aye and with Baliol being so remote in furthest southwest, Brix and his Pact may already have him surrounded by now."

Alain enquires angrily. "Then what legitimacy has this Pact, how can it be broken without the realm falling to a bloody civil war?" Wishart replies, "The Pact has formed a covenant and declared a blood oath to venture out on all occasions against all foes as one. With the exception of them giving their allegiance to the King of England should they gain the throne of Scotland." Wishart shakes his head disapprovingly. "As yet, we do not know for certain or have any proof that Longshanks is supporting this treasonous Pact, for he is currently residing in France." Leckie says, "Some o' our Nobles who wish a peaceful transition during the interregnum have sent envoys to meet with Longshanks. The Bishops of Jedburgh and Brechin, with Geoffrey de Moubray as their spokesman, they have already sailed for Gascony to seek out Edward Plantagenet and plead for him to intercede here to halt all of this madness, or at least to offer his advice and protections."

"What?" Exclaims Alain. "Have they lost their fuckin' minds? Longshanks must be supporting this insurrection by de Brix, if not publicly he will be pulling the strings in the shadows. If there are any English Knights flying English colours on Scottish territory, surely it is by the certainty that Longshanks gives his tacit approval." Wishart replies, "We don't know that yet, all we do know is that there are no English crown flags being raised. De Clare and Gilbert of Gloucester have recently had their lands confiscated by Longshanks, which would indicate they're not in his favour, and that slight alone would make any involvement by the English King most unlikely." Alain says, "Maybe de Brix has promised the Gloucester's and other English Knights, tract and title here in Scotland in exchange for their allegiance."

"That seems to be most likely," says Wishart, "But I cannot see Longshanks forcing an act of war on Scotland, that just doesn't make any sense. None would benefit from such a war, including the English." Alain enquires, "Then who stands with us against this Pact?" Wishart replies, "The Guardian army and all other twenty-six Earls and Barons, to be led by myself, Comyn here and Duncan the Earl of Fife." Curiously, Alain looks at Wishart. "I thought that you were a staunch friend of de Brix."

"I am," replies Wishart. "But I'll not support this naked aggression, I'm Scotland's friend first. If we the Bishops, do not bless de Brix, he will gain the recognition of but a few in the Christian community both home and abroad, and most certainly will not receive the Holy Chrism from the papacy Rome." Alain enquires, "How many levies has de Brix raised?"

"We're no' sure yet," replies Leckie. "We believe it to be roughly five thousand from Annandale, Carrick and Tweeddale, three thousand Irish and about another six thousand English mercenaries with de Clare, Gloucester and de Percy coming over the border." Alain enquires anxiously. "How many are with us?" Wishart replies, "Two thousand here and about the same number as de Brix, who at this very moment are riding toward the southwest in four battle columns." Leckie says, "The Comyn here is holding his peace Alain, but not for long I fear. At any time, both he and his brother could easily field over fifteen thousand men from the North, East and the middle-marcher lands. If Baliol truly is surrounded by the Brix pact, then Baliol will most likely declare the Galloway Kingdom at war with the house of Brus, and that will bring all the Gallóbhet and Ceitherne armies to the fore, numbering at least ten thousand, and who would or could lay blame upon him."

Bryce speaks, "Then it's without doubt that if the flames of war are lit, there shall be no mercy for the weak should the Galloway Gallóbhet of Baliol join the fight." Leckie says, "Baliol has at least ten thousand Gallóbhet in Galloway he could bring to arms, and the same number of men-at-arms from his Barnard Castle territories in the north-east of England. If this happens, the Comyns' will be honour bound to commit all their forces and that will set us an entire realm at war with itself, including a possible border war with the English."

"What are we going to do?" enquires Alain. "Have you a any plans confirmed to stop this happening before it's too late?" Comyn shakes his head defiantly. "If the Pact attacks and takes Cruggelton Castle and harm a hair on the head of our matriarch Devorguilla, then I warn yie all here, this will be an injury I and ma kinsmen cannot withstand. My house must then rise and ally with my kinsman John Baliol to fight against de Brix and his Pact. I have many allies in the North of England and Ireland too who will support us. If de Brix and the Pact are hell bent on this madness, they will leave us no other course but to war, for these actions de Brix perpetrates will be an insult of the greatest magnitude." Wishart says, "The Graham and the Douglas with Baliol's brother are going to stop more troops coming over the Border, then push from the east to contain the Pact before they take Dumfries Castle, and I have no doubt the Gallóbhet will be come at the Pact from the west…"

"What about the north-western boundaries?" Enquires Alain. Leckie replies, "Sir Ranald Crauford, he has a large garrison force and many patrols out and abroad that will block any Pact forces moving down from the north and west." Wishart says, "As the Guardian army, we must make all effort keep the peace and set ourselves between Brix and Baliol to prevent a civil war in the realm." Leckie says, "As is substantiated by the presence of Lord Comyn here who stands with us, he seeks no vantage, but soon he may have no choice except to exact blood honour if further provoked. We are all duty bound by our oath to the late Alexander to support the Comyn as he supports us now should he or his kinfolk be attacked." Wishart says, "If de Brix continues to confound the Guardians and also the church, he will bring a realms wrath to bear down upon his head and we must strike a mortal blow to the body of these Pact mercenaries he now employs, and we must utterly destroy them."

"Our other problem," says Comyn. "If it is true the Pact already has Balliol's land surrounded on three sides, we must presume the armies of the Gallóbhet are already raised in a prepared force of retaliation rather than caught in containment. If that is so, this will be a cruel, merciless and bloody war, for we are all aware there is no fighting force more cohesive, brutal and savage in all of Scotland than the combined Gallóglaigh and Gallóbhan armies."

"I've near a hundred good Gallóbhet, with me," says Alain.

"They're great tracker hunters and know every crag and fall from Carrick to the Rhinns and Galloway Machars." Leckie surmises, "We believe de Brix has set his force into four main Battles. De Burgh's Irish are coming from the southwest, de Clare and de Percy's English will come from the lower Southeast and de Brix will be attacking from Annandale in the mid southeast. We know his son the Earl of Carrick is already driving down from Turnberry." Wishart says, "Brus of Carrick will likely be passing Black Craig about now or may already have passed." Leckie counters, "Not unless he follows the old coast roads south into Galloway, which means he may already have been joined by the Red Earl of Ulster's men landed near the port o' MacGumerait out west or Invergarvane (Girvan) just south o' Turnberry castle."

Appearing concerned, Leckie brings the impromptu meeting to a conclusion, "Alain, there is no more time to be talking, we need you to make haste..."

Alain agrees and orders his horse to be unhitched from the back of his wagon, "I'll ride to Glen Afton immediately and raise as many men as I can, but by the time all are mustered about the Craig and Afton Glen, it'll be first light of the morn before we may follow you." Wishart pleads, "Do what you can Alain, for this is a desperate situation." Alain enquires... "Will we rendezvous at any particular point or do yie wish that we track you till we catch up? It'll not be difficult to follow such a large body of horse and your baggage train." Leckie replies, "Track us, for we've yet to find where de Brix and his main Pact army is located. We'll keep on the move with little break until we gain that knowledge." Alain looks around him. "Tam, wee Graham, William, Sean, Coinach... heed me." The men of Glen Afton gather round Alain. He enquires, "Did you all hear that delivery?" Everyone acknowledges they've heard the grave news. Alain continues,

"Sean, un-hitch the rest of the hunt horses, we need to get back to Glen Afton fast. Tam, you, wee Graham and the lassies take charge of the wagons and make your way directly home, for who knows what will happen and who is roaming the hills with vindictive malice of purpose." Wishart speaks. "We thank you for coming to arms Alain, we need everyone we can muster to halt this madness. We don't want to fight de Brixs' Pact, but we have to get between Brix and Baliol or this country will be doomed to a bloody war that will be more vicious than we can recall in a thousand years." Alain kicks slush on the fire embers. "Then we'll leave now Wishart. We're but a few hours fast ride away from glen Afton if we take the hunt horses over the Black hills." Alain sees that his men have already broken the hunt horses and tacked them. He continues. "With your permission my Lords, I will take ma leave o' yiez now."

As the two groups prepare to break camp to meet the emergency with haste. Alain calls out a command, "Tam… On route to Glen Afton I need yie to notify the hunter crews of Andrew o' Lowrie, and poste haste Alasdair mòr Blair as you pass their Clachans too." Alain turns and looks at his son. "William, you Coinach and Sean, I want you three to ride on with me. Now move and mount your horses… there is not a moment to waste."

Pulling on the horn of his saddle to mount, William experiences a feeling of extreme excitement and exhilaration flowing through his body as adrenalin kicks in. He says nothing to his father while containing these heightened emotions that he feels within his mind. Feelings he knows by experience will give him an edge on strength, stamina and a vigour that comes with the silence of attaining the perfect hunters mindset. All say their farewells then the two groups leave the crossroads with much haste. The air is filled with a tense but exciting atmosphere not felt in Scotland since the Norse invasions near thirty years before, but then it was an invading enemy from foreign shores that had brought it on and Scotland had a strong determined King as an undisputed leader, this time the enemy comes from within, now the threat of wars ominous visitation descends upon everyone.

The Wolf and Wildcat hunters gallop their horses recklessly but with great skill over the frozen snow covered ground towards Glen Afton, traversing fast flowing waters, deep and freezing boggy moorland and thick dense woodland in their effort to gain as much time as possible. It takes them less than three hours to reach the southern gateway to the fastness of Glen Afton, but they continually mete harsh encouragement to their horses, until finally, they thunder into the corral below the Wallace Keep. As they dismount, Alain issues orders. "Sean, you go and fetch all of your best dog handlers, then I need you to muster all our best trackers and hunters, we mustn't be short of our best men on this endeavour."

"Aye Chief," replies Sean. Alain continues, "Meet me at the Keep later when all is in order, then confirm to me that all of the Gallóbhet are understanding their duties. We must be ready to leave by the break of dawn. William, you follow me,"

On reaching the main doors of the Keep, William is startled when a stranger steps out from around the corner and looks directly at Alain. William watches the stranger with apprehension. He appears a most powerfully built character; similar in physique and height to himself, but slightly older, in his mid-thirties, with handsome sharp features and tied back long brown hair... "Bailey Wallace!" exclaims Alain in complete surprise. Bailey smiles, "Aye Chief, it's been a long time, too long..." The two men shake hands and warmly greet, then Alain is overtaken by the sense of urgency. "Bailey… I've no' got the time to be explaining all that's happenin' in any detail yet, will yie join with Sean Ceàrr and help to muster all our fighting huntsmen and trackers and prepare them to move fast with us by first light in the morn. Tell the hunters to pack all they may need for a long winters campaign." Bailey replies, "It'll be done Chief." Alain continues to explain. "We're not at war yet Bailey, but heaven help us if we're no' prepared for it." At that moment, Lady Mharaidh opens the door and overhears Alain's words. He continues. "Tá Bailey, I'll explain all to you in detail before we leave the morn."

"Chief," replies the stoic Bailey, he requires no further explanation; such is his loyalty.

The men and women of the Wallace Clan kith and kin have an instinct to act without question upon the given orders of someone they respect. Bailey himself is a veteran with a keen eye that few men possess; his loyalty to his Chief always give him the confidence to act and never to question. As Bailey leaves to carry out his Chief's orders, Alain clasps Mharaidh's outstretched hand, she notices the concern on Alain's expression and can feel the tension. "What is it Alain? Your spirit is so stern, it's frightening me."

"Ma darlin', come with me and I will explain all. But first, I must speak with the boys." Alain turns to see William and Coinach waiting to be told what their duties would be. He looks with authority into his sons' eyes. "William, I want you to be coming with me on this venture." William replies with excitement unguarded in his voice, "Aye Dá, ahm ready." Alain enquires, "Aye, but is your mind ready for this task?"

William stands proud before his father. "Dá, I was with you the moment we found out about this sorry business and when you set your mind to be with the Guardian army…"

"What army?" exclaims Mharaidh with deep concern in

her voice? Alain clasps her hand.... "A moment my dearest, for we have little time. I'll explain all to you when William and Coinach are given their orders." Alain turns to speak with the two young men. "Coinach, can you wait here with us a wee while longer?"

"Aye that I can," replies Coinach. "That's good," says Alain. "I'll have information and a requested order prepared for you shortly that I need you to deliver to your father the good Marchal. Now away with yie to the kitchens and get yourself something to eat, then go to the stables and tack yourself a fresh horse, I want you to return here to me and be prepared to leave here before dusk. By then I will have all your orders ready."

"Right yie are," replies Coinach. Turning to William, Alain says, "I want you to catch up with Bailey son, tell him to be setting out my finest hunters armour, and ma boy, whatever may fit you that is mine, is now yours. I want you to be using the leather-plate armour, for the iron and steel armour is too slow and cumbersome for the hills and forests about here. You're also to pick out whatever weapons you feel is first nature for your hand. Bailey will help you wie that, for he's experienced in our way of the craft."

William replies stoically, "Aye Dá."

Father and son look at each other. A rare unspoken moment of spiritual understanding and blood kinship passes between them, shared only between fathers and sons for all millennia who may ever go to war as brothers. The unspoken bond of pride fusing with exhilarating madness that could be the life or death of either or both, courses through their thoughts... Alain smiles, "Then away yie go son." Immediately William turns and runs down the path, following in the direction of Bailey. Watching William leave, Alain and Mharaidh both feel a pride, but also a great sense of foreboding. Alain puts his arms around Mharaidh's waist and looks into her eyes. "My love, we should go inside, for I have much to tell you. We must prepare for the worst, though I must believe that it is not inevitable." Alain and Mharaidh walk back into the keep of Wallace Castle where Alain will try to explain all to her.

Arriving at Sean's kennels, William can't see Bailey. He stands alone looking around the Glen watching the hustle and bustle of everyone in the dusky evening. Curiously, he still feels a great thrill and excitement coursing through his body. He clenches his fists with a strength he's never known before. His muscles become taught, like sinewy strands of pliant chord as adrenalin pumps through his body and an intense feeling of exhilaration soars in his spirit.

As he scans Glen Afton, he notices Bailey half way up the hill of s' Taigh am' Rígh mòr, near to the hunters obhain's, talking with a group of well-armed men. He sets to pace-running to where Bailey and the huntsmen of Afton and the Black Craig are standing. When he arrives and explains Alain's command, Bailey smiles, "Come with me then young Wallace, we'll get you sorted out for this foolish enterprise. We'll go up to the King's armoury and get you ready for the hop." Bailey and his young charge walk partway up the great hill of s' Taigh am' Rígh mòr to opposite the sentinel point of the Black Craig.

They eventually come to a plateau and stand before a large earthen tumulus. The man-made earth and rocky mound is so well placed in the landscape, it appears as though it is part of the hill itself. Surprisingly, William notices at the far side of the tumulus some men he recognises from glen Afton emerging from discreet thick heavy oak double-doors carrying lit torches. "I've no' been in there before," says William. "I've passed it often enough thinking it simply an ancient burial mound, but unless you know it's there, you wouldn't really see it, and you definitely wouldn't realise you could go inside." Bailey says "That's the point. It's the King's house… s' Taigh am' Rígh. This is where Alexander and his ancestors store their armoury for the Garda Rìoghail and Garda Céile Aicé in this part of the realm. Only the users of such fine weapons and armour that is contained within its chambers may know of its existence. Though I have never had the opportunity nor need for its contents before." The moss covered oak doors that appear strengthened with thick hammered iron bars and equally heavy iron rivets' lay open. William and Bailey walk forward and enter s' Taigh am' Rígh where he's amazed at the sight that greets him.

"It's like a grand wonderous treasure cave," says William. "Much larger inside than it appears from the outside." As he walks into the underground armoury, he notices multiples of cavernous chambers where he can see all types of amazing weapons and armour. Some of the highly polished pieces glint burnished reflections from the heavy pitch torch and candle flames. While in the armoury, Bailey properly introduces himself. "My name is Bailey Wallace, I'm your second cousin, I think, so you're William, Alain's son?"

"Aye," replies William. "Alain's ma father." Bailey smiles. "I have heard much about you, its good to be meeting with you at long last." William laughs, almost in embarrassment. "I'm sorry Bailey, but I've never heard of you, and your accent has me curious, where is it you hail from… Aberdeen, Inverness, somewhere up in the far north-east?" Bailey laughs, "Then that is good news to me ears boyo, for the less folk know about me and where I come from the better I be. But we'll get to know each other well enough as this venture unfolds."

The two Kinsmen look around the armoury as William relays all he has heard from the nobles meeting earlier at the crossroads.

Bailey speaks, "Then we had better get you well prepared. Now what's your weapon of choice?"

"Flights," replies William. "That's good," says Bailey. "And what do you like to use in close combat?" William appears slightly coy. "I like the bastard sword, but my favourite is the claymore, like that of Leckie mòr." Bailey enquires, "Have you ever used these weapons in any battle?"

"Naw…" William laughs, "Naw… I've never been in a battle before, just the occasional brawl down the village." Bailey grins, "You mean you have not killed anyone yet?" But he already knows the answer… "Naw," says William. "It's no' in ma nature. Fuck, I've never even thought that I would ever want too kill anybody." Bailey looks at William and sees that he really is green to battle, but there's something more in what he sees.

"Then, Master William Wallace, if we must execute this duty required of us with proper discipline, we should both pray me boyo that you never have to send anyone to a better place." William is curious, he enquires, "How d'yie know if there will be any actual fightin?"

"I don't, but I always prepare. Then when or if fighting comes, it's no surprise to me at all." William smiles and thinks, *'That makes sense.'* Bailey laughs then says, "C'mon, young Wallace, we'll search the armoury here and get you ready and prepared."

An overnight winter storm leaves the Glen covered with a thick blanket of snow and the freezing early morn is pitch dark as the Clan gathers round the fortalice of Wallace Keep. Coinach has been forced to remain in Glen Afton overnight, for it has been a stormy, sleet-driven and black moonless night. And would have been hopeless and probably fatal for him to have left before dawn. Alain is ready and mounted on his warhorse at the head of a Hunter Corrughadh (Hundred) from the Black Craig Wolf and Wildcat Gallóbhet. The noise of hooves clattering off cobble comes from horses that are excited, skittish and agitated to get moving is intense, the horses can sense a fraught atmosphere emanating from their riders. The horses breath anxiously, filling the dark morning air with a thick, hoary scented mist, as does the breathing of the mounted men, most of whom are dressed in pliant leather plate armour and heavy skin Brats, with each man wearing minimal metal armour, save for that on their shields breastplates and helmets.

William watches his father, who is dressed similar to his Uncle Malcolm the day he had left Ach na Feàrna on his way to Dun Ceann Orran. The only difference he notices is the dragon on Alain's helm and surcoats. This particular dragon clutches a spread sheaf of five golden arrows held in its two rear claws. William himself wears the winter double lined léine, a garment similar to full drop great plaid but with a shirt body and long sleeves attached. His leggings are made from layers of boiled pigskin, moulded dry to fit the wearer to shield his lower legs from the tearing of heavy thorn. Inserted between the pigskin and his bare skin is kitten pelt lined calf-leather breeks (trousers) protecting his legs from chaffing. William is also wearing his father's armoured leather battle-jack, comprising of thin square pieces of metal hammered and layered into the space between the linings of the battle-jack to prevent penetration by an arrow, or lessen the slash or pierce of any weapon. The piped runnels of the jack are stuffed with dry sphagnum moss, in the event of complete penetration into the body by an object; the medicinal properties of the moss would immediately enter the wound with the projectile head, whereupon the fine moss fibres clot the blood flowing from any wound.

Looking around the Glen, William is in awe at the body

of men gathering around him, for they are hardy tough mountain men. He can see many bare the scars of battles past. *'Fuck... these are real fighting men, and by the cut of their countenance I would no' be wantin' to be on the receiving end of their fury or vengeance. How the fuck am I going to stand shoulder to shoulder with any of these wild men if battle breaks out?'* As if reading William's mind, Bailey pulls his horse by his side, "You'll be fine Wallace. If battle breaks out, you stick with my men and me. Our single duty is to protect your father at all costs." Bailey laughs, "And so far, it has always been a most severe cost to others who would attempt to harm your father in my company." Bailey looks at William and smiles. He speaks calmly to comfort him. "You'll be fine." William says nothing by reply, but wonders how on earth Bailey knew what he was thinking.

Bailey continues talking without looking at him. "I know what you are thinking Wallace. You'll recognise how to read people without words soon enough. Now join with me, your father wants you close behind him on the ride out on this cold winter morning."

They walk-on their horses when William thinks of his friend Stephen, missing his companionship. Bailey and William draw their horses beside Alain, who dismounts and bids William to do likewise. Mharaidh comes from the Keep with Sean Ceàrr carrying a shield and helm behind her. She says, "I've brought you these gifts William at the behest of your father, and with the blessing of the Clan of Glen Afton and the Wolf and Wildcat Gallóbhet."

Alain lifts the helm and shield carried in the hands of Sean. He places the helm complete, with a blue and gold veined turquoise dragon, wings outstretched and claws clutching five golden arrows embossed in gold resting on the jaw-plates in William's hands.

The heart shield has the same design embossed into thick battle scarred bull-neck leather. "These here were your grandfather's helm and shield…" says Alain. He holds them out to William. "And now they're yours." William is speechless. He can't understand what has made him worthy enough to be given such precious iconic family heirlooms. He stammers. "But…"

"Try the helm on," insists Alain as he takes the shield from William and fixes it to the saddlebags on the rear flank of the horse. Alain, Mharaidh and the entire troop watch as William nervously accepts the helm with great pride, and greater humility. He runs his fingers slowly over the obvious strike marks made from weapons in battles past and glorious deeds. He gazes in wonderment at the beautiful ornate helm. Slowly he raises the helm and carefully places it upon his head. Alain enquires, "Well… what do yie think son?"

"It fits me perfectly," says William. "Dá… is this really the helm grandfather wore at the battle of Largs?" Alain appears surprised, he had never told William about his grandfather and the battle. "Aye son, it was his." William's heart fills with pride. "Then I hope I will be worthy of his memory." Alain is a little taken aback at William's thoughts and response, and then he smiles with a father's pride in his son. Mharaidh speaks, "You're a Wallace and you will wear it well, have no fear of that William, we see it in your blood."

Alain reaches towards the side of his horse then he turns back to face William. "This was your grandfather's hand sword and his belted scabbard." William looks at these precious gifts now passed on from his grandfather to his father, and from his father to him. As he accepts these treasured heirlooms, he exclaims, "I don't know what to say…" There is a brief moment as father and son look directly into each other's eyes, "Say nothing son, for I know you will wear our family colours well and with great honour too. Accept these gifts as intended, for this is your first venture out as a Ceitherne with the Wolf and Wildcat Gallóglaigh Corrughadh." William is again lost for words, now he is accepted as a Gallóglaigh Ceitherne? Alain nods toward Bailey who calls out, "All mount..." William mounts his horse with a humility and pride when Bailey pulls up close to him. "Wallace, the men and women of the Corrughadh would wish it that it is you who is to be leading us out of Glen Afton as our Dragon pursuivant." Bailey hands William a long lance with the furled pennant major from the house and Clan Wallace of Glen Afton. William proudly takes the lance from Bailey, for a moment he again feels overwhelmed. Only on the most rarest of occasions, has he seen these proud warriors, but now... now he belongs.

Nudging his horse forward while simultaneously raising the pennant high, William watches the pennant unfurl and flow, releasing a magnificent long silken tri-banner with a wheaten white background, revealing a flying blue bodied gold veined dragon with outstretched wings and claws that clutch a sheaf of five blue and white arrows with golden barbs, emboldened with a bright-diced blue and white border. The totemic symbol of the Glen Afton Wallace clan carries the fabled Guardians mark that fly's magnificently as the entire Gallóglaigh Corrughadh walks-on behind. William looks at the majestic pennant and his heart soars, for now, now it is his turn to carry the ancient colours and iconic symbol of his clan with pride. Suddenly war-horns blast in the distance. Alain looks up and sees the first glimmer of dawn break through the night sky, he nods to Grant the master piper of clan Wallace who marches to the fore leadin the Wallace out of the glen Afton with tunes of glory. "Don't you look quite the warrior now young Wallace?" grins Bailey as the

Wolf and Wildcat Gallóglaigh move southward, all leaving Glen Afton in a long proud procession. Coinach rides beside Alain, discussing the orders for the men of Marchal, while William rides ahead of his father flying his clans' colours, still in wonderment and filled with awe at the whole occasion, as the mounted soldiers, warriors, dog soldiers, fleetfoot, lightly armed trackers and the provision wagons move up the secretive pass at the side of s' Taigh am' Rígh.

At the front of this marvellous spectacle they are led away from the Black Craig fastness of Glen Afton by the clan pipers, playing with pride the marching tunes of the clan's past martial glories as dawn finally breaks. Looking up and down the spectacle, William feels incredulous at this sight. He'd heard about the clan and family regiments flying their clan, family and realms colours. He had seen them moving in all their splendour at pageants and special occasions, but now, he is a very real part of his clan's martial glory. The thrill is magnified by the inspiring sound of the bagpipes and war-drums filling his heart with pride. William will never forget this day for the rest of his life, for this is the day he feels he's respected as a man now stepping onto the world stage. On this cold winter morn, his people march to war, possibly eternity and into the folklore of his people, and he is a part of it.

As the column makes its way southward, William talks with Bailey for hours, both getting to know each other well. "I wanted to ask you again Bailey, You have an awfy funny accent. Where is it that you really hail from... the Northeast?" Bailey laughs, "No William, I'm Cymran. I'm from the border lands of Wales, within sight of England, I'm from a place called Shropshire." William enquires curiously, "What brings yie away up here then?" Bailey replies thoughtfully, "It's a long story boyo... It all started when the English first attacked

Wales and then murdered the royal house of the Llewellyn's. After that they turned their murderous intent upon all of our leaders. Finally, they visited their wrath upon us simple folk. The English brought much slaughter and rapine by such an overwhelming force upon our small realm, many of us knew then there would never again be an independent and free kingdom of Wales. And you Wallace's up here are our relations, so boyo, I decided to leave my native land and get as far away from English oppression as I could."

"So you're my relation proper?" enquires a surprised William. "Yes, that I am," replies Bailey. "Over a hundred years ago, some Wallace's went down to Wales and settled there, now it's my turn to come back." William thinks a moment; then he enquires, "Bailey, what do other folk call you as a Wallace, a Welshman?"

Bailey looks at William curiously, "Not by a Scot or in the Cymric language. Just English speakers or users of the Norman tongue. Why do you ask?" William appears contented with Bailey's answer. "Awe, no reason, I was just wondering." Before he can continue, the column comes to a halt. Just ahead of them they can see in the distance, wagons approaching. As the wagons get closer, William can see it's auld Tam driving the lead wagon with the rest of the wagons tied securely in train to the back of his wagon by the nose of their oxen. William hears Alain call out to auld Tam…"Where are wee Graham and the girls?" auld Tam replies. "Wee Graham's behind me sleepin'. He found a leaky cask o' craitur and the last thing he said was that he must save what he can. Now he's feckin drunk and passed out." Auld Tam pulls the wagon close to the troop as Alain enquires, "Where are Affric and the girls?"

"The girls asked me if they could take some o' the horses and leave for their camp down at the Corserine Gap." Coinach enquires with a sense of urgency, "You're sure that Affric has gone to the Corserine?"

"Aye, they were fair worried with what they had heard at the crossroads so they doubled up on each horse, I gave them provisions and sent them homeward. I hope it was the right thing to be doin'?" Coinach pulls hard the reigns of his horse upon hearing Tams words. "Aye, yie were right Tam," Alain speaks, "Tam, you keep heading for Glen Afton, and when you get back and wee Graham has his senses back in order, gather all the Youngblood and set them to fight training. Have them on full guard rotation all around Glen Afton till we return from this venture. I don't know how this situation is going to play out, but we best be safe."

Auld Tam nods, whips the ox reins and rumbles on towards Glen Afton. Alain and the troop watch as auld Tam trundles away, with his faithful, but very drunk and oblivious companion wee Graham sleeping like a babe between flour sacks and casks of wine and craitur. Alain turns and speaks to Coinach. "Make like the wind for your father's camp now Coinach. Tell him of all that's happened… and make sure to pass him the writs I gave yie last night." Coinach turns his horse when Alain suddenly grabs his reigns.

"Coinach, tell your father to send all his fighting Gallóbhet to meet with us at the foot o' the Silver Flowe lochan before nightfall on the morrow. I reckon the Northern Guardian army will be camped there. Tell him he's to send all the women and children to the safety of Glen Afton with much haste. It'll be safer for them there during this time of unrest. Leckie mòr told me armed bodies of men are moving into the Wolf and Wildcat Forest wie malice and purpose to eliminate all forester folk that could raise arms against the Pact." Alain pauses, then he says, "Bailey, William, you go with him…" Coinach raises his hand, "Naw Alain, I'll be much faster on my own." Alain commands. "Go then Coinach, and waste no more time," William and Coinach shake hands, then turning his horse southward, Coinach speeds away through the snow covered drove road into the distance. Alain issues further orders... "Sean, lead the heavy horse and wagons. I want the hunter horse to follow me; we'll ride ahead to see if we can catch up with the Guardians. We should be at the Silver Flowe about mid-day where we'll wait for the rest of you to catch up by eventide fall." Alain pauses, then says, "Bailey, you and William come with me, the rest o' yiez... keep your eyes and wits keen for anything other than Guardian army tracks." As William watches his friend Coinach gallop into the distance, he thinks '*Ah wish ah was going with yie... go safely brother*'

By late morning, Alain's Gallóglaigh hunters are approaching the camp of the Guardians, now resting at the foot of the Silver Flowe lochan as he had predicted. The Clan Wallace Gallóglaigh canters into the centre of the camp, where they are met and greeted by Leckie mòr and Wishart. Leckie enquires "Is everyone here Alain?"

"Our heavy horse, dog soldiers, fleetfoot and wagons are just a wee while behind us." Taking the tack and saddle pack from his horse, Alain continues, "I've sent word for Marchal ua Bruan's Gallóbhet to meet us here. With Marchals' fighters we'll number near two hundred o' the Wolf and Wildcat Gallóbhet." Leckie comments, "That's a fair call for such short time in notice Alain." Wishart approaches, "Co'nas Alain, from what I have been hearing, we will be needing every fighting Gallóbhet, Knight and levy that we can muster. Who did you send to call out the Marchal?" Alain dips a bowl into a cauldron of hot stew on the fire then he replies, "I sent young Coinach, his son, to raise the Marchals' clan. I reckon they should be here by dusk or first light," Alain pauses as he cups his hands round the hot pot of stew to heat his freezing fingers. He says, "I hope young Coinach got to the Corserine all right, for I have a bad feeling, that's why I sent him ahead to muster Marchal."

Dismissing his troop, Alain settles near the cooking fire with Wishart and Leckie. He speaks with concern, "I thought maybe Marchals' outriders would have been here already, their camp is not that far behind us?" Leckie replies, "Aye, they should o' been here, I cannae think there would be a problem though for all the unrest is to the west or south of us, not east." Alain enquires, "Did you no' pass his family on route to Glen Afton on your way here?"

"Naw we didn't." replies Leckie. "They may have followed the foothill road or taken the pilgrims route. It may be Marchal met with one of the other Guardian forces heading south." This information does not sit well with Alain; he says "Just the same, Marchal should still have made some kind of contact by now. Ah'v just got such a feelin' something is wrong…" Alain can feel it in his gut. He calls out, "Bailey, William, come here, quickly…"

William and Bailey rush over to Alain. "William, you know where Marchal ua Bruans' winter camp is don't you?" William replies, "Aye Dá, it's not far, maybe about ten or twelve miles behind us. They reside in a wee plateau halfway up the Corserine gap in the Rhinns o' Kells ridges." William points northeast across the glen. Alain issues a command…

"Bailey, you go with William, see why the Marchal is held up, then send back any news back to me by his outriders as soon as yie know anything, but mind, be cautious on yer route." Bailey enquires, "Do we stay with Marchal or come after you?" Alain thinks for a moment; then he replies, "I want you both to stay with Marchal and ensure he joins us with haste. If we are gone from here by your return, follow our tracks away from the Silver Flowe; that should be easy enough. I'll carry on with Leckie and Wishart here and help the Guardians to find the Pact armies." Alain looks directly into the eyes of Bailey, completely un-noticed by William. But Bailey knows exactly what Alain means by the fleeting glance. Should they run into trouble and it means giving up his own life for the safety of William, then Bailey would do so without a moments' hesitation. Alain notices that William is fussing and tending to his horse. He sees a young man standing proud in his colours and armour as a Ceitherne of the Wolf and Wildcat Gallóbhet, as he had once been by the side of Alexander as a youth. Alain speaks. "William, Bailey, go careful, be extremely cautious, if Scotland is on course for civil war, there are many who will strike out in fear before they question the loyalties of any strangers."

William grins confidently, "We'll be fine Dá, just don't you be starting the war without us."

Alain feigns a smile as he watches William and Bailey mount, turn their horses and gallop out of the camp toward the Corserine Gap. As they ride into the distance, Alain watches them till they are out of sight. He thinks, '*I hope and pray William, that you never find the war your impetuous youth so desires.*'

THE CORSERIℿE GAP

William and Bailey ride through sub-zero temperatures, thick snow fields and deep drift banks for almost half the day before they get their first glimpse of the mouth of the Corserine gap in the distance, a wilderness haven situated below the Rhinns o' Kells ridge. The vista that lay before them is breathtaking as the sun reflects from the brilliant white snow topped ridges, glistening as though millions of tiny starlets has been strewn by the deities from the heavens above, all sparkling and shimmering in the late afternoon polar sun. To William's eye, the Rhinns o' Kells ridge appears to be supported by spectacular ice clad waterfalls that surround the lower reaches of the Corserine, so Herculean in their majesty as they rise from the lower bowries as beautiful blue-ice pillars, supporting nature's very own cathedral.

Slowing their horses to a meandering pace, William and Bailey weave their way cautiously along the slender secretive path between the freezing treacherous bogs and marshlands. No words are spoken as they continue their journey towards the obscure gap that leads up to the Ceàrdannan encampment of Marchal ua Bruan's clan in the Corserine fastness. Bailey, riding ahead of William, senses an atmosphere that makes the hairs on the back of his neck prickle. William is keeping an eye on Bailey and notices him rise slightly in the saddle, as if he were trying to distinguish a faint scent in the air. Bailey slowly raises his left hand, waving gently, indicating that he's concerned about something and wants to stop. William edges his horse closer to Bailey who is straining his eyes and ears to see or hear anything that will satisfy his feeling of caution and trepidation. It's obvious he senses something is amiss... William is greatly relieved the experienced Bailey is with him.

They squeeze their horses flanks and move forward at a slow pace towards the Gap, watching, listening... then cautiously, they bring their horses to a halt, just far enough away from any deadly arrow flights that may be fired from the tree line at the foot of the Corserine Gap. For a long while they both stand completely motionless, again they watch... listen... and wait, both now with an acute sense of foreboding. William enquires in a whispering voice while he scans the tree line at the foot of the Corserine and Kells ridges. "D'yie feel somethin' odd in the air Bailey?"

"That I do..." replies Bailey. "Hold your horse still, for something's not right."

The two companions remain inert, waiting and watching. Their horse's ears continually prick forward, for they too appear to sense that all is not as it should be. As experienced riders, both kinsmen know that horses ears are as good as another pair of eyes. While they stand sentinel, the mist from the nostrils of man and horse is the only thing that moves in the crisp moorland air while they meticulously scrutinise the surrounding terrain for something, anything that will satisfy their senses of apprehension. Bailey speaks in a low voice. "Wallace, I want you to feel and see with your imagination for what you cannot see with your eyes." The atmosphere is unnaturally still and the creatures of the land are notice-ably silent.

The eerie absence of life confounds Williams and Bailey's senses with the contrasting panoramic beauty of the Corserine, the two young men know that the Glenside should be full of nature's music, but today, everything is silent…and deathly still. "William…" whispers Bailey, "Do you see those horse-tracks where the path emerges from between two large boulders, then splits south and east?"

"Aye," replies William. Bailey continues, "Move the horses up to the point where the tracks split, we'll look to see if they're fresh tracks. Maybe Marchal has already moved his clan away from the Corserine already." William speaks quietly… "Marchal wouldn't have taken those particular routes to join the Guardian army, if he had, we would've already met with his wains and women-folk heading northwest for Glen Afton."

They ease their horses forward cautiously, far enough till they can plainly see that many horses had recently left the Corserine gap. William leans forward in his saddle, scrutinising the ground around them. He whispers. "Bailey, that horse shit over there is no' yet frozen, and it looks as though many have passed by no' long since. Ah'v also noticed that these horses are all shod, Marchal's has no' got any shod horses… his are all native." Bailey nods in agreement. "I don't see any foot pad impressions in the snow or bog-mud neither. Does Marchal ua Bruan not have any footmen or fleetfoot?"

"He does," replies William curiously. "Many or most of them are masters of the long boar sticker, longbow and crossbow, so there should be plenty of fresh foot tracks about, but there are none here so fresh that I can see."

Both remain seated and silent as another few moments pass by, they keenly scan the tree line, then they both scrutinise a particular area of large scattered boulders around the gap mouth in particular. William whispers, "I don't like this feckn feeling Bailey... it's as though someone's definitely watching us. I don't know what it is, but something is very fuckin' wrong here." Bailey shrugs, "I'm with you on that feeling." Bailey then enquires, "Is the camp of the Marchal far from here?" William points, "Aye it's close, just up the Corserine hill there in a wee sheltered gulley." Bailey ponders awhile then he says quietly, "I can't fathom this unnatural silence." William nods in agreement. "Coinach should have been here by now, or at least someone here to greet us. I don't know why we've not met nor seen any signs of his clan responding to our presence." Both young men scrutinise the tracks again.

After a few moments, William raises his head and looks towards the Corserine Ridge. "If that wasn't Marchals' horses that left those tracks behind, then who did?"

"I wouldn't know," says Bailey, then he enquires, "Will it take us long to get to Marchals' camp?" William replies, "Naw, it's just through that gap there and up through a wee gully. From there we come upon a sheltered plateau where all their Obhainn's are situated. It'll not take us very long."

They edge their horses closer to the gap entrance, with both keeping a hawk's eye focus on the tree line, then William notices something peculiar and unfamiliar. "Look Bailey, look up there, follow the gulley track line up the Corserine pathway, about half a mile, near to that big bend to the hill beyond. Can you see what looks like smoke? It seems to be coming from where Marchals' sheilin' should be."

A translucent blue smoke can be seen rising from the depths of what appears to be an enclosed plateau. William continues, "That doesn't look like camp smoke, it's tinged a blue and black, it's usually white smoke from the camp fires." Feeling a cold chill run down his spine, Bailey looks up at the hazy smoke stack in the distance. He's seen this colour of smoke many times before in his Cymru homeland, and likely he knows the cause. He dreads that something haunting him from his past is about be revealed. His heart sinks while he prays quietly that he is wrong in interpreting his observations, but says nothing to William of his concerns.

"Move your horse slowly forward Wallace, very slowly, and keep our horses a distance apart and yours well to the side of me, should anyone fire arrows at us and miss, the other wont be struck." Bailey looks at William then he smiles. "Less of a target you see. And for fuck's sake boyo, keep your eyes, ears and especially your senses wide open." Instinctively, William knows exactly what Bailey requires of him as they separate and move their horses slowly forward, while cautiously watching the land ahead of them. The sloppy trudging through the mire of their horses' hooves is the only sound that's heard as they move closer to the track gap.

The strain of watching and listening soon increases the intensity of the silence now beginning to deafen William. Freezing crisp air brushes past his ears and starts to beat on his senses like great thundering drums... then he hears a faint noise coming from somewhere in the distance, like manic echoes raging down the slopes of the Corserine. He lifts his jaw-guards to listen more acutely. He whispers, "That's hungry snow-dogs or winter wolves not far away, can you hear them?" Bailey scans the hills intensely. "I do, its like rabid dog fighting, but that's an odd fuckin' noise."

William stands high in his saddle and listens. "It sounds like a big mad dogfight."

"Yes, but what's missing?" says Bailey. William removes his helmet completely; then he listens intently to the savage sounds in the distance. He mutters, "There's no cheering from any crowd... there's no even any voices to be heard at all. What the fuck is that noise?"

Confirming William's observation, Bailey agrees. "You're right, there's no voices, just hounds hollering, and that's a big fucking problem I reckon." William points toward the smoke rising into the sky. "Look, those are hooded crows, ravens and kites circling around the smoke stack. Why are carrion birds circling the smoke stack?"

"Dead meat, they're scavengers, when you see them birds circling, they're just biding their time to land safely. It looks as though they're waiting for the snow-dogs and winter wolves to have their fill before they can get to scavenging for the scraps."

Bailey becomes even more concerned, while William is also considering the worst, but neither speaks of their fears as they continue to move their horses forward at a steady cautious pace, till they reach the mouth of the Corserine gap. They squeeze their horses through a tight entrance between two great boulders where they see the path clearly opens up to a drove track leading directly through a gully and up towards Marchals' camp. As they study the route and surrounding landscape, they notice something unusual in the distance. William enquires… "What's that up ahead?" Bailey replies, "Whatever it is, it doesn't look as if it should be there." They strain their eyes to establish exactly what it is that lay across the path ahead of them, but they're too far away to distinguish the object.

Tentatively they move forward and around a sheltered bend in the track where they see two tired bridled horses standing forlorn and shivering in the intense cold. The object that holds the two kinsmen's curiosity lay spewed across the track not far behind the abandoned horses. Continuing with their cautious approach, the object that captivates both young men show's no indication of life, nor any definitive structure as to what it may be, though it becomes obvious that whatever it is, it cannot be deemed a threat. As they close on the standing horses, Bailey raises his hand. "Hold Wallace… Don't move, it might be a trap." Once more they sit for a long time surveying the scene all around them. William enquires, "I think those are the horses that auld Tam gave to the Ceàrdannan lassies yesterday?" Bailey replies "I can see that they have your father's brand on them." William enquires, "Then what the fuck is that on the ground up there behind those horses?"

Moving closer, William scrutinises the objects lying on the slushy freezing ground… Suddenly he jumps back in his saddle, appearing bewildered and confused. "Fuck Bailey, are those bodies lying out there?" Bailey reaches behind his back. "Go see what it is, I'll watch over you… and keep your wits sharp." Bailey pulls his crossbow to his shoulder and meticulously searches the nearby terrain while William dismounts and tentatively walks forward to examine what appears to be grotesquely mutilated animal carcass.

"WHAT TH' FUCK…" William cries, he cannot believe what he's seeing. Whatever he's looking at doesn't appear real, or of this world. He peers closer then suddenly he recoils in horror and cries out… "Fuck, naw… NAW…" He turns away from the scene and stares at Bailey with wildly insane eyes as his cry echoes around the hills. Bailey calls out with urgency in his voice, "What the fuck is it Wallace?" But he never averts his eyes from searching for anything that would indicate an ambush or trap. William remains in shock, simply staring at Bailey. "I… Bailey… it…"

Bailey cautiously drops his guard, dismounts and walks over with the horses on either side of him to give flanking protection while he investigates what had obviously shocked his young charge. He walks up beside William who faces away from the scene; then he examines what's lying on the ground. Bailey shakes his head in dismay; he can see clearly that these are human remains strewn unceremoniously across the track. Bailey looks across the skyline, still prepared for an ambush, but he sees nothing. Again he glances at what appears to be bodies in front of him, he then sees in horrific detail the slashed and dismembered corpses of four young women, all naked, their bodies cruelly ripped asunder with limbs hacked off or broken. Some of the girls' heads are swollen over twice their normal size by being repeatedly beaten while life remained in their poor broken bodies.

Bailey moves closer in the vain hope that perhaps one soul may remain alive in this carnage, then his eyes become witness to an ultimate atrocity. Even the experienced Bailey puts his hands to his eyes as the scene before him becomes tragically familiar with memories of his homeland. What is greeting the two kinsmen is a sacrilege so profoundly evil to have been practiced on these young women. Each of them had been violently opened from their womanhood to their upper-gut, their entrails pulled out and wound tightly round their necks like butchers offal. Their breasts have been brutally skinned and removed, revealing wretched bloody holes and bleach-white ribs, all of this defiling the very being of these victims of sheer atrocity.

William turns once more to look at the scene before him. The realisation shocks him to the core of his senses as he begins to truly understand the actions enacted upon the living bodies of these women. Losing all the strength in his legs, William collapses to the ground amidst the gory bloody detail. He mumbles incoherently, his voice almost a croak…

"I… I know these girls…" He continues in a trembling voice, "They're my friends from the Marchals' camp. We were all together in Lanark but two days ago. I can still see their smiling faces and I…" Bailey hauls William roughly to his feet. "For fucks sake man, bring your wits together, if the perpetrators of this evil are still in the vicinity of this here glen, I need you to be of a mind and prepared that we too do not fall to such barbarity." Bailey catches the reigns of both horses and thrusts William his leathers. Bailey continues to scan the track leading up towards the plateau while William stares intensely at the carnage before him. It's horrifically surreal for him to even try and rationalise the scene and connect it to his young friends.

With his senses reeling, William remains totally transfixed by the scene, he stammers, "She's not here…" Bailey enquires, "Who isn't here?" William replies, "Affric… my friend's sister… You know, Coinach, the wee fella we're supposed to meet." William raises his head to look in the same direction as Bailey. Both focus their attention on the inner track route and rocky slopes that lead to Marchals' camp.

"The shielin's…" Exclaims William. "Whoever did this might still be up there." Bailey replies, "No, I don't think so. Those top covering horse tracks are leading away from here, they're not going toward Marchals' camp." William enquires, "What should we do for the girls?" Bailey replies, "Nothing, not yet anyway. We mount our horses and ride on toward Marchals' camp. I just need you to keep a keen eye open for anything that moves or catches your wits attention, whoever did this may have left marauders behind to catch the unwary."

Cautiously, they make their way up the track till they arrive at what appears to be the outer entrance to the Marchals' shielin'. Bailey whispers. "Dismount, real slow, and keep your wits on edge." Moving forward, they hold their horses firmly to the outside of their bodies, affording some protection from any possible arrow or missile strike. They keep this protective shield flanking them till they are certain there will be no attack. Eventually they stand before an overgrown thicket of hawthorn and a willow coppice, indicating the entrance to Marchals' encampment is nearby. Bailey whispers, "Tie the horses under that Rowan and then nock an arrow tight... and keep your fuckin' bow string taught." He pauses while examining the terrain. "We should tread careful on our approach, there's something still not right up ahead of us, and we need to be ready for anything."

Bailey cocks his crossbow as they move towards what resembles a Ceàrdannan winter encampment. As they look through the thick coppice woods surrounding Marchals' camp, the scene is obscure and sinister in the stillness of the atmosphere. Then, much to their dismay, they begin to recognise the forms of many bodies hanging by the neck from tree boughs, with entrails spilling to the ground from opened stomachs. As they gain closer, they can see the guts are ice-locked to the ground, causing a macabre motion and turn on the bodies as they gently sway to and fro in the hillside breeze. The same breeze that now wafts an aroma of scented smoke down towards them.

Curiously, the scent reminds William of sweet bacon being grilled on a morning fire. Shaking his head to regain some sense of focus, William walks parallel with Bailey as they move closer towards the centre of the camp, they can see over the last high thicket perimeter that bow-wagons are still smouldering, some have been toppled over and wrecked. Most of the large Obhainn's had been burnt to the ground leaving a bizarre impression of charred willow and hazel stalks sticking up from the earth, like the burnt ribs from some fantastical creature. They see chairs; cribs and chattel are sitting all around the place, as though it is a drunkard's summer camp amidst the detritus of war. William becomes aware of crackling, hissing, spitting noises coming from a large central campfire; it's then they both see the source of the sweet smoke aroma. A large blazing fire hisses and spits from fat dripping onto the seat of the fire from bodies that have been unceremoniously heaped in layers upon it, like an enormous slaughterhouse pyre. It appears as though the hellish fire has been burning all night, kept lit solely by the fat from the bodies of the unfortunate victims of this atrocity.

William is transfixed by the horror of the carnage he sees before him. Bodies and human remains, or what he could make of them, are all blackened at the extremities. Body parts are strewn around the outside firestones like burnt twigs, intermingling with brain matter that has swollen and burst outwards from their victims' skulls from the intense heat. Stomachs had expanded and exploded, throwing entrails around the outside of the pyre, gluing most of the remains together in one bloody hellish mass.

Uncontrollable nauseating convulsions wrack William's body then he begins to retch violently. What he is witnessing is beyond the reason of normal men. Bailey knows what it is; he's no stranger to the sight of the butchery and killing of women and children in this manner, for a similar evil had been exercised upon his own family in Wales many years before. Bailey looks at William and sees that he is struggling to bring his senses under control as a witness to these ghastly inhuman scenes that lay out before the two kinsmen. The stench of burning bodies' cause William to retch till nothing remains in his stomach… Eventually he collapses to the ground, but still the painful retching continues, forcing him to curl up as a foetus to alleviate the pain. He turns over and lies on his back to lay prostate in the snow, weak and in a cold sweat, losing all sense of time as though in a drunken stupor.

Serenely he watches the soft white-grey clouds in the darkening sky and the continual circling of the hooded crow, kite and raven. He ponders over the timeless call of these winged scavengers. Soon, their cackling cries sharpen his senses as though calling for him to regain control of his emotions. Bailey is kneeling close by William's side, keeping a vigilant surveillance on the camp and surrounding area. He also knows what is going through William's thoughts, and why the scene is draining his young charge of strength and reason.

In a soft but comforting voice, Bailey speaks... "C'mon Wallace, I need you to be getting on your feet, there may be some still alive or in hiding that may need our help." William sits up, but still feels very faint. He looks away from the pyre, but everywhere his eyes meet with another atrocity, sights he could never have imagined lay before him... Dismembered bodies of men and women, disembowelled and decapitated. Bodies of teenage girls tied together by their arms, back to back. He doesn't understand as he scrutinises their dead lifeless forms, most with their hair burned off and throats violently cut, with breasts, hands and feet cut off and piled unceremoniously beside their lifeless bodies, all frozen together grotesquely. He winces upon seeing that their legs are opened wide and what appears to be the tips of wagon wheel spars sticking out from their lower parts.

Slumping his head between his knees William begins sobbing, he cannot fight against this confusion and utter horror as he sheds compassionate tears; then he begins to feel rage well up inside. Many of these people he had known, he had laughed with them, shared food with them. He can't understand why these gentle woodland people could warrant such a horrific defilement and destruction.

Meanwhile, Bailey is still observing the surrounding area in great detail when he notices someone in the distance sitting upright with his back towards them, near a frozen natural fresh-water spring, now coloured a black-bloody crimson.

Bailey looks at William and points toward the seated man rocking backwards and forwards with what appears to be a naked child in his arms. Bailey nudges William firmly but he can see that William is still traumatised by the scenes before him. Through the mist of anguish, William pulls himself upright. Wiping the tears from his face he is distracted by the source of the dogfight noises; he looks up and sees in the distance winter wolves, feral snow dogs and camp dogs fighting each other, competing mercilessly to tear the most succulent meat from the legs and lower stomachs of the corpses hanging from the trees.

Bailey nudges William forcefully, this time gaining his full attention. He points in the direction to where the man is still rocking back and forth. William feels some sense of wit return when he peers over at the man. He whispers to Bailey… "I think that's Coinach… but ah can't be sure…"

They cautiously approach the sobbing man, then suddenly, without warning, the figure spins around with sword in hand and lunges directly at the men he knew were approaching him. The wild man is between William and Bailey in a mere second. Bailey only just misses getting his skull split by the downward stroke of the sword. He quickly grabs the assailant's sword arm as it passes his face while William launches himself at the other side of the man, grabbing his other arm, then the two kinsmen fall on top of the flailing wild man. William rages, "Coinach it's me… William Wallace,"

"Stop him struggling," screams Bailey as he wrestles the sword from Coinach's grip. But William's maniacal friend fights like a trapped wildcat, resisting with the strength of ten men in his utter madness. William shouts again at the top of his voice. *"COINACH,* STOP…*it's ME… Wallace…"* Both William and Bailey struggle to hold Coinach down with their combined weight and strength. Eventually they manage to pin Coinach face down in the freezing bloody ground, yet his violent struggle is taking all their combined strength to subdue him. The deranged Coinach keeps resisting and fighting against the overpowering restraint placed upon him, until the presence of madness begins to fade from Coinach's blood red eyes. William speaks forcefully to his friend. "Now Coinach… if we let yie go… will yie stop fuckin' fighting us?"

"Wallace, is it really you?" gasps Coinach while attempting to lift his face away from the bloody snow, desperately trying to breath while spitting dirt and slush from his mouth. "Aye it's me," replies William, he continues. "Coinach, will yie calm down for fucks sake and tell us what th' fuck has happened here?"

The two friends ease their pressure on Coinach, enough for him to sit up and breath. He begins shivering and points to a lifeless looking body covered with a wolf skin. He says, "That's Affric is over yonder Wallace, she's still alive… the bastards have raped her… They've beat her near to death and left her naked bloodied body staked out for the dogs to finish off, but… but I managed to free her and keep her warm…" Coinach gasp's, "Affric's head is so swollen… she's almost beyond recognition, but she's still alive, she must be… Wallace, yie must help her. I had to leave her when I heard a wee wain crying." Bailey shakes his head forlorn, he's cradling the child Coinach had been caring for, but the child is long dead. His focus is shaken when Coinach wails, "Affric…"

William immediately runs over to where Affric's body lay in the snow while Bailey helps Coinach to get back on his feet. Coinach begins weeping; then he looks at Bailey and cries out. "They raped all the women and girls Bailey, the… the bastards stuck their swords, daggers and anything else they could find in…" "Whoa, Coinach," says Bailey. "Wait till we get you somewhere sheltered and get you warmed up."

Coinach wails, "But Bailey... my family..." Bailey deliberately cuts through Coinach's nightmare. "Do you know who it was that has perpetrated this evil?" Coinach sobs, "I don't know... I don't fuckin' know, how could I..." Bailey holds the wiry framed Coinach close. "Take it easy Coinach, we'll sort this out when our wits are cold for thought and not hot for vengeance." Coinach pushes Bailey away, but his body is weak and wracked by the freezing cold, his brain is driven to near madness by his witness to the massacre of his people.

Coinach stands erect; then suddenly he collapses forward. Bailey quickly reaches out and catches him then carries him over to where William is cradling his woodland lover. He says anxiously, "It's Affric, she's still alive, but she's unconscious." William sees that Bailey is supporting Coinach in his arms. Bailey says, "Coinach has passed out. I'll take him to a bow-wagon I saw earlier that looks like we could use for shelter."

William and Bailey carry Affric and Coinach over to the bow-wagon and bed them in the shelter of the wagon-well. They cover them both with thick layers of brats, furs and hides to keep them warm, then they hastily cover the top-ribs of the wagon with heavy sheets of flax hemp and cotton. They light fires in small cooking urns' filled with pitch oil, then place them inside the wagon to provide a little warmth.

Climbing out of the wagon, William and Bailey close the greased hemp sheet behind them. With dusk falling, William and Bailey think it best to remain in the basic shelter of the sheilin' that night and leave by first light of the morn.

For the rest of the short day, William and Bailey collect all the bodies and remains they can find of Marchals' ua Bruans' clan and place them on the fire for cremation, the ground is frozen and impossible to break the earth surface for burial. The two companions continue their search in the hope of finding any survivors of Marchals' clan, when William suddenly calls out… "I've found the body of the Marchal…" Bailey rushes over to see what has been a particularly savage murder. William cries, "They've fuckin' crucified auld Marchal to the back of a wagon… and the auld Chief is full of his own arrows. Fuck, his ears, lips and eyelids have been cut from him while he must have been still alive."

William puts his hand to his mouth when he realises Marchals' manhood has been ripped from his groin by dogs. He looks at the mortal remains of his old friend and forest mentor, he can see Marchal's throat has been slit under his jaw with his tongue pulled down to hang out and is now stuck to his chest. Bailey touches William on the shoulder, startling him. He points to just behind the wagon. It takes mere seconds for William to make sense of what he's looking at, perhaps this is the worst scene of all when he sees the woodland chief's beloved children… All are naked, and it's painfully obvious that most have been violated. Others have had their flesh torn from their small bodies by scavenging hogs and dogs. William and Bailey stand, silently staring at the barbarous result of minds that know no limit to heinous and sadistic cruelty.

"Bailey," says William, "I cannot believe what I see before me is real. It seems too fuckin' much for all that I have witnessed this day to be true. I cannot think that I'm even awake, for I've no fuckin' feeling anymore, or I cannot let feeling exist. I fear if I let my heart raise any compassion for a fleeting moment, I'll go ravin' fuckin' mad. I must be a base cold-hearted villain no better than the perpetrators if I feel nothing. If this is a nightmare Bailey, then my heart is black and I can't live with this evil inside of me." Bailey shakes his head, "I understand William, I truly I do. But this is not of your nightmares. I've seen this butchery before. If you fall to this madness, then our kinfolk who depend on you to protect them… then who will they have to come to their aid? That's why you feel so cold hearted. Believe me when I say this to you, we are lost if we allow our hearts to bleed to this reality. Men like us who witness these atrocities must use our given gifts to prevent it happening to others. I'll ask you again Wallace, who else will protect our kinfolk if we don't temper any thoughts of emotional recklessness to what we see… for if we don't then we're all truly fucked." Something in his kinsman's words rings true, William knows he must remain stoic as he thinks about Bailey's reasoning, but still he has his doubts about having a black heart. Bailey puts his hand on William's shoulder. "C'mon, we should be setting to task and see if any other has survived while we continue with our duty to the dead." William nods in agreement as they go about their gruesome task of caring for the dead.

The early winter eve darkness somewhat veils the scenes of utter destruction in Marchal ua Bruan's camp for William and Bailey. They have all but finished searching for survivors when they hear a bizarre howling coming from the direction of the bow-wagon, followed by an eerie silence. Suddenly a female voice shrieks out a name, startling both of them. The shrieking voice continues to echo round the hills, then suddenly ceases. Mere seconds pass by when the scream is followed by another bloodcurdling howl. This unnerving call of human nature William has only ever heard once before, when the mate of forlorn wolf bitch mournfully calls to a faraway mate whose litter has been killed by hunters.

Bailey enquires, "What the fuck is that?"

"It's Affric…" exclaims William. They both jump up and run through the snow as fast as they can towards the bow-wagon, where Affric howls so hauntingly that it sends waves of chilling fear through both William and Bailey, for a caring man's worst fear is to hear the sound of a woman's primal wail to the Gods upon the death of her children. Affric howls again as William and Bailey look inside the wagon where they see her sitting bolt upright. She begins screaming and fighting off the pelts and brats that seem to trap her. William reaches out toward her, trying to calm her down as she begins her primeval howl once more. Both William and Bailey want so much to close their ears to block out this deathly wailing of a woman demented, but they have to pacify her.

As they both climb into the wagon, Bailey slips and regains his foothold when he notices that Coinach is beginning to stir. William tries to cradle Affric who is screaming and flailing her arms and legs wildly, as if she is fighting invisible demons. He tries in vain to pacify her, but she punches and scratches him as he tries to calm her down, suddenly, Affric goes quiet and limp, without warning, she screams and sinks her teeth into William's neck, ripping and tearing at his throat and drawing blood. It takes all of his strength to close her down by wrapping her in a large brat... now he has no other choice but to pin her against the backboard.

Affric calms slightly, allowing William to pull away the brat, where he now sees that she has been badly beaten about the face and has many broken bones about her body. Her eyes are swollen and closed shut, locked behind a mass of bloody skin and blood-matted hair.

Suddenly, Coinach springs up at William in Affric's defence... he swings his fist blindly with all his might and catches William square on the bridge of his nose, splitting the skin, and breaking the bone while knocking William forward into the wagon. Bailey quickly reaches into the wagon and grabs Coinach by the shoulders and wrenches him back from William with so much of a force, both he and Coinach fall out the back of the wagon and land several feet away on the frozen snow covered ground. Bailey immediately rolls over on top of Coinach, using all his formidable strength to pin him to the ground once more.

Spitting blood and reeling from the searing pain of a broken nose, William, shouts out. "Fucks sake Bailey, hold him down till I sort out Affric in here will yie? Jaezuz Fuck… he's broken my fuckin' nose." Pulling himself up off the floor of the wagon, William can barely see for the blood and tears in his eyes caused by the impact of Coinach's fist. Bailey struggles with Coinach till he finally grips and locks him tight in a wrestling grapple by wrapping his legs round him and putting a choke hold around his neck… Bailey shouts desperately into the ear of Coinach while forcefully choking him into a semi-conscious state. "For Fucks sake Coinach, it's me, Bailey… fuckin' calm down or I'll choke you till I knock you out."

"Jaezuz fuckin' Christ," curses William as he clambers out the back of the wagon holding his broken bleeding nose. "Is Coinach alright Bailey?" Coinach gags as Bailey eases his grip, just enough to let him breath. Coinach screams in a muffled gargling voice from behind Bailey's iron grip. "Aye Wallace, am all fuckin' right." Coinach struggles violently to be released. He screams, "For fuck's sake Bailey, just ease up the pressure on me fuckin' throat." Bailey growls, "Do you know who is with you, Coinach?" "It's William and Bailey…" screams the spluttering, voice in reply.

"William and Bailey who?" demands Bailey. "William and Bailey fuckin' Wallace," replies Coinach. Bailey will not ease his grip, except that which stops short of knocking Coinach unconscious. He speaks determinedly into Coinach's ear.

"Now Coinach, I want you to listen to me very fucking carefully. I'm going to loosen my grip, but if you start struggling again, I'll knock you out good and proper boyo.

And when you come back to your senses, I'll knock you out again, and I'll keep doing this till you stop fighting us. DO YOU UNDER-FUCKING-STAND ME, COINACH UA BRUAN?" Coinach snarls, "AYE…" Bailey slowly releases the pressure on Coinach's throat while William watches closely as he nurses his bruised and battered face. As Bailey releases more pressure, just enough, Coinach suddenly springs free from Bailey's grip and rolls away a short distance in the snow, where he turns over onto all fours as a ravenous fighting pit dog, ready to savage any opponent. He glares wildly with such a venom and hatred in his heart that William has never seen before in any man. Bailey sternly enquires, "What's happened here, who has done this to your people?" Coinach simply glares at William and Bailey as they observe their friend who has the appearance of a fiendish mountain spectre.

For a long time, the three men just stare at each other.

Eventually, William speaks, though he's still angry with Coinach for the painful blow that has broken his nose. "Ach fuck this, Coinach, I'm going to tend yer sister. You watch ma back Bailey, make sure this fuckin' madman doesn't attack me again."

"I wont attack you," replies a lonely pathetic voice. Coinach sits in the snow and darkness a short distance away where the flames of the fire light the wretched features on his face. The madness in the eyes of Coinach has now gone from him, like an exorcism has cleared a murderous demonic spirit from his soul. Coinach slowly stands up. It's clear that he has all but lost his mind, but a sombre reality begins to appear in his demeanour. His long black curly hair, now a blood-clotted tangled mess, hangs like evil greasy rats tails about his face and shoulders. His eyelids are puffed and swollen from tears shed and a face spotted with dry specks of blood. His clothes are dishevelled, torn, filthy and wet. Coinach's weakened body shakes from both the extreme cold and shock overtaking his system. "Are yie back with us?" enquires William from the back of the wagon.

"I am," replies Coinach as he takes two steps forward, suddenly he drops to the ground from exhaustion. Bailey rushes over to Coinach, lifts and carries him over to the fireside, where rests him on a thick layer of deerskin and covers him with wolf pelts. Bailey speaks to William quietly. "I'll make a bed of hot fireside stones and wrap him tight here next the fire, but lets just keep them both apart for the moment. If either wakes from whatever hellish nightmare they are in, it'll be easier for us and them if we don't have to deal with them as before." William readily agrees. He lifts some hot firestones then climbs into the wagon to make sure Affric is covered and warm. He is much relieved that sleep has taken her, now he can safely examine her battered and bruised body. He reaches out and gently strokes her matted hair… "Ma poor wee Affric, how could someone do this too you and yours, ma bonnie wee woodland Aicé."

William feels tears well up from deep inside his heart. He pulls his brat tightly about him to keep out the freezing chill, but he can't stop his tears from flowing, causing him to hide away in the darkest bowels of the wagon.

A little while later, and regaining his composure, William calls out to Bailey… "Heat some more water in a wee cauldron for me will yie Bailey, I'll try and wash some of this blood away from Affric's face." Bailey calls out, "I'll do that; then I reckon we will have to examine them both thoroughly to see what injuries they've befallen."

Soon, the darkness of a long winters night completely envelops the entirety of the camp as snowflakes begin to swirl and fall heavily. Bailey walks up to the back of the bow-wagon and peers inside. He speaks in a low voice, "I'll salvage some more materials from this wreckage and try and build a warm shelter for us, but first we'd better bring all the horses up to the camp and get them grubbed, watered and fix them some kind of shelter too, if we lose our fuckin' horses, we will lose our lives out here too.

Throughout the cold night, William and Bailey search and gather more remains; then haul them to Marchal ua Bruan's clan funeral pyre. The grim task in the freezing temperature is taking its toll on both of them, but they work fastidiously till they can no longer function with any degree of strength or senses.

During the freezing moonless night, snow continues to fall relentlessly over the small glen in the Corserine while William and Bailey take turns looking after the welfare of Affric and Coinach. Thankfully both their Ceàrdannan friends are sleeping, though Coinach remains restless and screams sporadically. Affric makes no sound other than an occasional low sob that seems to come from deep within her soul, as though something in her spirit fights and clings desperately to life. Bailey builds a makeshift shelter and fire; then heats up more firestones. He has also found food for them to eat. He boils some water and cooks some fish and oats. William ensures Affric will be as warm and comfortable as can be. Exhausted, he makes his way back to where Bailey is sitting beside the fire.

Both of them sit for hours staring at the dancing flames and glowing embers, thinking of what they had witnessed in the Corserine. William says, "Bailey, I cannae tell you what is in my mind right now, nor what I'm thinking. Fuck, never have I nor could I have imagined to be seeing what I have seen this day. I feel I should be curled up in a corner crying like a wain or on my knees praying to any feckin deity for an explanation or reason for this. Or even hoping maybe that I may wake up and this has been but a hellish fuckin' nightmare." Bailey is mesmerised too by the fire that warms their chilled bones. He appears to speak, then he pauses a moment, as though he is in deep thought… then he says, "I've seen these sights before, and I felt then as you do now. So much senseless carnage having cruelly been visited upon so many innocent people, and for what purpose… I will never ever understand. I've seen too my own kin horrifically reduced to bit parts of scattered meat left as rotting food for the carrion beast, it just overwhelms your mind, just like poor Coinach there, you'll lose your mind awhile, or you be as we are now, bereft of feeling, yet so full of unanswered knowing. For whatever reason, if that be the right word, we are chosen to be witness."

"I, ah just don't fuckin' know," stammers William, "This, this is…" but he is lost for words. Bailey says, "We must keep our heads clear for the benefit of others."

William simply nods in understanding as Bailey continues. "I don't know why it is so, but for our own wits sake, we must remain so callously detached that most who would meet us at this moment in time, would render to all that we have no souls." William again nods his head in agreement, he says, "I don't know how I should be feeling Bailey, would it be I had just found Affric and no other, then I do know that I would be in deep mourning and in such a state as Coinach. But for so many people to die like this, I cant…? It's like my mind has casually accepted it or too easily my mind has shut it out. But I tell yie, in my heart, the latter is not true, for I see it all before me as though the night veil has never closed the scene away from my eyes. Aye, I could feel, but something in me chooses to be cold and heartless as my response shows, yet I know I am not heartless, I know I have feelings deep inside of me, but where are they?" William demands an answer from Bailey with a note of panic in his voice. "What the fuck is wrong with me Bailey?" Shrugging his shoulders underneath his heavy brats, Bailey replies, "What you've seen affects people differently, be it war, butchery or walking into a slaughterhouse as we have done this day. There's nothing you can say to me about how your heart being so cold that is any different from how I feel right now."

William replies, "Fuck Bailey, I don't know how I really feel." Bailey pulls his focus away from the tantalizing flames and looks at his charge. He's shocked at what he sees. William's demeanour in the low light of the firelight appears wretched and awful. Bailey rubs his eyes and looks again, yet still his young charge appears as an aged and withered old man, his face bloodied, grey and drawn in. The anguish and pain is displayed all over his young face.

Bailey thinks William looks worse than any winter beggar he has ever seen. But he has seen this instant characteristic and familiar change in many a man, in his own reflection once upon a time. He speaks softly to his young kinsman…"Here William, pack some snow in your hand and press it tight to your face, for it's a bloody mess where Coinach belted you."

Gazing at the fire William says, "I've no care for myself and I feel nothing Bailey." He wraps himself tightly with his great brat, pulling it over his head till only a slit is open to the dark outside world through which he observes like a reclusive hermit. He feels safe hiding away in his brat, with only the tiny thin space to see through. In this sanctuary, William thinks long and hard on what he has seen and experienced this day while he continues staring intently into the flames of the fire. In the distance he hears Bailey speak quietly… "About ten years ago, I too hunted the land of my homeland with my fathers as you do now. I don't know if you've heard of Edward Longshanks the King of England and about the English armies that swept through Cymru."

William shakes his head. "Naw, what about them?" Bailey continues, "The English murdered my people by the same method you and I have both witnessed here this day."

Shocked on hearing Bailey's words, William pulls back his brat and looks at Bailey, who still appears mesmerised by the fire as he continues... "That was only the start of it, for the English King embarked upon a plan to conquer Cymru by leading an army into our lands nigh on ten years ago. His first invasion proceeded along the North Wales coast to capture our true blood Prince of Wales, Llewellyn ap Gruffydd. Even though our Prince was the husband of Edward's niece Eleanor, Longshanks eventually caught up with Llewellyn and forced our Prince to do battle. Outnumbered five to one, the Cymrans fought the English valiantly, but we were forced to retreat and became trapped at a place called Aberconwy. After fierce fighting, Llewellyn eventually surrendered to the English King." William enquires. "Why did the Longshanks invade Cymru?"

Bailey looks into the fire. "I don't really know, some say Longshanks needed the bowyers of Cymru for his army and our resources to pay back debts he incurred in other wars. Others say he wanted our land for England's expanding Baronial class. He definitely needed our resources, for he takes them freely as his own to this day, leaving my land a barren wasteland devoid of native life. And do you know this William, could you ever guess what we people of Cymru got in return for his bringing of civilisation?" William looks at Bailey and shrugs his shoulders. Bailey continues, "Death, torture and virtual annihilation, even that of our women and children." He pauses and picks up a piece of wood and pokes at the embers of the fire. William enquires, "But what of your army and your King or Prince?" Poking at the fire awhile longer, Bailey appears lost to his memories. Eventually he replies, "Llewellyn's younger brother Dafydd, he rose up against the English while his brother was still held captive, when Longshanks marched another army into Cymru, then Llewellyn escaped imprisonment to rejoin the fight. Both royal brothers raised an army then stormed the English garrison castles of Builth, Aberystwyth and Ruthin, and we soundly defeated the English army on the Menai Straights up in Gwynedd. But William boyo, there were just too many Norman planters in Cymru by then. Finally Llewellyn was betrayed and killed at the Battle of the Iron Bridge, crushing any further hopes of our freedom."

Staring at the fire, William exclaims, "Fuck me, betrayed by your own people? Naw Bailey, that couldn't happen here… could it?" Bailey continues, "That fucker Longshanks had Llewellyn's head severed from his body then sent to London and stuck on a pole. Prince Dafydd tried to fight on, he led the Cymrans from the mountains, but he too was betrayed by one of our own and handed over to the English King."

William sits a moment, contemplating Bailey's story and thinking of betrayal. "Fuckin' betrayed again?" William groans. "I could never see any of the people I know who would stoop to betrayal." Then he enquires, "So what happened to Prince Dafydd?" Shaking his head, Bailey says, "He was tortured by the English then dragged through the streets of London by horses, after that they half-hung him. While he was choking on the rope, the bastards cut his balls and prick off then they threw them on a brazier in front of him. Next they cut a small hole in his stomach and slowly pulled out his guts and roasted them on the same brazier as the light of life still flickered in his eyes. They finally finished him when they sawed his head off with a blunted butchers blade and put it on a stake beside his brother's head on some place called London Bridge, supposedly as a warning to all Welsh people never to resist the English." William pulls his brat tight. "Fuckin' treacherous bastards. I'd rather die in battle than be betrayed and hung like a base creature for the pleasure of some cunt called Longshanks." He continues, "I'm just glad that couldn't happen here." Bailey shakes his head, "I sure hope not boyo."

They sit awhile longer in silence, then William enquires curiously, "So what did you do during the war?" Bailey smiles, "I practiced the art of killing English with the longbow, knife, stone, rock, rope and poison boyo, and any other fucking thing I could get my hands on to kill the bastards." William smiles weakly, "Naw, I don't reckon I could kill a man."

"You will kill men," says Bailey. "And you had better be good at it too, for what's happened here this day may fall upon you and yours unless you prove to be more evil by intent upon those who would perpetrate such a slaughter as this. Believe me, if this is the start of things to come in Scotland, and if you don't prepare, this evil will most certainly be visited upon you and yours a hundredfold unless you're ready to kill to protect your own?"

"I would if I had to I reckon" says William. "But only if my enemy could not be persuaded otherwise from this savagery. Surely this couldn't happen to a civilized people such as we are?" Sighing, Bailey replies, "My family were civilised…"

"What do you mean by that? Don't they miss you?"

"No," says Bailey. "They've greeted Coinach's family in a greater place than this." Bailey pokes the fire and appears to laugh. "It would seem to me that Coinach and I are now brothers in grief, for what has happened here this day was visited upon my own family by the English soldiery nigh on ten years ago." William exclaims, "This happened to you?" Bailey doesn't reply, he remains gazing thoughtfully at the fire, William is about to ask another question when he notices a tear running down Bailey's cheek. He is surprised and wants to say something, but he can't find the words, this private moment must be for Bailey alone. William ponders over Bailey's advice about killing men, but the thought of taking a soul from this life is something that isn't in his heart. He'd watched animals die slowly, seeing the blue mist converging in their eyes, sometimes that was upsetting enough, but taking the life of another man? He looks into the fire, then closes his eyes for a moment...

Waking up with a start, William can't think where he is. He lifts the great weight of his heavy brat hood from his head and quickly glances around to gain a sense of his location. He observes a scene of extreme winter beauty; the ground, bushes and trees are all covered in the most wonderful thick blanket of snow. He sees fresh rainbow reflecting icicles hanging from bough branches like a magical host of sparkling prism spears from nature's Fae armoury. William looks around and wonders if he's been dreaming, then he remembers his conversation with Bailey and realises where he is and what's happened... Instantly he jumps up, but his body is cold, stiff and aching. The sudden movement causes a wracking pain to course through his body. Then he feels an awful deep aching pain in his face. He turns quickly to get his bearings and sees behind him what looks to be a little old destitute man wrapped up and covered in snow, like a grotesque frozen woodland imp.

"You awake?" calls out a voice nearby. William looks closely at the form beside him; then he looks around to see Bailey fixing the last harness to the only remaining bow-wagon still functioning. He calls out to Bailey. "What's happening?" Bailey replies, "You fell asleep as dawn broke, so I've made us ready to travel for when you woke. I've sorted out Affric and Coinach, but we'd better get moving, we cannot be staying out here or Affric will surely die." Standing in the deep snow and shivering with the extreme cold, William solemnly thinks, *'So it wasn't a bad dream. I'm awake, and I'm still here.'* He looks up to find the ancient grotesque imp is staring at him, then he realises its Coinach. He enquires, "You all right?"

Coinach makes no reply, instead, he turns and stares toward the funeral pyre, for within it's ugly smoking remains, smoulder the bodies of his mother, father, brothers, sisters and all of his family, the good folk and children of his clan, including Affric's children...

Bailey calls over to William. "Help me Wallace, we have to get Coinach and Affric away from here, another night out here will kill them or maybe kill us all if the weather turns against us." William looks again at Coinach, but there is no sign of life save his breathing and his fixation upon the pyre. William walks over to Bailey. "What can I do?" Bailey replies. "I've Affric covered up warm and safe and I've packed some hot firestones inside her mantles. We just need to get Coinach onto the wagon and we can drive the horse and wagon out of here before we get trapped by another snowfall." William enquires, "How's Affric?" Bailey replies, "She's in a bad way. I checked her body this morning. It looks as if she has a broken leg, arm and some broke ribs, one of which is sticking through her skin. She's stopped bleeding though, and I've tied a whittle in her mouth to stop her from choking to death, I had to for her face is so swollen it's the only thing that will keep her breathing."

Feeling somewhat relieved, William says, "We should go back to Glen Afton and get Affric proper help there." Bailey agrees, "Lets get moving, Mharaidh and Jean may yet save poor Affric, but I don't know about Coinachs wits, he'll live, but I think his mind's gone..."

"It's not gone," comes a voice from behind them. Coinach

has silently staggered through the snow to be with his friends. "Just be helpin' me into the back o' the wagon and I'll be causin' yiez no more trouble." Bailey and William gather their friend up and lift him gently into the back of the wagon to rest him between a pillowed nest of hot firestones then they cover him with pelts brats and plaid to keep him warm beside his sister. William tethers their horses to the back of the wagon then they leave the Corserine behind. A place that was once a haven of nature in the wilderness and home to an honest loving clan, the Ceàrdannan summer walkers of Marchal ua Bruan, good and kind people who had loved nature, peace and bringing of happiness to all, now they are but a tragic memory gone to a better place.

***

Thirty miles southwest of the Corserine gap, Alain stands at the camp of the Silver Flowe with his men, embedded and committed into service within the ranks of the western Guardian army. He's torn between thoughts of war and where William could be. *'Is he safe? Would he be coming back alive?'* His thoughts are broken when he hears a warning from a guard. "Riders fast approach from the south." Heralds blow their clarion calls as Leckie calls out. "Rouse the men."

Gallóglaigh hunter-scouts ride into the camp and make fast to where Alain, Wishart, Leckie and Sir Bryce Blair are gathered. The lead scout quickly dismounts and immediately reports to Wishart. "De Brix has Pact forces laying siege to Dumfries Castle as we speak."

"This is grave news," says Wishart. "When Comyn hears of this, he will bring all his forces to the field for war. Where is the Northern Guardian army?"

The scout replies, "Earl Duncan and Lord Moray of the Northern Guardian army has sent a relief force to lift the siege." Bryce enquires, "What other news do you bring us, do you know where we must deploy our army?" The breathless scout replies, "We've found the main camp of de Brixs' Pact on the plains near Saint John's of Dalry. He has a few hundred cavalry camped nearby at Monadh-abh (Money-Ive). The Lords Douglas, Moray and Graham are holding Brix in a standoff with the main force of the Pact. De Brix makes gesture to parlay, but the Lords believe that he only plays for time while waiting on allies coming from England."

Wishart says, "We must combine the main bodies of the Guardian armies to stop de Brix on the plains of Dalry, or get between him and his southern allies before he can move his main force deeper into Galloway. If the Southern Guardians stall his English allies, we may force Brix and avert war." The scout continues, "Brix cannot move his forces south as there's a force of five hundred Capetians' landing at Baile na h-Uige to support Balliol. There's another larger force of three thousand Gallóbhet under the command of the MacDowell, MacDhuibhshíthe and near five thousand Gallóbhet with the MacDougal Chiefs waiting to greet them, then they'll come north to join us against de Brix."

Leckie mòr speaks, "This is good news then, de Brixs' Pact will not have enough men to both siege and fight a campaign with such formidable forces ranged against them, even with his English and Irish confederates should they make it through." The lead scout speaks, "Lord Duncan believes that de Brix may still be considering a confrontation with the Guardian army on the plains of Saint John's before this army or the Gallóbhet and Capetians can join forces with them on the plains." Wishart exclaims, "This misjudgement by de Brix could be to our vantage. He cannot yet be aware the western Guardian army is but a few hours from Dalry, or he may even believe that his attack on Dumfries will split and weaken our forces." The lead scout continues, "The Lords Duncan and Moray urgently require your presence at Dalry with utmost haste." The Western Guardian army commanders immediately give commands and orders to break camp while the Lords continue to discuss the urgency of affairs threatening to tear the realm apart. Alain looks toward the Corserine and Rhinns o' Kells ridges in the hope of seeing his son somewhere on the horizon.

As the Western army decamps, the Knights, cavalry and troops begin to march south towards Dalry. Leckie approaches Alain, sensing angst, he says, "Young William will be fine, have no worries about him old friend, to have both you and I as his mentors and a lifetime with Wishart and Malcolm…" Alain turns and looks at his old friend. "I hope so."

"Come Alain," says Leckie. "Bailey will look after him, it's time for us to leave here, for we must make haste to Dalry. If Brix is not stopped there, then all of our families will be at risk." Alain reluctantly walks with Leckie towards their horses. He knows they have a dangerous task ahead of them, but he's distracted by thoughts about William's whereabouts. He needs to know that he is safe. He thinks it could be that William and Bailey have returned to Glen Afton for some reason. If he's done so, Alain knows he'll be safe there.

Aware of Alain's persistent reticence, Leckie says, "I understand young William is still to the fore in your mind Alain. But I know the boy well, he's stout o' heart, just like his father, he'll be fine, you'll see." Sighing, Alain replies, "It's a strange thing we set our minds to do this day." Leckie looks at Alain curiously as they mount their horses. He enquires, "And what's that?" Alain looks towards the Kells and Corserine ridges one last time in the hope of seeing his son returning. Then he gazes up at the beautiful blue morning sky to see the ravens fly overhead. After a few moments, he looks at Leckie, displaying an expression of a man torn between heaven and hell. He shakes his head slowly that of a man who has foreseen his own death. He utters, "Leckie old friend, what kind of world do we bring children into, that in order for us to maintain peace in this life, we must go to war with our own people?" Leckie replies, "Ah know Alain, I do so wish it were otherwise…"

Acknowledging Alain's thoughts, they both meander forward to join the remaining Guardian commanders waiting for them at the centre of the camp. As they prepare to follow the Western army south to confront de Brix and the Pact, outriders approach them at speed. "Here's the Comyn now," says Bryce. Wishart mutters, "I pray to God that Comyn will hold his hand upon this news of Dumfries and Cruggelton Castles still being under siege. But I fear for his response to the attack on his kinsman's castles. There is none who could fault him if he raises his war banner to this insult and attack on his family to such a degree."

They all stand solemnly and motionless, watching and waiting with trepidation as the Lord Comyn and his magnificent northern retinue thunder into the camp.

Pulling his steed to a halt beside them, Comyn dismounts and immediately throws down his gauntlet at their feet. Wishart speaks, "I take it you have heard the grave news my Lord Comyn?" Incandescent, Comyn states… "By the great men and women of Scotland who have ever sworn to defend this realm for their Aicé, the Maid Canmore, true heir to Scotlands ancient throne… I swear to you all by saint Margaret and by my blood oath to our late Artur Ard Rígh Alexander, this heinous Pact who does siege my kinfolk in Dumfries and Cruggelton Castles, and who does now bay like famishing shite-hounds howling for the blood of my kinswoman Devorguilla... I will slaughter them all. This treacherous bastard de Brix has came to this realm from foreign lands to spill my kinfolks' blood... for why? The old fuck has thrown down his gauntlet at the feet of my family. I swear that I do declare to you all present here this day here and now, by the divine mother of the Tuatha De Cruinnè-cè... I will have the head of de Brix on a steak and his scrawny fuckin' carcass fed to all my hunting dogs, I swear... my Lords, I solemnly do declare to all of you gathered here this day... Scotland is now in a state of civil war..."

Sicut res propriæ nostræ

l-Malik al-Ẓāhir Rukn al-Dīn Baibars al-Bun-duqdārī... Baibars, the prolific innovative Kipchac ruler of the Mamluk Sultanate of Egypt and Syria; Magnificent defender of Islam and brilliant commander of the united Muslim armies, he inflicted a crushing defeat on our seventh Crusade... not once, twice but three times. He'd also destroyed the Mongol armies and their Armenian Christian allies at the Battle of Harod spring...' Edward Plantagenet, King of England, smiles as he reminisces over Baibars the magnificent, a formidable enemy who had made a lifetime impression upon him in his formative years after Longshanks himself had attained the title, prince of Jerusalem and Acre. Baibars influence has remained with him more than any other man, except that of his father King Henry. He reflects on his many years' crusading with Louis IX of France against Baibars Caliphate and formidable Saracen armies. Much to his everlasting consternation, Edward found the Crusaders to be more than matched militarily by the strategic brilliance of the Islamic ruler, and much to his dismay, he had also discovered the Christian armies intellectually retarded in all the human sciences by comparison. A humiliating fact that still rankles him as a shocking contradiction.

The more Edward studies Baibars and Islam, the greater his understanding and respect for both becomes. Baibars, a man of astounding singular focus, amended Sharia law by introducing public torture and the brutal execution of any who turned away from the faith of Islam. Edward thinks, *'No different to Pope Gregory IX who established the feared Catholic Inquisition long before Baibars, for the same reason and purpose.'*

During his rule, Baibars had shown a much greater tolerance and respect for other faiths than the Catholic Popes Margraves and princes. He had graciously permitted differing and often conflicting Christian orders to establish enclaves in the Holy Land, emulating the religiously tolerant political strategy of the old Roman Empire. Edward ponders, *'The religious benevolence shown to other faiths demonstrated by Baibars 'WAS' different to that of Pope Gregory and the Catholic hierarchy, who by comparison, had shown absolutely no tolerance nor mercy for other faiths and set it's Catholic imperialistic ambitions and fundamentalist zeal of the Holy Roman Empire on a course of destroying anyone who did not adhere to Catholicism. Yet Baibars had offered other religions the freedom to worship as they please..."* Edward reflects on his youth as a nominal prince of Jerusalem and Acre when he accompanied Charles of Sicily to a treaty with Baibars, where the Crusaders and Templar's agreed to a ten year-truce with the Mamluk.

Edward smiles wryly, remembering how magnanimous and affectionate Baibars had been to him during the treaties of al Haliq Bahrain. He reflects upon the time Baibars presented him personally with an exquisite Thuluth script Qur'an. He smirks thinking about the deep contradictions and the complex character of this wise leader of Islam as he gazes across the tall towers of his Château de Plantagenet. He laughs remembering when leaving the treaty precinct of Baibars to quickly discover the shrewd Caliph had ordered the disciples of Hasan ibn al-Sabbâh, the feared Hashashûn (Assassin) to kill him. Edward shudders thinking of when he was seriously wounded in the assassination attempt, only fleeing the Holy land in disguise dressed as a woman had saved his life. But still he maintains an admiration for the ruthless and benevolent effectiveness of the Mamluk Sultan who had been such a guiding light and great influence in shaping Longshanks as a King.

Baibars has long since died and now it's time to arrange new treaties with Al-Ashraf Khalil Qalawūn the eighth Kipchac Sultan, and also to treaty with many other Persian and Balkan princes he has met during his Crusading sojourn as a young prince of Rome. These Islamic leaders have also grown to become rulers and are now strategically fraternising with the Northern Kings Alliance. Diplomatic negotiations are also advanced with Nokhai Khan, ruler of the Golden horde, Mahmud Ghazan ruler of the Il-khanate Mongolians, Stanislaus' and his Balkan Cumans' The red Jew Khazarian's, and of no less of importance, Edward has made a secretive relationship with Osman Ghazi Khan, the Anatolian Sultanate ruler of the Islamic armies now ranging against the Constantinople gateway, from the land of the rising sun. Collectively these rulers are potentially vitally important allies to bring ultimate success to Edward's final Crusade... *the Great Cause.*

While residing in France, Edward masterfully plans to fulfill his Angevin Plantagenet destiny to be ruler of a new Christendom, inspired by his father King Henry's ambition, the visionary doctrine of Justinian, the Great's Renovatio Imperii and his own faith and righteous Césaric belief as Gods chosen emissary on earth. A firm alliance has already been established by Edward with disaffected Teutonic and Russo Kings, Margraves, low country princes and Balkan warlords, to whom they have ingratiated themselves with the noble title *the Northern Brotherhood of Kings*. Edward has all but secured Europe's most southern frontier Citadel of Constantinople with a dubious agreement prized from the pathetic Emperor of Byzantium, Mikhaēl Palaiologos. These strategic alliances' establish absolute, Edwards' foundation for a new martial Christian empire, ranging from the far northern Cyclopean stones of Henn Oglyd in Scotland, to the sun kissed sands of the Bospherus straits and Black sea.

Soon Edward will rule as magnate supreme and overlord of a new Christendom, this is the true unbridled ambition of Edward Longshanks and the house of the Angevin Plantagenet. Edward has good reason to feel just and proud in his strategic, political and martial achievements. Now only King Philip of France and the realm of Scotland stands in his way of fulfilling his imperious dynastic ambitious "Great Cause," to rule Northern Europe as Magnate Supreme. Edward continues to reminisce whilst viewing the vista from a parapet of his château de Plantagenet, when he hears a voice behind him... "Brother..." Edward turns to see his younger brother prince Edmund. "What is it that causes you to disturb me?"

"Sire, your council awaits you." replies Edmund.

Edward replies in a surly tone, "That may be so... Where are my good friends Burnell and Walter?" Edmund replies, "Walter continues to journey steadfast from Paris, but he still has not arrived sire." Edward enquires, "And Burnell?"

"Sir Robert is in the chancellery accompanied by mistress Julianna, they await an audience with you in private." Edward laughs... "Ah Burnell, our man of canonical law... What would we ever do without him Edmund?"

"I would not know what to do sire, for his astute working of judicial and clerical law is incredulous." He continues...

"There is none other as well versed in all of English law and literature. It would seem to me that Burnell has a mind born from the seed of Scripture in the womb of Canonical law... unmatched by any who would foster dispute against us."

"Or ever shall be..." concludes Edward "I believe it so that his intellectual strength and wit are the very reasons why the Holy Father will not grant Burnell elevation to Arch Bishop of all England, for which I should be eternally grateful. Thus it is surely the loss of the Vatican and most certainly to our gain. Burnells' resentment towards the pope is palpable and extreme Edmund. I do firmly believe that if God wishes England to have its own papacy, then it will be Burnell, who would surely relish his duty as our Pope of the English house of God." Edmund is slightly amused by this comment, "My lord, what you say, is it not heresy?" Gazing deeply into his brothers' eyes, Edward replies, "My dear Edmund, I am Gods emissary on this earth, there is naught I may say as an anointed King that could be deemed as heresy." Edmund appears surprised at the reply as Edward continues, "You're not getting religious on me are you little brother?" Edmund laughs, "It's a bit late for me to get religious now, though I suppose it might be a thought worth considering to be free of the yolk of Rome."

"Now that is heresy my Lord Edmund." replies Edward "I could have you torn apart and burned to a fine ash for those sacrilegious words, but you may be possibly correct in your considerations." Edward smiles as he considers the words of Edmund, "Perhaps another time?" The royal brothers walk along the parapet and enter the Château, followed silently by the king's personal bodyguard and sergeants-at-arms. As they approach the doors of their destination, they take off their heavy robes and make their way into the Chancellery deep in the centre of the château; they are met gracefully by

Edwards' old friend and ally Robert Burnell, his most loyal chancellor. Burnell immediately goes down on bended knee and kisses the royal hand of the King of England. Edward bids Burnell to rise up from the floor.

"Please old friend, there is no need for court formality here." Burnell replies, "Sire, I will always respect our friendship, in that you may never doubt my love for you as my sovereign lord, though I feel my loyalty is best served by my actions rather than my words."

Burnell has been invaluable to Edward for over thirty years as friend and personal council. He is much smaller than Longshanks, strong and stocky, his dark hair now greying, with the exception of his balding pate. He wears the religious statement of black satin cloth, brightened by his bold silver chain of office. Burnell is the legal and political mastermind behind Edwards's successful campaigns in Flanders, Burgundy, Ireland and Wales. He had also constructed the constitutional outline for the Welsh parliament of Rhuddlan and had previously re-written old King Johns Magna Carta, in order that Edward could avert a second expensive rebellion from his own English barons. But Edwards' international policy of constant expansionist wars has drained his royal exchequer, and is the primary cause of England's near bankruptcy.

Edwards attention is drawn to the corner of the room, where he notices a woman still in a royal court curtsy with head still bowed and holding her skirts aside gracefully to flow like silken butterfly wings. Edward warmly conveys his pleasure in this lady's presence. "And you fair Julianna, how wonderful it is to see you here too…" Lady Julianna smiles but remains bowed while still holding her skirts aside. Edward walks over and holds out his hand for her to kiss the royal appendage… "My lord…" says Julianna, mistress of Burnell as long as he and Edward have been friends. Julianna's youthfulness has faded somewhat, but she has grown into a fulsome woman and had borne Burnell three sons, two of which now serve in Edward's army. Their eldest son also named Robert, has become a leading chaplain in Rome and remains there as a vitally important contact and source of inside information for Edward, in the apparent service of pope Boniface.

"Julianna, my good lady..." Edward reaches out and clasps both her hands and brings her close. "You shall attend to my dearest Eleanor, for I fear she misses your company greatly, and your presence would be advantageous to lifting her health and spirit, much more than the finest of blood-letting leechers that do attend her now." Edward towers over Julianna, then he speaks softly, "Fair Julianna, we men have much to discuss and these things we must speak of are not for the delicate ears of one so fair and beautiful as you." Julianna flushes at such praise. She curtsies then walks backwards to exit the room "At once my lord." Julianna exits the chamber as Edward turns his attention to matters in hand.

"Now my lords, to the affairs of state. Burnell, what say you?" Burnell replies, "Sire, I would seek your permission to bring into this chamber, the venerable Bishop Bek of Durham, another eternally loyal supporter of your Kingship and an invaluable assistant to me. What I may be amiss in my fiscal and policy deliberations, he is not." A delighted Edward replies, "The Bishop of Durham is here? Why of course Burnell, pray bid his company to attend me."

As Burnell leaves the exchequer to fetch his companion, Edmund fills goblets of Wine for Edward and himself, he says, "This is good news brother, Burnell and Bek here together, this night will be a gathering of genius."

"This is good news indeed Edmund," agrees Edward "I

do believe that without these two loyal subjects and their unswerving vice-like wit for law, the Plantagenet dynasty would still be bourgeois vassals of Philip. There is only so much to be achieved by the swords of Gods army, but with the sword of gods blessing too, there is no limit to what is achievable, except that which man is blessed with in faith and imagination." Edmund sneers, "Much as I like Burnell and Bek for their wit my Lord, I do prefer the sword in my hand to do my talking."

"Yes dear brother, that may be so..." says a thoughtful Edward, "but that sword and you would both be silenced in the blink of an eye by the crusaders and Templar's of Christendom without the writ of papal approval. And there is the true value of Bek and his office brother, for you cannot have one without the other." The door to the chancellery opens and a guard calls out, "Chancellor Burnell and Bishop Bek Sire." Burnell quickly enters the room, followed by the portly Bishop of Durham, Anthony Bek. They rush over to Edward and kiss his hand, "Ah Bek..." exclaims Edward "I have not seen you since the parliament of Wales. I congratulate you on your work that day, for the poor miserable Welsh of no account have not yet the wit of a dung maggot far less any notional intelligence for the delicacy of law. Particularly when it is in the minds and scripted hands of such learned practitioners as your good self and that of my dear Burnell."

Flushing with the praise from his King, Bek says, "I thank you my lord but I am undeserving of such praise. It is nought if it is not in the cause of the Plantagenet Empire, and of course, the Great Cause."

'Empire...' thinks Edward, *'Perhaps Bek is right, for God must truly be on my side by aiding me in pursuit of the Great Cause, but I had never thought others may see my destiny as Imperial.'* Edward relishes the thought. He says, "Let us be

seated my lords, for we have much to discuss over these next few weeks. Then I must prepare to pay homage to this young rat-wit upstart the French King. I swear to you all that this will be for last time."

The four men sit round a great oak table that has been prepared with food and fine wine to sustain a long evening of planning and strategy. "CAPTAIN OF THE GUARD..." Edward commands. An officer of the Kings guard quickly enters the exchequer; "Sire...?" responds the captain while standing in starched attention awaiting his Kings further command. "Other than Walter of Hemingbrough and master of the lofts, no one is to be within ten cloth yards of this office, on pain of death... Save one who may call me directly on pressing matters from good Queen Eleanor, is that understood?"

"SIRE." replies the captain. He bows and leaves the room. Edmund follows him and secures the heavy bars and bolt fasteners of both the outer and inner doors to the chamber, making certain they are locked securely and also ensuring a soundproofed meeting is heard by no-one other than those present. Edward glances at his council sitting at the table. "Now Lord Edmund, chancellor Burnell, Bishop Bek... to the business at hand."

An enthusiastic Edward settles to deliberate with his council, for none in all of England has more power than these four men seated at the table in this French Château, with the exception of the missing Walter of Hemingbrough and Lanercost. Edward commands... "Burnell... open the proceedings. And please get directly to the intimacy of your agenda." Standing erect, Burnell picks up a swathe of velum legal writs from the table and holds them close to study the minutiae. He begins to comment on his findings... "My liege, and my lords... England is all but bankrupted by the recent campaign expenses in Wales, Burgundy and Ireland. More taxation demands arrive from Philip, Interest on past loans for crusade expenses and the levy of taxation by the Vatican does bleed us dry. Also, all monies expended ensuring the Barons loyalties do leave the treasury in a most delicate position. With more monies urgently required to support our allies in the Germanic kingdoms and Low Countries, including the cost of retaining our standing armies, fleet and your estates maintenance both here in France and in England sire, I am certain the conglomerates of Venice represented by lord De Lucca, will soon be demanding payment in full of all our debt and interest... Unless my lord, we can formulate a fiscal plan of action that will alleviate this great strain on our resources. Sire, I do concede that I have grave concerns."

"Sire..." says Edmund "I thought the holy father decreed usury a sin? And if that is so, then how is it we do owe the Church of Rome interest payment upon our loans?" Edward glares at Edmund as Burnell replies, "Vix Pervenit my dear Edmund... Usury and dishonest profit by any other means." Edmund looks at the table knowing his embarrassment has been spared by Burnell's timely reply.

Burnell continues, "The Holy Father recently produced a bull passed through the council of encyclicals, declaring usury to be damned by the sacred canons as an anathema detestable to God and contrary to the doctrine of Christian charity. Therefore his holiness forbids any money lending for gain, except through the Vatican's own bankers. His holiness in all his wisdom does make not money lending the sin and gaining from the transaction as un-Christian, abominable and heretical throughout Christendom. This Papal Bull allows the Holy Father and his bankers' complete control over all loan interest in Christendom by calling it an *Exchange charge*, made pure by holy sanction and blessing.

These variable exchange charges are now applicable in all Christian kingdoms and deemed necessary for the purpose of funding Crusades and the Holy administration." Bek sneers. "Yes, Those sycophantic bankers conveniently extract these exchange charges from monies that the Vatican loan out in the first instance to borrowers. Profit that normally comes from what you or I would call interest, the Holy ecumenical council do now call it charitable exchange charges."

Edward laughs at the bemused expression on Edmunds face. He expresses to his brother, "Dear Edmund, the difference is simply in the terminology, accompanied by the attachments of faith and Holy blessing. Profit for gain on debt interest is apparently Judaic and heretical in the eyes of His Holiness, therefore he declares it a sin, but to make himself a profit through exchange charges and using only his own bankers, this is seen as Gods will, therefore a demonstration of faith by the debtor to the Holy See, thus, Christian charity. The exchange charge is accepted as a nominal taxation that is set by the Vatican bankers and his holiness to be seen as a necessary but fair administrative charge for everyone, subsequently expounding that this particular interest charge is not a sin."

Edmund enquires curiously, "So Sire, let me understand this… His Holiness does make blessed exchange charges to collect gold and silver reserve incomes for his own Holy city bankers, and blessed by God, therefore legitimate, even though their interest charges are much higher in real terms to any interest rate a borrower would be charged for the same loan amount from the Jewry?" Edward laughs at Edmunds simplistic yet plainly accurate view of financial and religious politics… and banking. Edward replies, "Dear Edmund, the Vatican bankers do call it *collecting alms for the poor* and remove from any loan or exchange charges what they deem to be fair administration costs... is that not so Bek?" Appearing momentarily startled, Bek replies, "It is so sire, only recently the former Archbishop of Canterbury, John Peckham, laid stress and disdain upon Judaic moneylenders and sanctified the Vatican banking discipline regarding the sin of interest placed upon his own clerical flock, but it resulted in a great conflict between the church and our chancellery. Peckham's first Episcopal enactment during the Reading Council was to implement ecclesiastical reform on loan interest in all collegiate establishments in England by enforcing the Holy fathers Bull edict. In that, all borrowers agreements must be transacted only with the church not the Jewry nor the state. He heralded that all Christians would be damned to eternal Hell if they loaned from anyone but the Holy fathers bankers."

Edward scowls, "Peckham proclaims the Holy Fathers Bull as Gods will, for he is in so much debt to the Vatican Bankers himself, consequently he is under threat of excommunication unless he does repay his loans." Edmund ponders, "It would appear Sire that the underlying value of a Christian realm to the Holy See is no longer as much our armies, nor what little currently resides in gold and silver reserves in our own treasuries, our valued purpose now appears to be how much perpetual taxation and charges a realm may extract from its own people and pay to Rome indefinitely."

Edmund scowls at the thought, "I never did see nor did I realise our God given duty is now to be tax gathering serfs for His Holiness and be under threat of excommunication unless we continuously produce charge duties for Rome." Burnell speaks, "It is those same bankers who provide us with necessary loans and mortgage in the first instance for exchange charges gained by return..." A grim and bitter Burnell continues... "This naked robbery is orchestrated by a select group of priests ruling autonomously within the

Vatican bank." Bek is also incensed, "It is a travesty, now a sovereign realm can no longer trade openly in gold or silver thanks to the greed of the Vatican bankers, any realm of Christendom wishing to create a healthy home treasury must now either borrow the money from the primary lenders ordained to be through the Vatican's bankers, or truck secretively with the Jewry." Burnell interrupts, "…Or we must levy even more taxation upon our own Barons, subjects and simples."

"Bankers and Jews, Jews and Bankers…" exclaims Edmund, "this would rattle the mind of any honest man of God. There is little to define or differ between these two famishing twins of evil that I can see. It would appear that these two great parasitical leeches rule the world, and honest princes of Rome such as we, are constricted to act on behalf of both of these perfidious moneylenders. We should keep our own revenues and hold all that of our exchange and by God sirs, I would dare these pious pickers of pockets to…"

"ENOUGH…" commands Edward.

The room immediately falls silent. Edward appears ill humoured. "You think the financial situation of this great realm of Christendom gains us free time to discuss the difference between a Vatican banker and the Jewry?" Everyone looks to each other for comfort and shelter from Edwards glare, till finally, they look to their king once more as he continues… "Burnell, what plan do you propose that would alleviate these grave fiscal concerns you mentioned earlier? Speak now and without favour." Burnell replies with steely resolve, "Sire, your righteous zeal and conviction to further the dynastic claim of the Angevin house does outstrip all revenues gathered to support such endeavours, furthermore, the heavy burden of `exchange charges' due to the Holy Father and his bankers, has left our treasury nigh bare." Burnell pauses with apprehension, waiting tentatively for a reply from the king. Edward replies calmly "I am aware of this Burnell... I have placated De Lucca, he assures me his masters will wait a little longer for their exchange dues. I have faith Burnell, that you have solutions to remedy these temporary problems of our treasury, do you not? Brother Edmund here is quite anxious to bathe his blade in heathen blood and has armies are ready to enforce any law, writ or statute you propose, that I in turn may sanction to save the moment." Edward pauses and glares at Burnell "And...?"

Burnell continues cautiously "We... I mean Bek and I have prepared plans that if enacted, could clear our current interest and exchange dues, and also my lord, we may even establish large reserve equities for the next five years. These plans if approved by you will comfortably sustain your existing holdings." Edward appears somewhat satisfied. "You say Burnell... will these plans of yours be useful for prying the necessary finance we may require from the Bardi and Peruzzi conglomerate should we need their securities?" Burnell nods emphatically, "They will sire." Edward demands, "Then let me hear of your plans Burnell, for I shall make England great again and the wealthiest Kingdom in all of Christendom, indeed I desire it to be so, for we have necessity and urgency for England to be the wealthiest of all realms to enable the Great Cause. Heed me my lords, if we do not achieve these simple goals, there can be no legacy to pass to my children, and by virtue, that of your own seed... Should the broom of Plantagenet wither, then so it shall be so for all the vines attached, therefore the fate of all England."

Burnell replies, "My Lord, I have formulated a legal plan of taxation to be extracted from your Barons and territorial dependants... from the highest magnates, lords and traders to the most menial of simples who does own but a rats tail for his next meal… And a rats tail we shall tax for his privilege of dining under the protections you grant him Sire." Everyone laughs at the meticulous strategy of Burnell. Edward sits back in his chair and laughs aloud, "I do like your justifications for taxation good sir, but a rats tail as a taxable feast, indeed…" Burnell continues, "Sire, these proposals have already met with the Pontiff's approval and we are now in receipt of his blessing in principle. Equally important is a secure agreement of support with those of your loyal Barons Council in England." Burnell pauses to gain reaction from his King. Edward sits at the head of the table leaning back in his chair listening to every word intently…

"Continue Burnell, your findings are intriguing. In particular, your point of interest is in gaining the Barons approval. How so?" Burnell continues with confidence. "With a substantial increase on our levy of taxations on the native Irish, Cornish and Welsh, including your vassal states in France, and by imposing an import duty tax on Flanders and Scotch wool incorporating all their goods that use English ports Sire, we shall bring an additional sixty per cent income increase over and above your annual charges on all transactions from foreign traders, minus a minimal allowance of privilege that our tax collecting Barons shall benefit from by the same per cent above their own annual dues, this is a crown gratuity gifted to them for maintaining their position and provisions. Inasmuch Sire, each shire shall pay for standing yeomen to be in your service on any given Royal call-to-arms."

Edward nods in approval then enquires, "But what taxation vantage and benefits are to be gained from our Welsh campaigns?" Edmund replies, "Sire, we have already gained nigh on ten thousand yeomen, men-at arms and archers for the royal army from our Welsh campaigns, we do expect the same in cavalry and foot-soldiers from the Irish." Burnell says, "We also have the ring of castles in Wales now built in Flint, Rhuddlan, Builth, Wells and Aberystwyth, the *Iron Ring* will be complete after the building of castles at Conway, Caernarfon and Beaumaris, which are almost all but finished with their construction." Bek interrupts, "And all being subsidised by the Welsh exchequer through local taxation my lord and from the confiscation and auction of properties formally owned by the native Welsh and Irish which does bolsters your revenues greatly here in England."

Edward smiles as Bek continues... "The planting of your loyal subjects from the finest English aristocracy in Wales and Ireland, then selling them cheaply land and title including ownership of all the confiscated simples, serfs, peasants and their properties, is a great success Sire. There are other revenues to be gained from these planted nobles in our new territories of Wales and Ireland that will be a benefit the treasury two-fold sire. First, by elevating lower ranked English nobles to nominated positions of feudal Barons in their new individual dominions and Sherrifdoms, they do see this as personal reward for their loyalty and devotions. Second, these cheaply bought titles will create vast wealth of taxes through the selling of territorial natural resources, and of course, this policy ensures our new class of younger Barons will devote unswerving and enduring loyalty to you sire."

"...And the Barons council are in favour of this proposal?" enquires Edward. "Absolutely Sire," replies Burnell "these proposals sit well with your Barons for they see their sons having place, opportunity and responsibility... the Barons Council does favour expansion into new territories rather than to be constantly looking over their shoulder for the sharp end of a blade from their frustrated ambitious sons. It profits them in many ways Sire, hence the Barons Council have foresworn to give you absolute and unquestioned homage in exchange for royal patronage and titled position. They see that in return for their continued support for our vigorous programme of extending territorial lands, you will grant them title as trusted royal administrators." Edward appears pleased. "This is extremely good news Burnell, for the Welsh and Irish are of no consequence in reality and your establishment of planted loyal Englishmen in these new territories is surely Gods will without doubt, well done Burnell, pray do continue with your proposition."

Growing in confidence, Burnell continues, "A series of Laws of statute are to be enacted sire, pending your seal of approval of course, which shall forbid any native Welsh or Irish to own land or property within ten leagues of an Englishman's furthest boundary, this shall be known henceforth as Crown Property. Under penalties most severe, those same natives may not hunt nor trade in the same jurisdiction with any or all produce, movables and or chattel, unless by license, all of which may be exploited at the sole discretion of your appointed Lord or Sherriff. The same said Lord may also confiscate any native property that borders his land should he feel the said property or local peasantry does constitute a threat, or if the said land in question is not tilled or grazed to the full, the same lord may also deem it prudent to confiscate all the aforementioned with no recourse to fiscal or canonical action by the neighbouring tenants if they be native Welsh or Irish. All shall be confirmed by the Lord Chief justice, Barons Council and blessed by the Holy Archbishop of England."

Edmund speaks "Sire, when last in my home estate in Grisemond and also in my duchy of Lancaster residence I held local council, these charter proposals of Burnell and Bek were met with approval and great enthusiasm indeed from the Lancastrian, Yorkshire and South-western Baronages, in that, your proposed royal patronage of these small power hungry Baronial sons of England by elevation to a greater status, has them falling over themselves and much eager to support you in exchange for these favours. Their hunger to be little paladin princes is ingratiated by their lust for adventure and expanding family requirements."

Edward sits back with an intense look of satisfaction as Burnell continues reading his proposals from the draft charters, as though he is preaching to a flock of believers...

"We shall forbid any Welsh or Irish to marry or consort with any of true English of Norman blood under penalty of mutilation, drawing and removal of appendages, followed by appropriate form of execution. These same penalties are also to be applied to immediate and extended families by association. Nor shall any serf marry another serf without permission, ensuring that those race of vermin other than those at your disposal as your army and navy requires them procreates, this edict will wither the local peasantry and further free the said territories for your loyal and most obedient subjects of dynastic blood-lines. Furthermore Sire, all forests and woodland product, beast and livestock therein, shall be solely the property of the Crown, managed by the appointed Sherriff or Baron of the said Shire or Sherrifdom. And finally Sire, there shall be a trading taxation placed on all hides, wool, fish, livestock imports and exports in all your dominions and territories, these writs too have been approved and agreed by the Barons Council of England, Ireland, and now so too in Wales."

Contemplating Burnells' words, Edward enquires "And these proposals... they have already been approved and supported in principle by the Pontiffs representatives as well as the Barons Council?"

Enthusiastically Burnell replies, "They have Sire, they collectively believe in your enlightened considerations on parliamentary taxation is an example to follow. Therefore we have all statute writs and edicts prepared and ready to enact following your blessing and seal of approval." Edward leans forward in his chair and queries Burnell "And this new taxation and levies to be placed upon our dominions… they will square the interest and loans from the Vatican and Venetians? And will these acts you speak of clear all our fiscal ills?"

"They will sire…" replies Burnell "The revenue will increase annually and by a minimum of sixty per cent, within three years you will have opportunity to profit and gain most handsomely from all of these taxes and all territorial resources." Edward sits up in his chair intrigued. "The Northern brotherhood of Kings Burnell…they expect, indeed they require a fiscal sign of good faith from the house of Plantagenet. How do we sweeten their support if we can only increase our treasury by sixty per cent annually, and only after we have spent a great deal of time and monies putting your strategy to play. What sources of revenue can be left untouched we do not already extract?"

"The alliances you build sire," says Bek "they require a further annual payment of one thousand pounds of silver each, and that is not possible unless we employ other sources of revenue to pay for these alliances." Edward enquires, "Do any of you have solutions to offer other than these fiscal remedies you already suggest? What you say fairs well for the duration, but are there any other revenue sources available we may exploit freely?"

"There are sire." replies Burnell "Then what are they?" snaps an anxious Edward. Burnell hesitantly replies, "Sire, you must not wage war or employ a large or conscript army on any major campaigns or crusades for at least two or three years, if you do, we will never gain profit nor gain any vantage. It is proving to be too expensive my Lord." Edward glares at Burnell, but he also knows his loyal friend is correct in his clinical observations. Burnell enquires, "May Bishop Bek speak of his findings to you sire?" Edward looks at the bishop "Do you have a solution Bek?"

Anthony Bek, the Bishop of Durham and Sherriff to the northern English counties on the border with Scotland, is a life-long and faithful supporter of Edward Longshanks. Both he and Burnell had masterminded an elaborate series of continental alliances with Kings, Princes and leading church magnates, who readily favor Edward as a natural leader to that of Pope Boniface and King Philip of France.

"Sire…" says Bek "I do have solutions to offer for your consideration." Impatiently, Edward pounds his fist onto the table "Then speak man, what are you waiting for?" Bishop Bek, growing red in his portly cheeks, clears his throat… "The solution is in the collection of tax revenues from trade and property transactions from all the priests and monasteries in England and your fiefdoms and provinces…"

"THE CHURCH?" exclaims Edward in a raised but curious tone of voice. "Yes Sire… the Church…" Edward is clearly surprised at this inclusion to Bek and Burnells' devices. "You had better explain yourself precisely, and be succinct dear Bek."

"Sire, with your indulgence… may we urge you to consider my reply to that question on religious taxation to be the last subject on our agenda?" Edward sits back into his chair, intrigued. He thinks awhile then replies, "If you must. But what is it your spleen persists in telling to me before such an interesting subject of discussion?" Bek replies, "The Jewry sire."

"Ah the Jewish question." says Edward. "Yes my lord." replies Bek. Leaning forward in his chair once more, Edward enquires, "I thought we had drained their usury resources and curbed the silver clipping of the Jewry ten years ago?" Bek replies, "Sire we did, and although the Jews were made your personal property and branded to wear the yellow mark of David publicly, we gave them fifteen years to settle their business and leave England. Should it be that any Jew who wishes to remain in England under your protection, they must renounce their faith and convert to Christianity. The cost to the Jewry for your benevolent protection, is that all Jewry monies, property, possessions and debt owed, be passed to your treasury and crown as your personal property..."

Edward interrupts Bek, "Do we then cleanse this realm of all our Jewry?" Bek continues, "Yes Sire, any Jew that chooses to stay in England must reside in nominated monasteries in a state of Domus Conversum and make their conversion to Christianity, there they must remain in perpetual bondage under the severest penalties for any transgression. These Jewry converts must never be found in possession or ownership of any property, money, lending contracts, coin or clippings of the realm. Nor must they be found with any articles or images of Jewry faith under penalty of the heretical question and execution."

Spitting out words borne of frustration, Edward exclaims, "You dare tell me that there are still Jews in England bleeding our Kingdom dry whilst we struggle to provide an army that protects their greed and to follow their heathen faith... Perhaps these Jews would welcome another feast of Shabbat ha-Gadol and Pesach in another place?" Edmund, Burnell and Bek look at each other cautiously, for who is going to risk the wrath of Edward by providing an insufficient answer. Moments pass as Edward glares at his trusted followers.

Even though they are most secure in their friendship with Edward, they know that none are safe when an incandescent rage rises in his breast.

"Sire," says Bek cautiously "You magnanimously gave the Jews till the year twelve ninety to exodus the kingdom. A wise strategy I say, for it has allowed the Jews who remain here to continue managing certain trades and to gain what they believe to be a secreted profit."

Edward glares at Bek and enquires "For what purpose?" "Sire..." splutters Bek "They've hidden away their ill-gotten wealth surreptitiously, but it is known to us and now to our vantage..." Bek pauses a moment, becoming acutely aware of the silence, "Sire, my estimate in gold, silver, coin, clipping and property the Jewry have hidden in accumulated wealth, is a sum likely to exceed one hundred thousand silver pounds, the total taxation we have managed to gain from them over that period has been fifty thousand pounds. We also believe they have hidden away near thrice that amount."

"WHAT SAY YOU BEK?" Exclaims Edward.

"My Lord, I... Burnell and I have prepared for this moment." replies an anxious Bek. Burnell quickly comes to Beks' aid. "Sire, the Jews are still your personal property and subsequently they are not protected by the Christian Church nor any Laws of this land... and as King of England, the law decrees the Crown can enact any edict upon them at ant time, in that an example would be that all Jewry property and all outstanding debts and contracts owed to Jews may be transferred to the King's treasury immediately." Burnell can see he has momentarily contained the flame of Edwards' passion. Edward enquires "And can I apply this edict in England and enforce it on my Jewish possessions here in France and in all my provinces, without need for approval from Philip... or the Pontiff?"

"By canonical law, you may sire," replies Burnell. "Legally you are correct in your reference to our earlier edict regarding the *Statutum de Judaismo,* forbidding any Jew the trade of usury or lend for gain. They Jewry were granted limited power to engage in commerce and provincial handicrafts; they were also permitted to farm for a period not exceeding ten years. Bek and I have scrutinized French law, the edict is yours to freely enact at your discretion without obligation to the French King, or his treasury." Confirming Burnells' account, Bek concludes, "This is correct sire, you may enact these law's and taxes in all of your territories, for there are none who will protect the Jewry."

"Perhaps the Scotch might sire…" says Edmund "They are the only Christian kingdom which has no history of state persecution against the Jewry, and it is known the Jews of the Baltic and Varjag traders Guilds also reside openly as freemen in Scotland's towns and cities." Edward replies, "No… the Scotch will not protect them, the Scotch will soon have too many problems of their own to be troubling themselves with the protection of the Jewry. Edmund, how do you fare in martial readiness if so required?" Edmund replies, "I have my armies well prepared sire." Bek says, "Sire, it's imperative that the particular edicts required should be applied with great diligence and with immediate haste here in France, and they must be concluded before Philip is made aware. Should he intercept any thoughts of what could be achieved and the financial gains to be made; then it is certain Philip will apply this same Christian Justice upon his own Jewry by law. This would mean that as the Jewry are your property, all revenues gleaned from them become taxable as stock and trade to Philip."

"I concur Sire," says Burnell. Edward enquires, "What revenue would our French Jewry bring to us?"

Bek replies, "I believe over one hundred thousand silver Pounds over what we would raise from our Jewry back in England sire, for the Jewry here have never been subject to the same taxation as those placed upon your Jew properties in England."

"Edmund...?" ponders Edward "When could you start the seizures and expulsions of the Jewry on my French estates?" Edmund replies, "We are ready and prepared to move immediately Sire, we simply await your command. Bek and Burnell have been keeping me apace should you require an immediate remedy to the Jewish question here in France."

Intrigued, Edward enquires, "And what would our ethical Christian reasoning be for enacting this edict upon the Jewry?" Bek replies, "Sire, we conclude that the ethical Christian reasoning for the expulsion of the Jewry would be that, as a non Christian heathen cult, they have neglected to follow previous edict's as agreed by both parliament and the Council of Barons constituted in the *Statute of Jewry* you placed upon them... and Sire, we would gain much popular support for this act if we did enact the edict in methodical stages over the next three years, which would follow your original Edict of Expulsion time-line, then we further a final legal statute of Jewry, namely the *Edict of Expulsion.*" Bemused, Edward looks at Bek "And what exactly was the minutiae in the Edict of Expulsion Bek, do you forget the *Charter of Joseph?* Whereby the all Jewry may move about England privileged and freely as my own property... *Sicut res propriæ nostræ...*"

"Yes Sire, I do remember and I do understand," replies Bek, "but by this method we would rid England from the curse of Jewry forever... Which we know would be popular with your trader subjects and meet with no resistance from your Barons. It would also be legally binding and also complimentary with the Judaic statute blessed by Canon law. Furthermore, it shall be a requirement for all Jews in the kingdom before the final expulsion to reside only in the towns where Archae are placed for receiving all their monies and valuables. The Jewish Statute will be enforced absolute, requiring the continued wearing of a distinctive yellow mark in the form of a star or circle to be worn by all Jew males aged seven years and over."

Sitting back in his chair, Edward smiles, "Finally, we have found a profitable solution to the Jewish question... do tell me Burnell, what specific punishments for those who continue to follow the Jewish faith who may remain in England, and for those that would give them succor and shelter?" Burnell replies, "It is proposed the removal of hands, feet, nose and lips and their eyes scarified by the blessed scalpel sire. Rabbi's will be burned at the stake as heretics or traitors, with the subsequent confiscation of the same goods properties and debts owned and owed to the Jewry being passed to the Crown by example." Edward commands, "Then make it so, we must cleanse this holy land of God from this pestilence." Edmund enquires, "Shall I prompt my army commanders?" Edward replies, "Make it so..."

Pleased with Bek and Burnells plans, Edward enquires, "How soon may we confirm these edicts in law?" Burnell replies, "By morn, Sire. I have drawn up the necessary statutes requiring only your scrutiny, approval, signature and seal. Then it will be law in motion. The Jewry here in France will be stricken by the sword of God before you wake my Lord." Edward queries Bek, "And what of the Flemmards who are little more than the Jew themselves in all but name?" Bek replies, "Alas sire, they are of the Christian faith and have certain limited protections, therefore a pogrom cannot be affected upon them." Burnell says, "Sire, if we apply retrospect taxation tariffs immediately upon the Flemmards here in France, perhaps twice or thrice that of our English traders, this will serve to give our burgess coffers great vantage. If we employ a foreign trade tax upon the Flemish traders in England, who under penalty for resistance, shall also be put to the question, this will allow your chancellery *Right of Seizure* upon them, as is with the Jews, including imprisonment of all Flemish traders and their families till all debts, ransoms duties and dues are paid in full. Together with confiscation of their properties, we believe half as much may be gained in revenue income from this source as we would collect from the Jewry in England sire."

Edward enquires, "And you have prepared the necessary documentation to effect this immediately?"

"We have Sire." replies Burnell while he unfolds velum writs of prepared edicts. He lays them carefully upon the table for Longshanks to view, sign and seal. Edward begins scrutinising the documents. Edward appears pleased, "Then let us not waste any more time."

Bek holds sealing wax over a nearby candle, preparing for the seal of Plantagenet to legally confirm rights of taxation and subsequently, the murder or removal of the Jewry and Flemish communities in England. Edward speaks, "Edmund, open the windows and make to have sustenance brought to us for I have a great famishing. These two master cooks of law and God's will have invigorated and whetted my appetite."

Refreshments are quickly brought to the small gathering. When the servants retire, Edward says, "Well my lord Bek, I am intrigued… Now you must tell to me of how you intend to apply taxation of the priests and Catholic Church in England, your stratagem must be explained regarding this most unusual inclusion of nominations." Edward signals a brief gesture of approval towards his loyal lawmakers, he knows that a glance of appreciation approving of their diligent applications is enough to make Burnell and Bek ecstatic. Edmund opens the windows and walks back toward the table. The silence of the moment is broken by the faint heavenly sound of voices singing in the distance. "Ah…" Edward sighs, "the choir from the monastery of Angeriacum St John in the village."

Pausing for a moment, Edward savors the delightful music that wafts with a slight harmonious echo, sweetening the music to the ear. "How appropriate…" says Edward. "Pray tell me of your plans for taxation of the church Burnell. How do we tax the Church more than they are due in kind to pay to Rome? And also avoiding the potential for censorship or conflict with the Pontiff?" Burnell replies enthusiastically, "Sire, it is not the church to which we propose to tax, rather it is their priests, nuns, Friars monks, but specifically, not the ruling elite Sire, for in them being exempt from taxation and favoured by you, it does gain their vigorous support. This tax exemption for the church governors ensures they will not dare challenge your crown authority. In exchange for this dispensation, they will absolve all our measures, as they shall thrive personally, for there are non wealthier in all of Christendom than these monastic communities who are already divided amongst themselves."

Edward comments, "Not taxing the Bishops you say… are you not wealthy Bek, especially when our realm pulls in its belt from the grip of austerity. How many knights do you employ in your retinue?" Bek flushes at this question, he hesitates… "Well Bek, I am waiting?" says Edward… Bek replies, "Forty knights sire." Edward makes no response other than to continue with his questions regarding taxation. "And what of the Vatican, how will they react to this additional taxation upon their minions?" Burnell replies, "Sire, if we target the

Christian sanctums less favored by the His Holiness, then all of the priest-hood over a longer period of time, we believe that two years may pass before it would it be challenged by the Dicastery of the Roman Curia and His Holiness, and we would gain the support of the Vicariate General. And of course Sire, our reasoning for this taxation would be as is theirs... to provide monies for the protection for the Holy Church and the funding of crusades, which would be a valid judicial and ecumenical argument that could take many years to resolve."

"The Holy Father does need our protection doesn't he?" smirks Edward, "Its only twenty odd years since Guyuk Khan demanded homage from Pope Innocent in train with all the princes of Rome as an act of submission. The threat of facing the Mongol hordes at the gates of Rome is a risk the Pope cannot once again risk. Had not we and the Mediterranean Kings Brotherhood came to the aid of the Holy See, he would not exist today." Burnell says, "My lord, once we have dealt with the Jews and Flemmards then it should appear to the Holy Father that ultimately he will be the supreme and ultimate beneficiary from these punitive but necessary taxations." Bek blurts out, "I wish we had the treasury of the Scotch at our disposal sire, for their main trading port of Berwick alone returns an annual income of almost one third of England's entire exchequer income." Edward thinks long on Burnells' words, he enquires, "That much revenue could be raised from the Scotch?" Burnell replies, "As much as the Jews and Flemmards in all of your territories sire."

Noting Edwards interest sharpen, Burnell continues, "If we could gain control of Scotch taxation Sire, you will have all the necessary monies you need to immediately buy outright all sympathies necessary for the Great Cause from all of your influential allies in Europe, in particular Adolphus and the

Germanic Low Country princes, which would eliminate any obvious thoughts of a Holy War with the Northern Brotherhood from the Vatican. The Holy planners would prefer to follow your lead by example sire, but they would never admit it." Edward sups some wine then speaks in a low voice, "The Scotch question is at a very delicate moment in time my lords, but we shall deal with them soon… and their wealth." Edward pauses then he enquires "And should we withhold all of these particular new taxes and charges from Rome?" Burnell replies "It would be courageous to enact sire as they cannot excommunicate us for raising charge dues for future crusades and his holiness protection."

"A very risky business though…" says Edward thoughtfully, he enquires, "But it could be done?" Burnell replies "It could Sire." Edward says, "Ah, but we only surmise Burnell, though I see that both yours and Beks' solution to the Jewish question invigorates the very depths of your collective wisdom. I compliment you both on your use of astute taxation prowess in demonstrating clearly that these tax edicts will ultimately benefit the Vatican. It will wrest a perplexity of debate that will take the Holy Fathers bankers many years to deliberate, and any unfavourable reaction from them in any measure is futile. There appears no outcome for us other than ultimately favourable."

A confident Bek continues, "It is widely known the great affection his Holiness has for you sire, be it from your reputation as a stalwart supporter of his very existence through your political and military genius. We are certain these factors will eliminate any thought of a punitive conflict with His Holiness." Stamping his signet seal on the last document, Edward straightens himself up, his muscles and bones are aching from such a long day deliberating and diligent application to the duties required. "We shall talk more on this subject of taxation later this eve my lords," He continues, "Though I must congratulate you all most sincerely upon your endeavors." Burnell speaks, "Sire, there is one other question that we must once again wish to put upon you before we retire, a question that did not appear on the agenda, but a moment ago was mentioned by Bishop Bek. We believe it is vital that we discuss this particular subject..."

Looking at Burnell curiously, Edward enquires, "And what is this question you wish to ask of me with such reservation in your voice my lord?" Burnell and Bek look at Edward, then Burnell utters nervously... "I know you said it is in hand sire, but we must discuss our situation with Scotland." "Ah Scotland..." says Edward knowingly, he smiles wryly as he replies, "with the expulsion and elimination of the Jewry... I shall make it so that it will be the Scotch peasantry who shall replace our Jewry, for they are destined to be my next *Sicut res propriæ nostræ*... The Scotch will soon be my own personal property to do with as I will..."

BEN BUIE

awn breaks over the Wolf and wildcat hills, revealing a wonderland scene of heavy snowfall that completely blankets the glen of Afton in beautiful wind-sculpted snowdrifts. Below the heights of Black Craig, the hearth fires glow in a snow clad Wallace Keep as Mharaidh and auld Jean work through the morning in the warmth of the kitchens. The day is uneventful with only concerned thoughts for the safety of their men and the situation of a possible civil war being uppermost in everyone's minds. Suddenly Auld Jean's foundling grandson, young Jamie, comes running into the house shouting wildly, "Granny Jean... Granny Jean..." He continues in a fluster, "there are strange looking big men coming towards the Keep, ah think they might be forest Ettins' maybe... come see, quickly." auld Jean enquires, "Jamie ma bonnie boy, what's all this fussin' and commotion about?"

"Come on..." insists Jamie "Yie must be coming to the door, quickly, they look really scary. ah saw them coming on horses through s' Taigh am Rígh pass from the Wildcat hills... they're scary lookin' big fellas." Auld Jean and young Jamie walk cautiously behind Mharaidh as she opens the door, but they are met with swirls of light snowflakes and a chilling breeze sweeps through the room. They all huddle together and peer outside, but a grey winter flurry obscures any view more than a few feet from where they stand. Mharaidh shivers and peers into the snowfall a few moments longer as auld Jean wraps her plaid around young Jamie, takes his hand, and ushers him back in to the warmth of the busy kitchen fires. She says, "I didn't see anybody out there Jamie, I think you've been dipping too much o' the sweet honey son, maybe you're imaginin' those bogey men out there?" Mharaidh continues to search for Jamie's bogeymen till she is certain that no one is there; then she too turns back towards the kitchen, closing the door behind her.

Suddenly the door crashes open and a fearsome looking giant of a man in snow covered ice-clad pelts barges in, sending auld Jean and Jamie reeling back in fright. Mharaidh quickly grabs a large iron skillet and strikes the intruder a heavy blow on the back of the head as Jean smashes him in the face with her flour baton, young Jamie bravely kicks the intruder repeatedly on the shins... "STOP, stop hittin' me, fuck me jaezuz..." yells a pained a voice from below the snow covered brat. "It's me Mharaidh... it's William." He frantically pushes back the hood and pulls at the brat-muffle protecting his face from the subzero wind chill outside.

Shivering and shaking with ice crystals clinging to his beard and eyebrows, his lips blue with the cold and skin pallor a deathly white, William gasps, "Hurry Mharaidh, I need your help..." He struggles through the pain of frostbite to pull off his gloves with his teeth, then, with a single sweep of his hand, he clears the table to place upon it a snow covered bundle of frozen pelts. Auld Jean enquires urgently "What is it William, what's wrong?" William doesn't reply as he frantically tears the thick layers of frozen pelts away from the bundle on the table, he pulls the last pelt off to reveal the injured shivering body of Affric. Auld Jean exclaims, "Oh Affric, ma bonnie child..." Another crashing sound startles them as Bailey comes slamming through the door like a giant Caledonian bear, he too quickly sheds his winter brat and mantles to reveal a semi-conscious Coinach sheltering under his arms. Mharaidh calls out "Shut the door Jamie... quickly." Auld Jean reaches for warm plaids to cover the lifeless looking body of Affric. Katriona arrives to see what the commotion is all about. Auld Jean calls out to her "Boil some water Katriona... quickly, then fetch me plenty o' goats milk, honey, whisky, and lots of sfaggy. (Sphagnum moss) Crush it well and mix it with may-butter, egg white and lard a' plenty, then fill a large bowl to mix a poultice with fiongeur (Vinegar)"

Mharaidh and auld Jean remove Affrics frozen blood-soaked clothes, they immediately see many serious looking slash and gash wounds on her body, "Jamie," says Mharaidh, "go fetch some hot firestones from the inglenook." Wee Jamie runs for stones as Mharaidh continues... "Pack the warmest fire-stones next to her body, that will bring her blood nearer to the skin." As Mharaidh tends to Affric, she glances over at William, Coinach and Bailey, now standing in the fireside inglenook, shaking uncontrollably with cold and mild frostbite, desperate to gain heat into their frozen bodies. Mharaidh calls out to them as she and auld Jean continue tending to Affric... "Boy's, wrap yourselves in plaid from the firebox at the window, we'll get you something warm and dry soon." Mharaidh fills an oat-supping bowl with a hot honey-whisky broth; then she enquires urgently, "William, is your father with you, is he all right?

William can barely speak he is so cold. Bailey replies, "He's fine Ma'am, it was just us that befell this evil misfortune." Grateful to hear the news from Bailey, Mharaidh soon sees the full extent of Affric's injuries, "Oh my bonnie wee darlin'"

Auld Jean glances at Mharaidh and shakes her head forlorn, as though there is no hope for the Elvin Ceàrdannan princess. Coinach notices auld Jean's gesture and panics,

"She's not going to die is she? Please don't let Affric die..." Coinach breaks down and begins to weep. "She'll be fine," replies auld Jean "but we must get her to a soft warm crib and tend to her wounds. Immediately." Mharaidh cleans a deep wound on Affric's breast then she calls out, "Katriona, break some eggs and separate the yolk, we'll use the whites to paste the deep wounds, this will help clot the bleeding, and fetch more fiongeur..."

Auld Jean looks to Mharaidh "We'll be needing the cauterising irons before the blood returns. It's a blessing o' sorts that she's so cold or she would surely have bled to death by now, oh my, but the pain of the hot irons will be tenfold upon the wee lass." Mharaidh replies, "I know, but it's best we do this now though, while she's unconscious... it's her only hope." At that moment, Auld Tam and wee Graham rush in through the door. When they see the seriousness of Affric's condition, they are shocked. Immediately they carry her to a small warm room where Mharaidh quickly makes up a warm soft crib up as Katriona hastily builds a large peat fire in the hearth. Auld Jean boils up linens, medicinal moss and herbs. Mharaidh calls out, "Wee Graham, I need you to be heating the cauterising irons till they're near white-hot." Wee Graham knows exactly what to do for he has known life after the hot irons that sealed his own mortal wounds in times past.

For many long hours, Mharaidh, auld Jean and Katriona tend to Affric's wounds and injuries, bathing her in vinegar, setting her broken bones and covering her in a body poultice. The screams from Affric as her wounds were being cauterized has long since passed, much to everyone's relief; now she lay in a deep comatose state. The young men have hot-washed and changed their clothing, William has had his broken nose reset by auld Tam while Mharaidh apologetically tends to the large growing lump on the back of his head where she had struck him hard with the heavy iron skillet.

Later that night, everyone sits around the kitchen table and fireside, discussing everything the three young companions have witnessed. Coinach spoke, "I came upon the track o' the Corserine Balloch'... but I knew something was no' right, everything was unnaturally quiet and I had this awful feeling inside o' me, gnawing at ma peace. There were no birds flying or singing, no beasts grubbin', the whole place was deathly still, no voices, no music or beatin' o' hammers on anvils. I started up the track when I noticed a couple o' horses wondering towards me with their tack hanging loose." Coinach stammers, "Th... that's when I noticed behind the horses, the girls lying on the ground... when I saw their broken violated bodies... ah knew they were all dead... then I realised, I had to get to our Balloch, to my family. I thought, surely my kinfolk couldn't o' known the girls were there. I rode as fast as I could up to the Balloch, praying that the folks up there had missed the girls, for it would mean that my family were still alive... but as ah got closer, ah caught the smell o' death..." Coinach raises his hands in the air and pleads, "Why was I too late... why was I the one to witness this... why not take my life and spare the children?"

Coinach starts sobbing and shaking. Auld Jean wraps her arm around him "Here Coinach, have some hot Toddy." (Hot whisky) She reaches to pull a shawl from her back and places it upon his shoulders as he sits with tears streaming down his face. Coinach drops his head into his hands, sobbing uncontrollably. Mharaidh sits beside him and pulls his head to her bosom. Bailey speaks, "It was almost identical to when I found my family in such a condition, the same betrayal of humanity befell them..." Coinach tears himself from the warm sanctuary of Mharaidh's bosom and scowls at Bailey...

"Its not the same… How could you know how the fuck I feel?" Bailey sits back and glares at Coinach, but he doesn't respond to the jibe, for he sees Coinach is in a grievous state of shock. A moment later Coinach says, "I'm sorry Bailey, I didn't mean…" Bailey lifts his hand and smiles, "No matter." William, sitting morosely beside Bailey, comments, "Affric said Du Berry, or something like that, over and over…"

"De Percy," says Coinach "she said the name de Percy." Auld Tam looks up, "That's the name of a powerful English family just over the border marches in England." Coinach continues to recall what he saw, "I thought everyone in the Balloch was dead, so I started to pull all the bodies I could find to the fire, for the wolves and wild dogs were no' going to feed upon my people. I just didn't know what else to do, ah just couldn't understand why would anyone do this… I kept trying to make sense of it all or thinkin' ah must be goin' fuckin mad, then I heard faint sobbing coming from behind a burning wagon and ran to where the sound of life was coming from… it was there I found Affric, lying naked on the ground and her wain lying beside her crying."

Coinach sobs, "I noticed Affric's hand holding on tight to a dangling bloody foot, pressed to her cheek; then I saw a brutalized mangled body nailed to a fuckin' wagon wheel… I recognised my father… the bastards crucified and defiled him… I don't know how long I stood there … his face… what they had done to him…. though ma head was spinnin' I knew I had to keep Affric and the wain both warm and hoped that they knew I was there for them. I don't know how long we sat there before you both arrived."

"De Percy," says Bailey "I've known a Henry de Percy, he's a northern English knight of king Edward, a cruel and barbarous man that he is, but he usually hides behind the justification of English Law to carry out such deeds, that's what he did in Wales, I've not known this defilement from him without the pretext of Law or warrant. But then this is Scotland, he wouldn't have the right of warrant for such deeds up here, would he?"

"Naw," says auld Tam "that wouldn't be possible, not without starting off a border war." Graham spoke, "Maybe that's what the bastards are after Tam." Mharaidh enquires, "Did Affric say anything else?" William replies, "Affric's only words that made any sense at all were De Percy, that's all she said." He shakes his head and cups his hands towards the fire. "I've hunted this land near on a year now with my father, and ah'v seen outlaws and bandits industrious, but never have I seen anything like this before."

"Aye" Sighs wee Graham, "I've been here peacefully nigh on thirty years and never heard the likes." Auld Tam sneers, "That kinda barbarism was a favorite terror the Norse used to employ on their victims when they were about to invade a realm. To brutally murder innocents or defile them in such a way that the message they left was to spread terror amongst the local population... or it had them fighting amongst themselves first to soften them up before an invasion, Aye, brave men those Norsemen." Wee Graham, with obvious disdain for past enemies' retorts, "Aye Tam, brave killers o' monks, women, wains and well practiced in the arts o' the buggeration o' alter boys and fat sheep."

Auld Tam laughs while staring into the fire drinking his toddy. "Aye Graham, they sea-fairin' fellas feign honor and then they like to write great Saga's of heroism for themselves, aye, those bastards have many faces, and none good to look at... As bad as all o' those fuckin Christians that..." "TAM..." exclaims auld Jean sharply, "you must not talk like that." Coinach suddenly throws his Toddy jug against the wall of the kitchen, smashing it to pieces. He stands up and throws his plaids to the floor and storms towards the door shouting, "Talk about anything you want, but it won't bring my Clan back…" Coinach spits out the words "I'm going to find the evil bastards who did this, and when I do, I will take a long fuckin' time stripping them of skin and life. I swear by A'nnan the Goddess o' the hunt… I will have my revenge." Bailey calls out, "Wait Coinach, we should leave in the morn, and then only to seek out Alain and tell him of this, he will know what is best to do."

Mharaidh, all flustered at the thought of them leaving so late and in such treacherous conditions, spoke out, "You boys have not yet slept nor got your strength back… and it's waist deep in snow and dark outside, you cannot be leaving till it is good light." Bailey says, "We should leave as soon as the dawn breaks and warn Alain and the guardians about what's happened." Coinach states, "If we don't track and gain close time on the bastards who committed this atrocity, then the same fate may befall many others who are unaware of this wanton butchery. We've got to warn everyone we can find to be guarding against strangers who wear arms foreign to our lands." Auld Tam nods at Mharaidh, "They're right yie know Mharaidh." Bailey speaks, "We should tack up the horses now William, for it's near the dawn breaking now." Coinach growls, "I'm coming with yiez…I have no injuries 'ceptin those I carry in my heart."

Everyone feels and understands the chill of emotionless conviction in Coinach's voice. They also know in themselves, that they would be as Coinach is now in seeking revenge on the perpetrators of the Corserine massacre. Bailey speaks, "Mharaidh we'll go and get the horses ready, if you could arrange vittals that we can take with us?" Mharaidh replies "Make sure you take extra winter brats and mantles with you then, we'll get you plenty of winter vittals ready for the journey." Coinach says, "Lets go… Now." He storms out the kitchen door towards the stables, quickly followed by Bailey. William looks to auld Tam and Wee Graham, before he leaves the room, he enquires, "Will you see to the defense o the Craig?"

"Already sorted young Wallace." replies auld Tam. Wee Graham says, "Alain had a gut feeling to be on our toes, but now we will be especially vigilant and double our guard." William looks at Mharaidh, but before he can utter a word… Mharaidh smiles, "Affric will be fine William, her fever has eased and she is being well cared for, as if she were a wounded angel who has thankfully fallen to our healing bosom."

"She'll be all right," agrees auld Jean. Mharaidh clasps William's hand, "Now hurry William while we get your vittals ready." William puts his arms around Mharaidh in a tight embrace, no words are spoken as they hold each other closely, Mharaidh pulls back a little and looks up into William's eyes "You'd better go William… go on and help Bailey and Coinach, we'll prepare everything here for the leaving." reaching up on her tiptoes, she leans forward and kisses William gently on the cheek. He smiles at Mharaidh then leaves to join his friends and make ready for the long journey. Tam calls out "Take the Garron ponies with yiez too and no' be takin' the cobs or Connemara's, the Garrons they're best footed for these winter conditions."

"Aye, ah will do," replies William as he closes the door behind him. The three companions quickly pack for the journey, dressing three horses for the ride and three more as packers. The Garron pony is a strong sturdy and thickset breed, famed for its hardy and stoic temperament and best suited for the long winter trek ahead of them. William says, "Ahm going up to the big house tae see if the vittals are ready."

"I'll go," says Bailey, "you two finish here then bring the

lead and pack horses up to the Keep." As he is about to leave the stables, Bailey looks back at William and nods in the direction of Coinach who hasn't noticed the glance between them. William watches Coinach struggle with his saddle and girth straps, "Here Coinach, let me get that. You fix the pack horses in line then lead them up behind Bailey, we can load the vittals straight onto the horses from there."

Coinach glares at William then walks over to the tether the packhorses without uttering a word; curiously, he keeps staring at William, making him feel very uneasy. William has noticed Coinach's glare for a while and it's beginning to unnerve him. He thinks to himself *'I am no' your fuckin' enemy Coinach, but I'll take only one more dirty look from you, and I swear I will feckn have whatever is bothering you out in the open.'* Coinach finishes tying the packhorses in line as William secures the girth straps on the horses. The two meet up at the door of the stables and Coinach is still gazing at him with a cold strange curious look… "Right that's it…" says William "ahm gonnae…"

"What happened to you?" Enquires Coinach pointing into Williams face. "Yie have two black eyes and a broken nose by the look of it?" William looks at his friend in disbelief, "Are yie fuckin' jestin' me?" Coinach replies tersely "Do I look as if I am in a fuckin' humour…"

William shakes his head, realising Coinach doesn't remember, "Nuthin' happened, ach fuck, I'll tell yie later, lets just get going before the weather turns bad on us." Coinach moves away muttering to himself as he leads the horses out the stable door, he says, "It must o' been a mighty big hefty whack of nothing that did your face in then." Coinach walks outside leading the packers. William shakes his head then laughs to himself. He calls out, "I'll follow you up in a wee while Coinach, I'll just be grabbin' some extra bags o' horse grain then I'll secure the stable doors behind me." Watching his friend leaving, William stands bemused and bewildered. He thinks of Coinach's question, knowing his friend wouldn't understand what happened to his face, especially if he didn't remember that it was Coinach himself who had broken his nose. He shakes his head as his friend leaves the stables.

William stands alone, thinking what he would do if this massacre had happened to him and not Coinach, he shivers at the thought. Grabbing two large bags of grain, William hangs them on his horse and follows Coinach's tracks up to the old Keep, Wallace castle. He soon reaches the back of the kitchens where Bailey and Coinach are outside loading the packhorses with an Obhainn Beg (Small tent) and vittals.

The three friends enter the kitchens then go to the bedside of Affric before their departure, hoping that she may be recovered when next they meet. Bailey and Coinach leave the room, but William waits awhile longer beside Affric. Lovingly, he lifts her hand, clasps it and swears an oath that he will exact revenge with Coinach, he leans forward and kisses her gently on the forehead, then he walks back to the kitchens to say farewell to everyone. Auld Tam asks which route they intend to take. William replies, "Ah reckon we should take the drovers road up the ravine of Ern Cleuch towards the summit, then head straight through the Wolf and wildcats to Blacklorg and down between the Polskeoch and Corlae hills. We should arrive at Ben Buie by nightfall and make camp there. Any fires the guardian army make will likely be seen from its summit at night."

"Aye," sighs Tam, "that would likely be best." William continues, "From that vantage, I reckon we can strike out in any direction, though Dá said that everyone would likely meet at the Silver Flowe lochan, so it shouldn't be hard to find them." Wee Graham says, "Mind and tell your father that we might take everyone up to Gillebrighte and into the old fortalice at Loch Dhùin. If its no' safe there, we have also got the old hunters Crannog's on the hidden inch at loch Fionlas for the women and the wains. Third choice would likely be at the auld Motte up at Dame Helens auld toun. (Dalmellington) But only if we think that stayin' here at the Craig or at Gillebrighte is too much o' a risk." William replies "Aye Graham, I will say to him." Impatiently, Coinach demands, "C'mon you two, we don't have time to be wastin."

The three companions bid their farewells and set off from the warmth and safety of Glen Afton on their perilous journey. Although the early morning is bright in sunshine, the ground is frozen and sheet ice lies perilously beneath the snow. The route they are about to take is the quickest to the southern mid-west of Scotland but it would probably be the most dangerous underfoot. In the kitchens of Wallace Castle, the conversation is of concern for Affric's condition and that of William and his resilience. Auld Tam sits back from the fire and reminisces, "It's only two or three days since young William left us as just a boy…"

"Aye" says wee Graham "Now look at him, yie can fair see a difference in him comin' through as a fine young man."

Mharaidh watches as the three young men disappear into the Wolf and wildcat hills before she closes the door behind her. She looks at auld Jean, Tam and wee Graham and speaks with great concern in her voice "I hope the boys stay away from trouble." Wee Graham, in a soothing voice spoke, "Ach they'll be fine ma'am, don't yie be frettin' none."

"Aye," Continues auld Tam, "Bailey told me that William acquitted himself very well at the Corserine, even in his having never witnessed such wanton brutality before," Auld Tam shakes his head "It's such a tragedy… Who could have committed such an evil on Marchal's people?" Wee Graham says, "We will likely have to wait till spring before we can say for sure." Sighing as he sups his favourite nectar from a horn cup, Wee Graham continues, "Aye, we watched a young lad leave us so full of the joy wearing his fine armour and flying the Dragon pennant o' our people only a few days ago, now this new day we are watching a young man leaving his home with a mans intent set in his heart." Nodding in agreement, Mharaidh sits at the fireside with Tam, Auld Jean and wee Graham.

They sit awhile at the fireside in thoughtful silence, then Mharaidh reiterates her concerns. "I just hope they will be careful and that they all come back home safely. What worries me the most is that young Coinach looks to have black murder set in his heart." Auld Tam shakes his head, "William and Bailey will no' shirk their responsibility to be by his side Mharaidh. I just hope they finds his father first, then they can deal with it wie the guidance o' an aulder wiser head from there, Alain will lawfully seek out the murderers of Coinach's family…"

Suddenly a scream is heard coming from Affric's room, auld Jean and Mharaidh jump up and rush through the door to see Katriona tending to Affric who's desperately fighting to escape the constrictions of the blankets and bandages that wrap her tight. Katriona struggles to tend to the badly injured Affric. She calls out with urgency, "Affric's having nightmares and she's in a state of great fever," Auld Jean immediately attends Affric and begins changing the moss and may-butter poultice on her wounds before pulling the scattered shawls up to cover her naked body, she utters "The poor wee soul…" Auld Tam looks through the room door where Affric hovers precariously between life and death, he speaks quietly to wee Graham, "She has Great Spirit and fight in her, and that might just be the saving o' her."

Wee Graham nods, "Ahl make her a wee Toddy... does any o' yiez want one while I am there?"

***

An extremely long, cold and excruciating day takes it's toll on William, Coinach and Bailey before they reach the foot of Ben Buie, the journey taking almost thrice as long as what it would normally have taken on a summers hunt ride out. As the dark night of winter sets in around them, they laboriously make their way half way up the Buie through snow drifts as deep as the mid-flanks of their horses. Finally they reach a sheltered hollow on a flat outcrop midway up the Buie, familiar to all the hunters of the area. They settle in to make camp using willow and hazel strips, large animal skins and wool felt taken from the pack horses, then hastily they set about building a small winter Obhainn with a small peat fire lit inside, gaining warmth and shelter for the night.

Once everything is secured, wind and watertight, the three friends lay out their sleepin cribs then Coinach fills a pot for boiling water with oats and sleech, (Brine-salt) William lays down rolled skinned eels enclosed in mud and wild garlic around the fire to slow cook, He pulls a thick brat round his shoulders then speaks, "I'm going up to the top o' the Buie to see if I can spot the Guardians camp-fires anywhere in the lower glens. It's a clear night now, so we should see any major fire glow within twenty miles o' here." Coinach jumps to his feet and slaps Bailey hard on the shoulder then he pulls on his thick winter brat round his shoulders, "Wait Wallace... we're coming up there with you."

It takes a long time to trudge through the snow and reach the freezing summit of Ben Buie. Once there, a full moon winter panorama lay before them. William Coinach and Bailey scan the vista, but there is nothing visible or any sign of any campfires in the distance… then William exclaims "Awe fuck…". Bailey enquires, "What is it?" William replies, "Look to mid-south and tell me what you see?" Bailey looks to where William is pointing, "I can't see anything… oh fuck…" Coinach frantically enquires, "What do yiez see?"

"Ahm no' sure," replies William, "I cannae quite make it out." Bailey sighs, "I can."

"Then my eyes are no' deceiving me," says William. "There are least three large camp fires away over there in the direction o' Saint Johns, and lots of smaller ones too by the looks of it?" Coinach calls out, "I see them. One… two… I count three major fires." Bailey ponders, "If it's the main fires of two armies by the size of them, where is that? And who has the third fire going?" Coinach replies, "It's the main crossroads where all roads meet near a place called Saint Johns Kirk of Dalry." William says, "The Guardian army has likely met there as it's the only passing place for fifty miles in this country, especially at this time of year."

"So who is who then?" mutters Bailey, "I thought the main fires would be two or four?"

"What do you mean"? Enquires Coinach. William replies, "That sight means there are likely three small armies down there, spread throughout two glens… but ah don't know who they all are." Bailey spoke "We wont know till we reach the closest fire first." Coinach enquires, "Do you think that it may be Brixs' forces Bailey?" Scanning the panorama in front of him, Bailey replies, "I don't know Coinach, but we have to assume it might be though, we'll be sure enough when we make our approach tomorrow." Shivering in the sub zero wind, William mutters, "Jaezuz it's feckn freezin', we should get back down to our camp before we get caught up here in this feckn wind-chill." Bailey agrees, "Aye lets get back to the camp."

The three friends wrap up and make their way back down the Buie to their Obhainn beg. Later, when sheltering from an arctic winters chill, the three companions talk about what they've seen. Coinach enquires, "What dyie make o' the camp fires then?" William replies, "I reckon they're as far as the Kirk o' Crauford and Saint Johns at least. If each main fire is surrounded by a hundred smaller fires, then there's some amount of men gathered there."

Bailey nods in agreement, "If it's two armies down there, one from the Guardians and the other from de Brix and his Pact followers, then we could be in trouble if we run into patrols from the wrong one." William replies, "When first light breaks, we should strike camp and go see..." Coinach states with conviction, "Me... I'm goin' to hunt down De Percy and take pleasure in killing his whole fuckin' family in front of him, I'll keep him alive a long time tearin' him to fuckin' pieces." William says "Yie don't know if the murders were committed by De Percy, we need to be sure first."

"I know it," replies Coinach with venom in his voice. William shakes his head, "If de Percys' in this country, we'll find him Coinach, and whoever else perpetrated the killings, we'll find the murderers eventually." Coinach says, "I'll follow him to the ends of this fuckin' earth Wallace, no matter where he may try and hide." Bailey says, "You two wont be in a fit state to find anyone if you're up all night blethering, get wrapped up double warm and get some sleep, for we must be moving out of here fast by the first light." The three friends huddle round the small peat fire to try to stay warm in the freezing conditions, burying themselves deep underneath layers of skins, Brats and mantles, sleeping close tight together inside their little Obhainn.

A chill Morning breaks below a clear blue sky over Ben Buie. William, Bailey and Coinach have already packed away their camp and stand keenly observing the beautiful endless snow blanket that caresses the landscape that lies before them. Bailey enquires, "Do we go east and join the main road down to where the armies are camped or will we try and gain time by going directly over the hill tops to the west of us?" William looks and thinks long on the choices open to them. Coinach replies, "That's the west Manquhill's Bailey... If we travel directly over them, it'll be feckn treacherous, but it'll save us near on half a day." William agrees, "Aye Coinach's right, travelling over the top of the hills would be the fastest route, but there could be risk of snow bridges on the climb or drop, which is likely, and we wouldn't see any o' them till it was too late. Ahm no' sure... what do you reckon Coinach?"

"There's a middle route we can take," says Coinach, "There'll be the fast flowing river courses and massive snowdrifts to go through, but if we follow in track with the river, we should reach the plains on the far side of Saint Johns much quicker than by any other route. The tree lines and willow banks should provide us shelter enough to get us onto the pilgrim's road, but if we find it any way impassable, we will have to cut all the way back then climb up and over the Manquhill to the west of us."

Looking to where Coinach is pointing, William ponders, "That would mean we would have to take the long way round past the Garroch hill and down the southern slopes near Craigendarroch to get to saint John's, I reckon the middle route will be best right enough." Coinach scans the peaks to the west, "Aye, there are plenty o' Balloch's and shielin's up there hidden in the braes o' the Manquhill, mostly belonging to the Galloway Ceàrdannan, we could get assistance from them if we need it." Bailey says, "Lets follow Coinach's route."

"Then what are we waiting for?" Enquires William "I'm

feckn freezing up here." Pulling on the reigns of his horse, William begins to canter down through the snow packed slope of Ben Buie, dragging his packhorse behind. Bailey and Coinach quickly follow, driving down the Buie till they come to the banks of the Dalqhaut river ford. The three companions precariously cross the river and begin weaving slowly and carefully down the western riverside of the Dalqhaut towards the lower slopes of the Manquhill. William is thinking of when Stephen of Ireland talked about how the Norman settlers had driven Ireland to a state of almost perpetual provincial war. His thoughts are broken when he overhears Coinach speak with Bailey… "Do you know of this Lord Robert Brix then Bailey?"

"I do…" replies Bailey, "he's a hardy veteran of many wars and campaigns, learning his trade and earning his spurs as a loyal soldier of the Pax Plantagenet. I remember my father telling of when de Brix was greatly honoured by Edward Longshanks by elevating him to the position of the first lord chief justice of the royal Bench in England's history. Apparently he had fought in the Barons rebellion in England many years ago and had saved King Edward Longshanks when he was but a young Prince. De Brix also saved the throne for Longshanks many years before that during the first English Barons revolt."

"Fuck, you really do know him," exclaims Coinach. Bailey appears somber "No… I don't know him at all, I'm more acquainted with his soldiers and his evil doing's." William turns and enquires, "What do yie mean?" Bailey continues, "Brix commanded an army for Longshanks when the English set Wales to destruction by fire and sword." Looking curiously at Bailey, William enquires, "I thought de Brix was a Scot?" Bailey smirks. "No… he's Norman English, one of those Norman families who came to Scotland to supposedly bring you lot civilisation." William is surprised, "So Brix fought against the Cymrans for that Longshanks fella?"

"He did," replies Bailey, "the last I heard of Robert Brix was that he'd been appointed by King Edward as his paladin warden to lord it from the borders of Scotland to Mercia in the mid-west of England, keeping the peace in the north of England and to quell any more Welsh uprisings." William says "Ma Dá told me de Brix served as a regent of Scotland during the minority of Alexander III, but when King Alexander died, ma Dá said that de Brix demanded the throne of Scotland as his birthright and that's what this fuckin uprising is all about." Bailey frowns, "De Brix was the commander of the troops that attacked and massacred all the people of my home valley in Wales, that's how I know of De Brix. The English were sweeping through our country, raping and killing, they fucking destroyed everything, that's their way of bringing peace." Bailey pauses, "I will tell you this Coinach, what has happened to your family at the Corserine… it also happened to me and mine."

"You mean…" started Coinach. Bailey continues, "My mother, father, brothers, sisters… my whole family were tortured and slain at the hands of de Brix's men." Shocked to hear this, William enquires, "But how did you survive and yer family didn't?" Bailey replies, "My father told me to hide away in a small coal bing up in the hills above our village. He told me to wait there and he would come back for me later, but he never did. By the time I had the courage to go back to my home, it was too late… I saw that my family had been murdered by the English, and I saw what you saw Coinach, and I felt as you do now…"

"Fuck," Exclaims Coinach, "I didn't know…" Bailey says, "How could you boyo." Coinach enquires, "How did you manage to get away then?" Bailey replies "It was De Brix."

William exclaims "What…" Bailey, looking ahead, continues, "I had spent many days in my valley doing as we did at the Corserine, bringing in the bodies of my family to a great fire and sending them onwards. I hadn't eaten food nor drank any water for many days, I must have looked like walking death when an English patrol swept into what was left of our little hamlet and caught me unawares." Surprised to hear this, Coinach enquires, "So what happened when they caught you?" Bailey replies, "They had their fun knocking me about, whipping me and beating me awhile, then they decided to hang me by the neck from the tips of an old cart."

"Fuck," Exclaims Coinach. William enquires, "What happened? I mean you're still with us… so what happened, how did yie get away?" Bailey smiles, "I didn't get away… the bastards had a rope round my neck and pulled me up till my toes were barely touching the ground. I was choking as the rope tightened round my neck and I couldn't breath. Fuck, it was like someone had placed my head between two large crushing rocks, I thought my head was going to explode; then suddenly they dropped me to the ground. It was then I saw that De Brix had ridden in to the hamlet and ordered them to stop."

"De Brix told them to stop?" exclaims Coinach. William is intrigued, "But why?"

"I don't really know why," says Bailey "but he did… maybe he took pity, I don't know why, but that was the first time I ever saw de Brix. Then an old English sergeant at arms took care of me and nursed me back to health."

"I don't understand," queries William, "I mean…" Bailey laughs, "I didn't understand neither, but they knew somehow that I was an apprentice bowyer and that I made good longbows, so they set about tasking me to make longbows and arrows for them. They told me if I lasted twenty five years in their service, then I could become a token Englishman…"

"So what did you do?" enquires William. "I stayed with them awhile didn't I, and like you Coinach, I wanted vengeance, no, I needed vengeance on those who killed my family. I wanted to find all of the fuckers who were responsible. But in time I found out that many of the ordinary English soldiers were decent folk and they had no choice but to follow the orders of their knight or baron, or what they did to the Welsh would befall them and their families back in England if they refused." Bailey continues, "Just the same though, there were plenty of the English who relished their chosen work, and I took many of them out of their boots before I left their service."

"What dyie mean?" enquires Coinach. "Well," says Bailey with a grin, "I waited many months before I could strike back. I moved about the English army to try and find the murderers of my people, but it just wasn't possible, so I thought to take my revenge from within on what was available to me, and I got some satisfaction in that."

"What did you do?" Enquires Coinach. Bailey continues, "I got my first chance when our troop were sent into the mountains to hunt down Welsh outlaws as the English called them, but in reality the English just robbed killed anyone Welsh folk they came across, near on every man woman and child they met was put to death one way or another, that's why I decided to take my vengeance upon them all from within. I knew the English were really scared of the Cymran brothers attacking them at night, so I set about them on nightly occasions by waiting till the old sergeant was asleep, then I would slip out at in the dark of night and dispatch a few of the English in their cribs, then get back to the sergeants' tent before the alarm was raised."

William exclaims "Fuckin' hell. That was risky."

"Not for me it wasn't" replies Bailey, "Like Coinach, I didn't care, I just wanted revenge." Coinach enquires, "So how did you manage to dispatch them without getting yerself caught, I mean, what did you do, how did yie do it?"

"Ha" Laughs Bailey, "I learnt damn quick boyo, I remember well the first one I took out. I grabbed him from behind and stuck my blade deep into his throat, just here..." Bailey leans forward and sticks his finger into the side of William's throat. "Then I held him by the chin and I cut out the way... And what a fucking mistake that was... as I dropped him and ran, I could hear the noisy gasping and the rasping sounds coming from his throat all the way back to my tent."

William enquires, "What d'yie mean, you could hear him?" "Well," sighs Bailey "Cutting a mans throat can be a very noisy affair, well his was, that's certain. The noise that came from his throat were his lungs still trying to breathe, but it sounded more like two wet hemp or leather sheets flapping together in a gale, it was fucking scary too boyo's, so I changed my tactic after that." William enquires, "What do you mean... What did you do?" Bailey laughs, "If you have the nerve to chance it, grab them from behind with one hand over their mouth, then you ram your blade hard, rapid and as often as you can into their skull. Do it any way you can, be it up through the chin, through the eye or into the ear, then stir the blade and mince the brain so they drop in a second. But keep a hold of them, for they sometimes wriggle awhile... but it's silent and does the trick." Bailey pauses a moment then continues, "And not so many weird fucking noises escape them."

"Fuck me," exclaims William, "Remind me not to annoy you then fall asleep." Coinach enquires, "So how is it you didn't get caught?" Bailey replies, "Luck and good planning." William enquires, "How did they not know it was you though?" Bailey laughs "Ha! My Cymran brothers would often sneak in at night and do the same as I was doing. I just joined them on every occasion that I could, but I always returned to the camp where I stayed, as the English trusted and never suspected me." William shakes his head, "I know I've asked you this before Bailey, but how did it make you feel taking a life?" Bailey thinks a moment, then he replies, "Nothing prepares you for taking a life, but when you cross that line, there's no turning back... ever."

William and Coinach ride onwards in silence, thinking of Baileys experience, then Coinach enquires, "How long ago is it since you were with the English army, and for what reason did you come up here to Scotland?"

"I came up here about a week ago," says Bailey "I was in North of Wales with the English soldiers that I mentioned, but by that time, between me and the Brothers of the valley's attacking them piecemeal, there were only about a dozen of the original group I first met left, and all very jumpy they were too, but I knew that some of them were now beginning to suspect me, and it was only a matter of time or their nerves would go and I would be killed anyway." Coinach enquires, "So what happened, did you just slip away?"

Bailey sits in thoughtful silence; then he replies, "No, it was an odd incident that forced my hand. I took a chance one night to get a few more of the bastards, which I did, but on the way back to my tent, the old sergeant at arms caught me cold. I could see by the look in his eyes that he knew what I had done." William enquires, "What happened then, if he knew?" Bailey sighs, "I had reached the tent, and as I bent under the flaps to slip back in, he was sitting there waiting for me, he just stared at me awhile, then he asked me, '*why*'..."

"Why?" repeats William curiously. "Why... I know," says Bailey "It's a curious question... just that one little word and I lost control completely, one small fucking word '*Why*' and my brothers, sisters, mother, father, friends... all their voices screamed into my head from the heavens above for vengeance." William enquires, "What did you do?" Bailey smirks, "What could I do? I liked the old bastard, for he had been good to me and he'd saved my life..." Bailey pauses a moment, lost in his own memories, then he hears William's voice "And...?"

"Oh" says Bailey "I rushed at him and rammed my knife under his chin and as far up into his skull as I could push it. I pulled the blade out then cut through his windpipe with a quick deep slash and we both landed in a heap on the floor. But what a shock I got then boyo's, for he was still full of strength and still trying to fight back. Would you believe it? So I rolled over on top of him and I held him down and plunged my knife repeatedly deep and rapid into his heart and twisted the blade with all my strength, and still I had to hold him down awhile before he passed. I really did feel sorry about that one though boyo's, but it had to be done. I wanted his death to be quick, after that I knew that I couldn't stay, so I packed up all my kit, stole a couple of horses and slipped away from what was left of them."

"Fuck me Bailey," exclaims William, "I hope you don't mind us asking you all these questions?" Bailey didn't answer straight away; then he replies, "Wallace, it's hard on my heart to recall, but sometimes it helps the healing greatly to talk. I survived because I knew my enemy; you must strike at them harder than they would ever strike at you. If you ever have to fight the English, remember this, they like to fight with numbers on their side, but if you strike at them unexpectedly or when they think they're safe, that's when they'll fear you most. Always choose your own time and choose your own place, never theirs." William nods in agreement upon hearing this advice.

Coinach enquires, "How many family did you lose then?" Bailey replies "All of them." Coinach exclaims and blusters, "All of them?" Bailey nods, "At first just my immediate family, which was three brothers, five sisters, my mother and father, but I found out later that the English had killed all my people of our valley. The only living family that I knew that were still alive was up here in Scotland." Coinach exclaims, "Jaezuz Bailey, I didn't know… I am so sorry for all these questions."

"Me too." agrees William. Bailey sighs, "Your all right boyo's." Coinach then enquires, "Didn't they try and track you down, or didn't you want to stay in Wales?" Bailey replies, "Ah, it wasn't so easy getting out of Wales, but I had to get out. I didn't want to leave the land that I love so dearly, but I couldn't have survived English rule had I stayed any longer, for they would surely have caught and killed me eventually, though I would have taken as many of them with me as I could. And I almost went to do it once without a care, then I remembered when I as a young boy, when your father Wallace and your uncles came to Cymru. Then there was one time we all came up here with our family to see your Father, but you weren't in Glen Afton then."

"Aye" Replies William "That's sure a hard story that one." Bailey continues with a smile… "So Coinach, I had a long time to think, but I needed much longer to be thinking in peace about what I should do, and now… well… here I am." William smiles, "Aye and here you are Bailey… and right back into the thick of it by the sounds of it."

"I didn't want this," says Bailey "I've seen too many good men of peace take up the blade to avenge, and none have I met or ever known who made this turn have lived a life free of malice or pain. But maybe my hurt and my experience will help heal others of the same pain. That may be my life as God has planned it for me, so now I've elected to seek out justice rather than murderous revenge... though it did have its moments I must admit." Curiously, William enquires, "You still believe in God after what's happened to you?" Bailey replies, "Of course, if you don't believe in God what can you believe in?" William thinks to himself, *The Aicé, Danu, A'nnan, Mother Nature, the Goddess... The Bible sez many times that Christians should commit murder upon non-believers, and all in Gods name, but I don't think Bailey wants to hear that right now.'*

William wanders forward on his horse, trudging onwards through the snowdrifts and lost in his thoughts of what Bailey has been telling him, he stops and turns his horse to look behind him, "Bailey..." says William. "What is it?" enquires Bailey. "Did you never catch any, even one of the murderers of your family?" Bailey replies, "No, I never did, or none that I know off. But there are a few hundred now toes up in the valleys that I have taken as down payment. And by the mantle of justice God has placed upon me, it may be that one day I will meet up with them... or the brothers will."

"A few hundred!" exclaims William, "Fuck me... I couldn't take one life never mind a few hundred." Bailey laughs at his young charge's comment, spoken in all innocence. Coinach brings his horse up beside Bailey. William watches the two stop together for a moment, then sees Coinach reach out, "Will you take my hand?" Bailey sits back on his horse and looks at Coinach with a slightly confused expression. Coinach continues, "I've been so wrong to have thought that you cared naught about me or my family, I cursed you and caused offence between us Bailey... now please Bailey, I beg your forgiveness."

Knowing what Coinach means, Bailey hadn't realised till this moment how much he had appeared emotionally detached and aloof from Coinach's suffering, though he knows it was only to protect his own heart from breaking as a witness to a pain he knew so well, a pain that Coinach must surely now endure. William watches as the two men shake hands and embrace; then he notices tears well up in Bailey's eyes. He smiles to himself then turns his horse once more and nudges it onward, leaving his two friends to share the private grief they so obviously own. He prays to himself that this would be one of life's experiences he would never share with his friends. Lost in thought William wonders over a rise into a small clearing and stops his horses abruptly, a pause that goes unnoticed by Bailey and Coinach.

"Toes up," laughs Coinach, "I like that expression." Bailey smiles as the two friends spur the horses into a canter to catch up with William. They ride on the little distance together, laughing and talking, while following Williams tracks, suddenly their horses spook as they almost run into the back of Williams pack horse.

"What the fuck…" Exclaims Bailey. "Fuck sake." says Coinach. They see why William has stopped his horses. Only a few feet away from them are a man and two boys hanging by the neck and lifeless from the high bough of a tree. It's plain to see that they had been shot with many arrows and emasculated. William whispers, "I didn't want to shout out or move in case there is anyone waiting for us in ambush…"

The three companions sit awhile, searching the thick snow covered woodland for any signs of life, but there is none apparent. William and Coinach dismount. William says, "Lets cut them down Coinach." Drawing his crossbow, Bailey keeps a watchful look out. William says, "This is fuckin' terrible," Coinach agrees. "I know these folks Wallace, it's the Fletcher hunters… old Torquill and his sons."

"Ah know them too Coinach, fuck me man, who is doing this?

The bodies are frozen solid and rigid in the freezing morning air as William and Coinach struggle to cut them down. Bailey says, "Look to the arrow shafts for any maker marks. What kind of flights are they? Maybe we will know who killed them by the marks." William and Coinach examine the arrows, then William replies "It's their own arrows Bailey, whoever shot them used the arrows of the hunters."

"Fuck," exclaims Bailey, "That might have been a way to find out who's behind this, it's a way to find out who you may be up against if they ever leave their mark behind."

William enquires, "What will we do with the bodies?" Bailey replies, "Its too cold to bury them, too wet to fire them as they're frozen like ice. We can't put them on the back of the packhorses… Just wrap them up and pull there bodies high into the tree boughs." William agrees, "Aye that's likely best. We can come back later and bury or burn them, at least this way the wolves and wild dogs wont defile them."

It takes the three of them all their strength to wrap and pull the three frozen bodies high up into the treetops. When they had completed their duty to the dead, Bailey mounts his horse and says, "We had better get out of here. It's not safe to be dallying as we gain closer on the gathering armies down at the plains. There must surely be many patrols out, and though there may be many who may favour us, I reckon there will be more than a few who wont." William is looking ahead, "I can see many tracks in the snow, should we follow them?"

"Aye," Replies Coinach, "But they're spread out in many directions and there's been more than one troop or squadron that's passed this way recently." William says, "Maybe it's time to follow the tracks heading up high ground and over the Manquhill pass. We can make our way from there to the Guardians camp, staying here in this woodland is no' safe."

Struggling through the deep snowdrifts, the companions leave the Dalqhaut Riverside and soon climb up the Manquhill, painstakingly making their way ever closer to the plains of Saint Johns. When they ride high enough up the Manquhill, they occasionally get a glimpse in the distance of the gathered armies and also get a faint scent of the smoke from camp fires, but it feels like they are never going to get through this remote wilderness mix of moor, woodland, gorse thickets and snow-banks to join their kinfolk.

Bailey enquires, "What do you call that place where the third army is camped on the far side of Saint Johns?" Coinach replies "That's Monadh-abh." Bailey looks at Coinach, "Fuck, what does that mean?" William replies, "Land o' water or water of life, depends on who's telling you." Bailey half laughs as his horse sinks gut-deep in the boggy ground, he exclaims, "They were not fucking jesting then… and I thought Wales was a wet boggy fucking realm." Coinach points… "It looks as though the pilgrims road is clear down there by the river." Coinach spurs his horse and drags his packhorse into a canter the half-mile down to the riverside, quickly followed by William and Bailey. When they get down by the river, Coinach turns with a hapless expression, he shrugs his shoulders and says, "Sorry Fella's…"

They look down at the fast flowing river to see that it is deep flooding the old pilgrims' road, William exclaims, "Jaezuz Coinach, the whole place is flooded and in spate." He shouts at Bailey and Coinach above the noise of the spey. "This is a madness, we're never going to get to Saint John's by this route, we're going to end up miles to the east or fall in that feckn river." Coinach shouts to them, "We have to go back up high, we'll never get through here. I know it too well, the whole place will be flooded for miles." Bailey blows warm breath onto his cold fingers, "Either way, we are going to freeze to death if we don't get across or find some way out of here soon." A disgruntled Bailey curses, "Fuck Coinach, I thought you said there was Ceàrdannan Balloch's on this route where we might get some help?" Coinach replies, "There is, but we should go back up to the crest of Garroch hill, just over yonder." William points, "It's just up there a mile or so Bailey. From there we should see Dunveoch, that's where the camp of the Fletcher clan is cooried up in a wee coppiced woodland. We could get up there and try and spot another route down the Glen o' Lee from there, that should take us too Saint John's." Coinach agrees, "When we get up there we could ask the Fletchers for a guide. But it's going to be a hard talk in hell with the Fletchers clan, for that was their chief and his two sons we found earlier." William shakes his head "It has to be done Coinach."

They hastily leave the deep spey of the river and make their way westwards and up towards the crest o' the Garroch. The snow is deep and the ground underfoot is soft and boggy, but they begin to feel the warmth of the open sky replacing the chill felt beside the fast flowing river. After a few hours climbing, William and Coinach see in the distance a peculiar looking woodland set in the depth of a hollow in Dunveoch hillside. Coinach points, "That's the Fletchers Sheilin over there." Bailey looks across the skyline but can see nothing except the occasional bushes of low growing hill scrub. "Where?" he enquires. "Just over there," replies William. He points across the hillside towards a large Willow coppice, about half a mile away. Coinach says, "Fuck fella's, I'm sure no looking forward to letting the Fletchers clan know what's happened to old Torquill and his boy's."

"I know," says William "They're real tough fuckers, there's no way of telling how they may react." Nobody utters another word as they make their way up the side of the Garroch towards Dunveoch. William says, "You'll never come on a traveler's sheilin or Balloch easy Bailey. They build their homes and shelters into nature, rather than tearing nature down to build a home." Bailey says with a smile, "I kind of like the life you Scots live up here."

"Aye, me too," laughs William, "I've learned so much from the Ceàrdannan folks since moving to Glen Afton with ma father, they're great folk to be knowing."

Travelling slightly ahead of them, Coinach pulls his packhorse close and smiles hearing the words of respect used by William and Bailey about his kinfolk, but then the pain returns, thinking his kinfolk have forever joined with nature at the Corserine. He stops for a moment on high ground of the Garroch, then points and shouts out, "Look… down there, they're facing each other off down on the plains of Dalry." William says, "At least they're no' fightin, yet…" Bailey retorts, "Aye, not yet…" William says, "Lets get goin' to the Fletchers Sheilin. We can find out from them if they know a quick route down before we miss everything."

As they pace-canter towards the shielin' Bailey enquires, "William, what do you think the Fletchers will do when we tell them about the bodies we found down at the river… will they believe it's connected to us this foul deed?" William replies, "This won't be easy Bailey. As gentle as they are, equally these Gallóbhet are the most feared fighters in the Kings army."

"Gallóbhet?" enquires Bailey curiously. William explains, "Sorry Bailey, the Gallóbhet is what the rest of Scotland call the fighting folk of Galloway, partly in scorn and partly through fear. Galloway was its own separate Kingdom until very recently, they only joined the estates of Scotland after the death of good King Alan about fifty years ago." Bailey enquires, "What's so special about them?" William replies, "The Gallóbhet are made up of Scots and Irish Clans, like the Fletchers, Marshalls, MacDougall's MacDowell's McWilliam's, Scotts and many more, even some o' us Wallace from the Rhinns and Machars. They're a fiercely independent mercenary gathering o' people, the men are called Gallóglaigh (Galloglass) and the women are called the Gallóbhan, (Gallovan) collectively, Gallóbhet." Bailey says, "It would seem then to me that someone is trying to kill off these Gallóbhet quickly and quietly." Coinach pulls his horse round, "I'll tell the Fletchers what we found. Though they know and trust you Wallace's, but they will not doubt my word as a brother Ceàrdannan."

William and Bailey nod their heads in agreement, then the three friends spur their horses into a hard canter. As the snow thins on the ground they speed toward the Fletchers hillside coppice home on Dunveoch. The free canter cheers the spirits of riders and horses as they turn the canter into a gallop towards the Fletchers Sheilin. William, having been here recently, races ahead and in through a narrow concealed entrance in the dense overgrown coppice ahead of Bailey and Coinach. Only slowing down his horse a pace as he approaches the entrance, William canters on into the Sheilin when suddenly his horse spooks and rears. He struggles to regain control of his horse and packhorse when he notices swarms of small creatures scurrying everywhere. He mutters, "Rats?"

Bailey and Coinach soon ride in behind him. They halt and look around the enclosure where everything appears normal… everything except the multitude of rats and the eerie stillness. Even though soft smoke wafts through obhainn roofs, the Shielin' appears totally deserted. William enquires, "What the fuck is that smell?" suddenly his heart sinks, he glimpses something in an Obhainn doorway and realises its rats gnawing the fingers off the bloody hand of a child sticking part way out the door. Coinach jumps from his horse and runs to the main obhainn belonging to Torquill Fletcher, the clan chief. Coinach kicks' open the door and disappears inside. William dismounts slowly… "Bailey, that's the smell o' opened guts and fresh blood isn't it?"

"I reckon so," replies Bailey. "I fear we've arrived into another bloody nightmare." Dismounting, Bailey surveys the Sheilin' as William walks over to the obhainn where the bloodied child's hand is sticking out. Bailey keeps a watch, then he notices William involuntarily turning his head away, coughing and retching, he looks across at Bailey. "They've been butchered Bailey, all have been bound, their throats have been cut and stomachs opened."

Bailey looks to where Coinach had ran, only to see him stagger out of the Chiefs obhainn and collapse to his knees and putting his hands to his head in great angst. Bailey runs over to Coinach and then on inside the Obhainn, only to be greeted by carnage. Holding his sleeve over his nose he searches for anyone alive, but it's in vain. Torquill's wives and entire family all had their throats cut, some had been skewered in the chest by sword or had their skulls split. Bailey leaves the Chiefs' obhainn and pulls Coinach to his feet.

"William, Coinach… check every obhainn, Bothy, hut and bow-wagon for anyone that may be left alive." William and Coinach show no emotion or reaction to Bailey's order. "NOW," commands Bailey… "MOVE…"

The two companions are suddenly sparked back to their senses by Bailey's commanding voice. They quickly investigate everywhere and anywhere in the Fletchers sheilin where they might find any sign of life. After a short while William and Coinach meet back at the horses, Coinach looks at William and says simply, "None…" William simply shakes his head, then he to replies too, "None." The two friends stand in silence looking all around the enclosure, in the hope Bailey will return with news that someone is still alive, they hear angry gruff curses then they see Bailey walk around the corner of a small roundhouse, kicking at fleeing rats. They know by the look on his face that he too had found none alive.

"Get mounted," orders Bailey. "We can't say here. Did you both notice that many of the bodies are still warm? We've no time to lose… if we move out through the main gate, we may see fresh tracks that'll lead us to whoever perpetrated this evil. Maybe it's the same bastards who visited the Corserine, NOW MOVE… there's nothing we can do here."

Coinach springs onto his saddle and spurs his horse on. Both William and Bailey follow him as he makes his way out of the enclosure, they pull to a halt just outside the shielin' where they examine the many horse tracks at the entrance. "Which ones?" Enquires Coinach. Bailey replies "Follow the freshest cut tracks." William pauses for a moment, examining the tracks, he says "We've ridden in from the North, the western track looks old and frozen, but the ones heading east… look, they're the freshest, it looks like many riders having passed through this way only recently." Coinach calls out, "C'mon." "Wait…" says Bailey. Coinach demands impatiently, "Why do we waste time here?" William replies, "We're near the camp of the Guardians Coinach, I can make out their marker flags from here, we should go there now and report everything to ma Dá."

"He's right," says Bailey, "but we must be cautious, if the battle takes off before we get there and they go to fight it out, the last thing we want is to be caught in the wrong place and not to be recognised as friends." Coinach reluctantly agrees. They pull on their horses and continue their perilous journey toward the Guardians camp.

It's been a long arduous day since they packed their camp halfway up Ben Buie to where they are now. With a lack of sleep and what they've experienced these last few days and the addition of the severe Scots winter chill in their bones, they're now feeling the debilitating effects of the freezing temperature dropping drastically. Despite all the warm clothing they wear, the combination of factors is near to reducing their body movements to a minimal degree of control. "Look over there," exclaims Coinach, "we're gettin' close, ah can make out the flags and Pennants of the Guardians." "Aye," says William, "I see the Wallace clan flags away to the left flank of the camp."

"Lets get down there fast," urges Bailey "I don't like being caught out here in the open like this. If there are skirmish patrols out here and this battle commences, then we could be in a difficult position with no cover or defense against any attack." Spurring their horses forward through the snow and on down towards the woodland surrounding the plains, Bailey thinks to himself that William has shown himself to be reliable under the most trying of circumstance. His baptism with the Corserine massacre and his resilience to keep going impresses Bailey. Another vital asset William is beginning to show is his reading of the land situation and a natural sense of leadership in making sound decisions. Bailey's thoughts are lost as they push their tired horses till they can run no longer, then they begin to meander along the pilgrims' road, each of the friends are thinking solemn thoughts on what they have seen and experienced, not noticing that their concentration and alertness is not as it should be because of cold, hunger and a creeping fatigue.

Losing any sense of caution and awareness of their surroundings, they enter a large thicket of gorse and dense woodland that slowly begins to engulf them, all they are aware of is the slight warmth the woodland gives them away from the freezing wind-chill of the upland moors and finally closing in on their destination. Suddenly, without any warning, mounted Knights charge out of cover and ride directly at them with needle-sharp quicksilver lances lowered for battle. From behind the three friends comes another four mounted knights, also riding at speed directly at them with lances pointed at their backs, there's no time for them to react, no time to maneuver... the heavily armoured knights thunder towards the three beleaguered colleagues with razor sharp needle tipped lances, aimed directly at their hearts... there's nowhere to run, they're trapped...

PLAINS OF DALRY

Warlike Knights pull on their reigns to halt their steeds with lance tips mere inches from the faces of William, Bailey and Coinach, they're caught totally unprepared by these mounted warriors. William curses under his breath as he places his hand on the hilt of his sword. He notices Bailey bring his arm up slowly behind his back, searching for his crossbow. Coinach has already pulled throwing blades discreetly from inside his battle-jack. William's senses prickle when a crack of a breaking branch causes him to look to his flanks, he watches as ancient looking warriors emerge from the gorse thickets on either side of them. These enormous looking mercenaries encircle the three friends. William studies these warriors who wear heavy Highland bull-skin brats over full-length chainmail habergeons and very odd-looking rust covered conical helmets, topped with Eagle feathers upright. The strange looking helms are large and leaning back at a slight angle, the rear sloping leatherneck protection runs deep down the nape of their necks.

The features of these warriors are obscured by a long nasal bar and broad jaw guards, their faces are half masked by large unkempt beards, though by the look of these wild men or what could be seen of them, their faces have taken the brunt of all battles these fierce looking men had ever fought in. Each warrior holds a lethal looking spartaxe and carries a large shield, ornately inlaid with the most intricate knotwork.

"Innis Óglaigh… Gallóglaigh," mutters Coinach quietly, "Island and Galloway mercenaries…" The lead Knight raises his lance away from William's face, but the flanking Knights and Gallóglaigh keep a focus on the three companions. Thinking fast, William turns and fixes his gaze on the lead Knight, a tall and broad shouldered man, similar to Bailey in his powerful physique, greatly enhanced in appearance by his battle armour. It's obvious that he too is experienced in warfare with his scarred ruddy face. The Knight removes his helmet, revealing his long black pleated hair. William could see it's tied and platted in the same fashion as his father, then he notices the coat of arms on the shields and horse caparison of a brilliant white background with a thick blue bar running along the shield-head with three white stars affixed inside the bar, William has seen this before, but where?

Another Knight moves his horse forward and closer to William, but this Knight wears a much different coat of arms. This Knights' shield also has a white background, but with three yellow scallops running inside a black bar and a distinct black crescent moon in the centre of the shield. Again this is repeated on the caparison of this knight's horse. William is familiar with this armorial coat of arms too, but he can't remember where he has seen it before. If these are the men that have been committing the atrocities at Corserine and Dunveoch, William steels himself and prepares to take as many of them as he could. All he has to do is wait out the impasse and strike at the slightest given opportunity. Glancing at Bailey and Coinach, he could see the same thoughts are in their heads, both waiting on his next move…

"William Wallace?" enquires the Knight who appears to be the commander. "Who's askin'?" enquires William gruffly while gripping and pulling slightly on his grandfather's sword. The Knight laughs, "Touchy young fucker?" much to the amusement of the surrounding troop and Gallóglaigh. William replies with contempt, "Put your lance down and face me on foot and I'll show you who's fuckin' *touchy* ya old bastard." Bailey sighs, "Ah fuck, here we go then…"

Everyone looks at William who is refusing to take his piercing gaze away from the lead Knight who laughs out loud once more, then he stares menacingly into William's eyes, but says nothing. The silence sends a chill through Williams mind. The Knight senses the brave but impetuous nature of youth in William, he also knows by experience that a deliberate gaze and taking time to think, is more effective at unnerving a young mans bravado than simply fighting without the thought of cunning. The Knight eventually replies, "Aye, ah reckon that you would fight me alone young Wallace, even though you're aware my men could skewer you all like hogs before I finish this sentence." A defiant William replies, "Well you had better make it a good fuckin' skewer old man… for I'll still reach you… and ma grandfathers sword here will slake it's long thirst in your boney fuckin' face."

The Knight sits back in his saddle, slaps his thigh and laughs aloud again. Bailey keeps his eye him now that everyone is in no doubt of William's intention, futile as it may be. The Knight is all the three companions can focus on in their tunnel vision. Coinach sits coldly staring at the older Knight as though at any second he will spring at him barehanded, such is the tension running through his body. At that moment, another Knight moves his horse closer to William and pulls off his helmet, revealing a strong sharp-featured young man about the same age, with his long brown hair simply tied back. "Wallace, it's me…" says the young Knight with a smile. William recognises something in the smiling eyes of the young knight. "Wallace don't you recognise me... From Crossraguel?" William stammers. "What... Who...?" The young Knight smiles at William again, momentarily disarming the three defiant companions. William is puzzled trying to remember who this handsome young knight is, and from where he knew him? Suddenly he raises his eyebrows in recognition... "Graham?"

"Aye, It's me Wallace... John de Graham o' Dundaff."

"Fuck me," exclaims William "it really is you..." He smiles as he recognises a childhood friend. Graham dismounts and walks towards William, removing his armoured Gauntlet and reaches out his hand in friendship. The older Knight enquires, "Is that big runt young Wallace right enough?"

Aye," replies Graham. The Knight sighs, "I should have known it. A typical Wallace... all fuckin' attitude and no fuckin' brains." Graham laughs, "Aye, he is all that for sure, and he's much bigger now than I remembered him, but I couldn't mistake that look of an inbred bastard for any other than an Ayrshire Wallace."

The Older knight laughs, dismounts and walks over to William. "You look so much like your grandfather Billy, he had the same attitude too boy." William dismounts and embraces his friend. "John de Graham?" Exclaims William, "Feck I didn't recognize you, not till I saw that smiling face of yours... and that hasn't changed much 'ceptin you're a lot more wrinkled now... just like your mother."

"Fuck off Wallace," laughs Graham, "You've lost a bit of the bloom of youth yourself... How many years is it since Leckie Mòr belted us both?" William grins, "Ha Leckie... now there is a man to avoid on a good day." Graham stands back and looks at him, "Good to see you Wallace, but where have you been? We've been patrolling for the guardians and keeping a look out for you for nigh on two days, what kept yie?"

While William recounts his experience, the horse soldiers' raise their lances and the wild looking Gallóglaigh disperse, all talking amongst themselves. Bailey feels relief; he sits back in his saddle takes off his helmet and breathes in the crisp air that renews his life force with every intake of breath. Suddenly he hears a woman's voice behind him, calling out to Coinach. Both Bailey and Coinach look round to see a tall auburn haired woman sitting on a bay-brown black-leg hobyn as she emerges from the woodland. Then they notice three other women on dun-brown hobyn's follow her out of the dense green gorse and dark golden bracken, each carrying a taught horse-bow with three viciously barbed drop arrows in their pull hand. Bailey had seen the knights on horseback and sensed the presence of the wild Gallóglaigh on his flanks… but he had no awareness of these women who now emerge from the woodland. The fact these riders had been invisible to both his eye and his senses irks him…

'*Fuck*,' thinks Bailey, '*How could I have missed these women hidden in the woods?*'

"Faolán…" calls out Coinach, "Lihd, Eochaidh, Fiónlaidh…"

"Co'nas Coinach," replies Faolán, "Fuck…" Exclaims Coinach. With one bound, he leaps off his horse and runs over to embrace each of the four women, though Eochaidh keeps her bowstring taught and a vigil on William and Bailey, for she trusts none. Unexpectedly Bailey notices a flirty glance from Lihd. She's small and of athletic stature, with long shining brown hair and hazel eyes, carrying a horse bow and full quiver of arrows as do Eochaidh and Fiónlaidh. He also notices that each of the Gallóbhan carry on their backs two sgian-lùbach, short curved swords.

Lihd smiles at Bailey over Coinach's shoulder, curiously he feels a wave of excitement at the glance from this beautiful woodland creature. Then he sees Faolán winking at de

Graham. He studies Faolán's beautiful features, with her long Auburn hair plaited back and her piercing sky blue eyes. Her skin glows as alabaster and her feminine frame is scarcely concealed by her woodland clothing. He also notices that these female warriors of the Gallóbhan wear a style of earth brown coloured léine, similar to that worn by the Gallóglaigh warriors. Their bodies are protected by dark brown light-weight leather plate-armour instead of chainmail, with thick box pleated dark brown hooded brats, accentuated by loose interwoven rags, making these warrior women virtually invisible when in the dense woodland. He also sees Faolán is carrying a horse-bow and full quiver of arrows, with two of the long curved sgian-lùbach tucked into her waist-belt at her back.

Fiónlaidh is dressed in similar garb, but she is smaller than Faolán with long thick wiry red-blond hair tied back, her hazel eyes and features are as the description of the praetorian noblewomen of old Rome, she also carries a small deadly crossbow with a quiver of quarrels and another larger quiver with five short javelins hanging by her saddle.

Bailey also couldn't help noticing the beautiful features and athletic movement of these women, who emit an overwhelming sense that they're well experienced and more than confident in the arts of war... "Bailey," shouts Coinach "Come over here, I want to introduce you to my cousins from the Machars of Galloway."

"Thought you'd never ask boyo." replies a jubilant Bailey. He quickly dismounts and joins Coinach with this strange mixed band of Warriors from the deepest untamed wild hinterlands of Galloway. "Wallace," Says Graham, "May I introduce to you sir William de Douglas... or 'Hardy' as everyone calls him, he's our commander and a long time friend o' your father."

Hardy smiles and offers an outstretched hand in friend-ship… "Co'nas young Wallace, I'm pleased to be meeting you at long last. Your father Alain told me you would be coming soon and I was to look out for you and bring you all back to the plains of Saint John's." Hardy scans the tree line. "We should no' be wasting any more time here lads, for there are many patrols about, and not all from the Guardians. We'll take a cut straight through the woodland directly onto the old pilgrims road, that's the fastest way back for us, and it should free us clear from any marauding bands of Pact patrols."

William shakes Hardy Douglas by the hand, "I am honoured to meet with you sir William…" Hardy scowls, "Young Wallace… call me hardy or Douglas, for there are too many fuckin' Williams in this mans army. When anyone is to call out the name *William*, I ask yie Wallace, how many men would be distracted looking around and singing, *Aye* like some mad choral ensemble?" William laughs, "Aye Hardy, ah know what yie mean." Hardy places his hand on William's shoulder, "And I will be calling you young Wallace." William replies, "That's fine by me Hardy." Hardy smiles; pleased that he has found Alain's son, but now he wants to get back to the Guardian camp and deliver him safely to his father. As he returns to mount his horse, Hardy commands, "We should leave this place now young Wallace and afford our friends on the plains our fine company."

"Ha Wallace…" says a cheery Graham. William replies with a grin, "Ha, to you too Graham… feck but it's good to see you after all these years. And I'm sure glad that you recognised us though." Graham smiles "Well apart from you being the ugliest big fucker in the Wolf and wildcats, it was the Dragon on your chest piece and shield that told us who you were long before any words were spoken."

Graham pulls his own horse and mounts, "You'd better call your men Wallace, Hardy waits for none, look see, he pulls out with his troop and the Gallóbhet already."

'My men?' Thought William, *'Promoted already and I haven't done anything?* ' He laughs to himself and calls out to Bailey and Coinach, who come running over immediately. Bailey enquires, "What's happening?" William replies, "We're going to the Guardians camp with Hardy Douglas and his men, and we're leaving right now." Bailey hesitates; then he enquires, "If it's all right with you William, I'll ride with Coinach and Faolán there."

"Who?" Enquires William

"Faolán… Lihd, Eochaidh and Fiónlaidh are the leaders, or Aicés as you fellas like to call them." Bailey points to Faolán, looking magnificent and regal in her martial garb, holding a natural poise as a fighting warrior of merit. William notices Lihd smile at Bailey, who says quietly to himself, "Lihd, mo shíorghrá" (my eternal love). William laughs out loud "Fuck, you're fair picking up the Ghaeltacht twang already Bailey." He smiles at Bailey as he continues; "you seem to have fallen off your horse for that bonnie wee Gallóbhan over there." Bailey looks at William with a child-like innocence "William boyo, I think I'm smitten…"

Watching the female warriors, William could see they are from fine Gallóbhan stock by their proud appearance. He has also notices that Faolán their Chief, has her eye on Graham, then unexpectedly, she looks directly at William. For a moment, there seems to be a spark of recognition between them as she lowers her head and smiles, *'My God'* thinks William, *'what a gorgeous smile.'* Faolán glances at him one more time then she turns her horse and canters away. William glances at Lihd then he speaks to Bailey, "A fighting Gallóbhan Aicé there that may be a match for the fightin Bailey Wallace? You'd better be watching yourself with those women Bailey, for it's true their love making is as fearless as their warfare, and that's lethal enough, and an extreme mistake to be making is for those who would think these women to be of the weaker sex... and I should know Bailey, for I have been romancing Coinach's sister Affric for long enough, and she's a ranking Aicé of the Gallóbhan herself." Graham approaches then he says, "Ride beside me Wallace, for we have much to talk about."

Mounting their horses, William and Graham ride to the front of Hardy's mounted troops to join him. Running alongside them at a fixed pace are the feared and notorious Gallóglaigh warriors. Men of immense physical prowess and stamina, all born to fight for the old Kings, clan Chiefs' and warlords of Galloway and from Donegal in Ireland with extreme brutality, and without any thoughts of mercy upon the vanquished. Bailey rides beside Lihd, but he is unable to hide his curiosity, he enquires, "I've never seen or heard of women like you Lihd, certainly not in England or Wales... where are you from?"

"Ha," sighs Lihd "We're the Scots-Irish Guardians of this wilderness. Our people are sometimes called Gall-Ghàidhil (Goll-Gael) by townies. We've made this remote wilderness of Galloway our own since time began... a dangerous place for any outsider with ill intentions on their mind." Bailey is more than happy to be conversing with anyone other than William and Coinach, He enquires further "So tell to me Lihd, what's the difference between the Gallóglaigh and Gallóbhet... apart from the obvious?"

"I'll tell you," says Lihd, "The Gallóbhet are men and women together, the combination of our most ruthless fighting men the Gallóglaigh, and the assassination stealth of our finest women the Gallóbhan Aicé's, those qualities combined are called the Gallóbhet, we're despised by most when not needed, but we're the finest of warriors to be hiring when the nobles require some dirty work done, here, England or in Ireland. The Gallóbhet have borne themselves a reputation over time that's reached into Europe as a feared mercenary elite... for anyone who dares to hire our services." Coinach, listening nearby, sighs, "Aye Bailey, the Gallóbhet still merit the honoured position of standing directly in front of the Scots King in times of war." Bailey is curious, "I've never heard of the Gallóbhet in Cymru nor...?" Lihd interrupts with a cheeky smile, "That's because you Cymrans still use big shovels to dig wee holes for coal and have no need of swords... but most surely a need for an education."

Bailey's face lights up in surprise at this answer from the sprite-like Lihd. She spurs her horse onward, leaving Bailey slightly confused, but most definitely feeling alive as a man.

The troop led by Lord Douglas, soon ride onto the old pilgrims route to Saint John's of Dalry and onward. William glances behind him to see Bailey, Lihd, Faolán and Coinach in deep conversation, following up at the rear are Eochaidh and Fiónlaidh, both keeping a hawk-like vigil for any would-be attackers behind or around them. "This is a tough looking troop o' warriors you have here Graham, especially with these Gallóbhet in our company. I thought the men of Carrick and the Wolf and wildcat Gallóglaigh looked fucked in the head and incorrigible, but these warriors make our men look like angels by comparison."

"Aye," Replies Graham, "They're no' the people to be fighting against if you've any choice."

William laughs nervously as he observes these fierce looking warriors, "They have a look about them as though they were feckn disappointed we were not to be the focus o' their retribution." Sitting back in his saddle, Graham replies,

"Wallace, these mad fuckers are grown from childhood like the ancient Spartans as a fighting force. Mainly they are orphans or bastards from Clan chiefs or foundling sons and daughters hailing from Galloway, Antrim, Ceanntyre and the Hebrides, men and women who train together as wains at the Rhinns ynch fort o' the Aicé at Dùn Reicheit, or up in Dun Sgiath on Skye." William admires the attitude and pride attributed to the Gallóbhet as Graham continues, "Since Brix and his Turnberry Pact began attacking all the small Shielin's and Balloch's all over Galloway, Carrick and along the eastern Annandale marches, most of these men and women have had their clans slaughtered by marauding bands of English mercenaries, brought here by de Brix from his lands and compatriots in England. It's been a long while since the Gallóbhet rode out in service with the Guardian army and it's their families left behind that has paid the ultimate price, now the Gallóbhet rightly claim the blood tax… and they aim to get it."

"Ah can understand Graham," says William. "What's the point of being a Guardian when you can't even guard your own family?" Graham continues, "They're resolute oath warriors Wallace. Anyways, where have you been? We've had patrols out looking for you for two full days now?" William sighs, "We weren't very far from here. We'd travelled less than thirty miles out o' Glen Afton, and I tell yie, what we've seen up at the Corserine Balloch of Coinach's family was a bloody massacre, someone murdered his father and butchered his whole Clan." Graham looks at William horrified, "Fuck… Coinach's whole family?"

Pausing a moment, William explains, "Graham, all of the Marchal's clan were slaughtered, and ah mean slaughtered, I still cant take in what I witnessed. There was one sole survivor, young Affric, Coinach's sister. It was the same bloody business we saw at the Fletchers Sheilin up at Dunveoch. The entire Fletcher clan had been massacred only this morning. Fuck Graham, two Gallóbhet Chiefs and their entire clans murdered, and we don't know by who or for why? I've never dreamt such atrocities could ever be committed by any man." Graham shakes his head… "Wallace, there's been a score or more of such massacres that we know off already, I have seen sights that will live in the darkest shadows of my heart forever."

"I feel the same," says William, "when we left the Fletchers Balloch' we were following what we thought were the perpetrators' tracks when you came upon us. Did you meet with any troops or pass any soldiers before us? We thought we might catch up to the perpetrators."

"Naw," replies Graham "we saw you coming down from the high moorland we thought you might be spies sent by de Brix, but I'm sure glad to see it was you. De Brix has been the cause of much slaughter in Galloway Wallace, the Gallóbhet are a proud race o' folk and they want their vengeance. They demand payment in blood, not justice. Their hatred for the house of Brix is all but under control for the sake of the greater good, but who could blame them if they do not accept any peace deal that Wishart may broker, I don't know how we will contain the blood feud that boils in the veins of these Gallóbhet if peace is restored."

"Fuck… this is grim tidings whichever way you look at it," says William "And you said Wishart? Is he down there?"

"In all his finery" replies Graham "even though you can see his fighting armour underneath his black robes, he leads a delegation of peace negotiators, including abbots from Glenluce, Dundrennan, Tungland and the Priory of Taigh Mhàrtainn." William says "I hope they broker a settlement with Brix and his pact."

"And I," replies Graham "I've never witnessed so much killing nor such brutality in all its manifestations. It's put a cold feeling around my heart."

"Ah sure know what yie mean," says William, "since I set my path on this cause with my father only these last few days, what I have seen and what I feel now leaves me cold and confused. Ah'll tell yie this Graham, I don't like the feeling afoot in the realm, its like something far beyond our ken is present and bodes a greater evil we must run with. It's like this malignant air will not stop till it's seen out its course, no matter what we do."

"Have you ever killed a man Wallace?" enquires Graham, "Naw," replies William "but whoever has committed these deeds should be brought to equal measure, I don't think I would flinch at seeing justice meted out to them as they have dealt out such savagery themselves, be it from town, Gallóbhet or Breathaim law... Have you killed anyone yourself?"

"Naw, me neither," replies Graham, "but I will if needs be." William enquires, "Do you know what the fuck this uprising is really all about for I don't?" Graham glances curiously, "Don't yie know?"

William runs his hand down the mane of his horse, "Naw, no' really, I only know what my father has told me. I don't have any ken about this uprising nor anything about who would or should be wearing the treasured crown of Scotland." Graham smiles, almost in disbelief. "I'll tell you Wallace, at least then you will know when you get killed what it's for." William laughs as Graham continues, "Lord Robert de Brix of Annandale and his son de Brus, earl of Carrick, both refuse to accept the maid of Norway as our rightful Queen, Brix is making an attempt at usurping the throne of Scotland by instigating this uprising, but John de Balliol lord of Galloway has right of ascension before him."

Somewhat perplexed William enquires, "Who the fuck is John Baliol?" Graham replies, "He's a Norman Scots baron, the hereditary Lord of Galloway. He also has vast possessions in England and France, but the Lord Baliol only rises to protect his lands in Scotland from de Brix's attacks. His own senior claim to the Crown is his by the right of descent from queen Margaret, his maternal grandmother… and his mother 'Queen' Devorguilla, daughter of King Alan, the last King of Galloway. But in fairness to Baliol, he's a loyal supporter of the Maid of Norway's rights to the throne and vehemently opposes the claim of the Brix for that reason, it is de Brix who raises the flag of war and Baliol raises arms only in defense."

"I know well the lineage of the maid of Norway," says William "But how does that play for the Brixs' claim for the Crown of Scotland?" Graham continues, "Margaret was the eldest daughter o' David, the Earl of Huntingdon, brother to William the Lion, King of Scotland. Her sister Isabel was the second daughter o' David and she's the mother of Robert de Brix. Now de Brix wishes to subvert Alexander's granddaughter from her rightful ascension to the throne. De Brix and his Pact utterly reject being subordinate to a woman so he's asserting a blood claim, stating that the throne of Scotland should be his." William exclaims, "Fuck, you're losing me…"

Graham continues, "Wallace, you'd better be finding yourself right damn quick then, if this uprising cannot be ended in peace or by an agreed treaty, Scotland will fall to civil war, and then you must choose yer side." Graham continues, "There are thirteen claimants, fourteen including the King of England, and if we cannot keep the peace now, I don't know what will happen to Scotland if they invite in the English King."

Willaim says "I know where I stand Graham and that's with our Aicé the maid of Norway, then Baliol through the blood of Devorguilla. I'll follow my family and my heart and that is given to the rightfull Queen of Scotland. And should she for any reason refuse the throne, then I must follow the bloodline, which means that John Baliol would be my liege lord by right of matriarchal lineage."

Graham smiles and holds his hand out, "Spoken like a true guardian o' the Aicé mo chara." William grins then reaches out and accepts the gesture of goodwill. "Graham... how do you know of the Aicé Guardians?" Graham replies, "Dyie see that tattered old worn-out blue Dragon of the Wallace on your battle-jack and shield?"

"Aye, what about it?" enquires William. Graham reaches inside of his breastplate and pulls out a piece of furled material, "What's that?" enquires William. Graham unfurls the material to reveal a long tri-sided pennant with a background of emerald green running full length down the bottom half of the pennant, with a matching pastel saffron panel running along the top half. Centered and embossed with meticulous fine needlework flows a two-legged ox blood red Dragon. "That's amazin'," exclaims William. Graham laughs, "The Wallace are not alone in their love of the Aicé."

"You're Céile Aicé too?" enquires a surprised William. Graham replies cheerily "Me a Céile Aicé... why of course Wallace, yie don't think your mad wee tribe are the only ones who love the Aicé and Magda Mòr do yie?" William laughs, "Then you too have a wee granny that would sort this mess out in moments then?"

"Aye Wallace, that I do," replies Graham. William smiles at Graham, knowing that it's not just his own grandmother or `wee maw' that rules the roost in a clan. William exclaims "Feck me, would yie believe it?" Both he and Graham laugh loudly at the thought that they both share the same joys and terrors of a wee maw in each Clan of the Céile Aicé Garda Bahn Rígh. "Gwydoddan," states Graham proudly, revealing his Aicé lineage. "Morríaghan." replies an equally proud William. Graham exclaims, "Fuckin' Normans indeed..." as he rolls up his pennant and places it back between his Breast-plate and his heart. "What?" exclaims William appearing surprised, "I thought you Grahams' were of Norman stock?"

"Fuck off," retorts Graham "It was my Cruathnie ancestor Grammas mòr, Artur Ard Rígh that knocked the shit out of the Romans up at Rossie Law, when your lot were holding the sweet tails of your women at the brawl o' alt Cluid Goram." William laughs out loud, "Aye, and It's good to see the fightin' women armed to the teeth back there too Graham."

"The Gallóbhan?" Replies Graham, "those particular Gallóbhan are feckn ruthless Wallace, Faolán is their Taoiseach (Elected Chief) and the wee ones, Lihd, Eochaidh and Fiónlaidh are all Aicés too, fuck Wallace, they can throw a longdart and shoot a crossbow better than any man I've ever seen." Laughing, William says, "Oh ah know what they're like fine enough, Coinach's wee sister Affric and I have been woodland lovers awhile now..." William hesitates; then he continues in a serious tone as he reflects on recent events...

"Affric is the only survivor from the Corserine massacre Graham. We took her to Glen Afton before we came here, that's what kept us back so long. Whoever attacked her people brutalized her and left her for dead." Graham nods his head solemnly, "A few days ago we caught a group of English marauders' who had committed slaughter on a Balloch near the old fort of t-Seann Chathair (Sanquhar) it was a terrible sight Wallace, men women, wains... then Hardy let Faolán's Gallóbhan loose on the English marauders, fuck, such a cruel and barbarous venture as I have ever witnessed, the next time those Gallóbhan are close-by, look to their waist belts, you will see what looks like little silk sow's purses hanging from…"

"Awe naw," exclaims William, as he checks his manly tackle. He winces at the thought. "Coinach's sister Affric is lethal with the sgian beg'" Says William, "she used to tell me stories about the girls trainin' from a young age as assassins for the Kings of Galloway, and many stories about ancient legends when the clan Olambh Rígh spoke in rhyme, telling of the Gallgael history and singing songs about the legendary Lillith and her daughters. Many a night I slept not sure if my prize possessions would be still be there in the morn if she was no' in a humour with me before ah fell asleep."

Graham winces as he too checks his manhood to give him comfort at the terrible thought, "Aye right enough, I've bedded a few of those bonnie Gallóbhan or they've bedded me… but I sure do know what you mean."

William grins, "I noticed that the tall dark haired lass has her eye on you?" Graham laughs, "She has more than her eye on me Wallace." William smiles then enquires, "Is she your woman?" Graham laughs again, "Don't say that out loud for fucks sake Wallace, unless you want her bonnie fist breaking the rest of your bonnie face. She says I am her man, in that order, and for the sake of that bonnie broken nose of yours, don't forget it." Graham pauses then he enquires, "So what happened to your face anyway?"

"Ach nuthin' ahl tell yie later," Laughs William. He continues, "It's good to see real fighting women with us though, and that Fiónlaidh, she has such a bonnie sparkle in her eyes, wee bright eyes that one." Graham laughs, "She would have your head cut off and your sack sown into a purse before you felt the pain; wee *Bright eyes*." William smiles "Ha, I hope not. I am glad they're here though and they've survived the papal bulls for women to desist in the arts of war, especially when everywhere else in Christendom has their women chained in the breeding stocks and cook houses? What a stupid fuckin idea that is, what a waste of fighting talent. Feck Christian dogma ma arse."

"Ah totally agree with yie," says Graham, "when Galloway joined the crown estates of Scotland the Christians gained the opportunity to impose their ban on women attending battle, but the Gallóbhan refused and continue their ancestral rights to keeping their faith in the Goddess as daughters of the Macha and guardians of the Macha Aicé ban Rígh. With the support of the Gallóglaigh Chiefs, the Gallóbhan refuse to disband. They still keep their spiritual home intact at Dùn Reicheit near Glenquhan on the shores o' the Rhinns. I've seen them in action Wallace, and for sure I am certain that any man who would abuse those bonnie lassies, breathes his last shortly thereafter, they're a tough breed the Gallóbhan."

Nodding in agreement, William says, "Aye, wee Affric suffered injuries that would have killed most grown men Graham, she's one tough wee lass with strong fightin' spirit and she fears no man. I hope she'll be o' better health and recovered by our return." Sitting back in his saddle, William thinks about Affric. "Feck aye," sighs Graham "All of the Gallóbhet have suffered Wallace, the men losing their families and the women suffering sinful terror, rapine and unspeakable torture at the hands of de Brixs' mercenaries, if they're caught they are shown no pity nor mercy." Suddenly another squadron in full armour with lances at the ready approaches them as they near the end of the pilgrims' road. Hardy speaks with the captain of the squadron while William watches closely, then he sees through the trees in the distance, the rear part of the Guardian army's massed ranks gathered on the plains of Dalry.

"Wallace," says Graham "Aye what is it?" enquires William. Graham comments with a smirk, "I couldn't help noticing your broken nose, with all the swelling and your big yellow black eyes, go on… go on, tell me what happened to yie? Did you get kicked in the head by a horse or did you just annoy a wee Gallóbhan?" William smiles, "Naw, it was feckn Coinach." Graham exclaims, "That wee fella with Faolán, he did it?" William pulls up his horse and stares at Graham. "Aye, that wee fella back there. Coinach has arms like the back legs o' a bull and fists as hard as any anvil."

Graham looks round to take the measure of Coinach, "Fuck Wallace, your appearance would make another man consider you have been hit by a lump of Aberdeen granite or kicked in the face by a mad Galloway bull, but that wee fella…?" Before William could reply, Graham walks his horse forward, he sighs. "Ach well… he must have had his reason for it." Graham notices Hardy waving his squadron onward. "Come on Wallace, that's us into the Guardians camp as soon as we clear this woodland."

Still pondering over Grahams' humour that Coinach had a reason to break his nose, William rides up behind Graham as they exit the woods and onto the northeastern end of the plains of Dalry. As he canters into the open plain, a surreal scene appears that takes his breath away. He pulls his horse to a halt and gapes in wonderment at the spectacle before him, he's completely engrossed and doesn't hear the horses of Coinach, Bailey and the Gallóbhan pull up beside him. "Would you look at that" exclaims Coinach. Bailey says, "Well boys, I have to admit, even in Wales never did I see such a sight as this."

In front of the three friends, the plains of Dalry is host ground to many thousands of men in great martial ranks and clan regiments, with hundreds of house and clan banners flying high and proud in the breeze, akin to thousands of white and beautifully coloured birds of the Machars and Rhinns marches raising as one great flock over the endless sand-flats of the great Solway Firth. Squadrons of brightly coloured and armoured horse troops pace and canter to and fro behind the regiments of the Guardian army, all in order to confuse an equally massed army opposing them, denying certain knowledge to the opposing camps as to where and when the hundreds of mounted warriors will strike out should battle commence. William speaks to Bailey quietly... "Did you notice something earlier that may have denied us our attendance and opportunity to witness such a sight?"

"I did," replies Bailey "and I'm sorry about that." William looks at Bailey curiously, then he says, "It wasn't just you Bailey, it was all three of us. If it hadn't been Hardy and his Gallóbhet that came upon us and it had actually been those we were tracking, I don't think we would have stood a chance after being caught so easily."

"It won't happen again." says a remorseful Bailey "It won't," replies William with a stern look on his face, "I'm supposed to be the hunter who knows this land and for you to rely on my knowledge, it's me Bailey who offers you an apology." Suddenly the mood breaks when Graham comes galloping back to them, looking magnificent in his armour with pennant flying high, the caparison on his horse flanks waves and flows gently like bleached white swan's wings in flight. The sight impresses William as Graham pulls his horse to a sliding halt in front of him. "Wallace, why do you sit and gawk here? Follow me and I'll take you to our pavilion to meet with your father."

Walking the horses forward, William enquires "Do you think there will be battle today?" Graham replies, "Only fools would fight in this winter hell, but for the sake of our kingdom, and if it is our destiny to stop this uprising from spreading through the realm, then I will lead my people to war by the side of my Guardian brethren if I must... as the bravest fool in all of Scotland... Now follow me Wallace."

They spur their horses into a canter toward the pavilions of the Graham and Hardy Douglas. As they ride through the bustle of the war camp, William could see in the middle of the plains between the two armies, three large rings of many gathered warriors. The outer ring of horsemen are mounted squires holding the banners, flags and pennants of those gathered. The middle ring are the mounted Guardian commanders, with' lances pointing skyward and holding a riderless saddled horse of their Chiefs and Lords to their left flank. It appears the dismounted riders are standing in front of their horses, forming a great and perfect centre circle while debating.

At the centre of the gathering, William sees the Flag of the late king Alexander, *Am Bratach rìoghail na h-Alba*, the Royal War flag of Scotland, as it waves proud and effortlessly in the breeze, its colours of the golden field is bordered by double red border bars with attached Lilies, representing his Aicé, Queen Yolande de Dreux. Centered within the golden field is the proud and rampant red Scots mountain Lion of the fabled Breathaim Rígh warriors and noble King, William the lion of Scotland. Alexanders' war flag flies proudly high at the center of the parley... "That's the parliament of magnates and chiefs," says Graham, "Our fate and our future are now in their hands."

A dark grey noon sky hangs low and heavy over the plains of Saint John's of Dalry, while thousands of men at arms and knights prepare to do battle in conditions that no army has ever fought in living memory. Lord Robert de Brix and the Lords of the Turnberry Pact impatiently watch the distant stirring of the Guardian armies from the doorway of their warm pavilions, while their own armies stand at the ready in the cold freezing winters mid-day chill. Robert de Brix, Lord of Annandale and Guisborough, peers across the plains to see the Western army of the Guardians facing him, led by Bishop Wishart. He glances to the southeast and sees the Northern Guardian army approach, led by the Lords Duncan of Fife and Comyn of Badenoch. To the Southwest is gathered against him the army of John Baliol, Ingram de Balliol and Lord Herbert de Maxwell.

"We will wait." Mutters de Brix quietly to his son Robert Brus, Earl of Carrick, "They're marching in from the east and the west," says De Burgh of Ulster, "and there are thousands of Baliol's Gallóbhet coming in behind us from the southwest. Our scouts inform us that more of Baliol's forces from his Barnard Castle estates in Yorkshire are now approaching from the border marches, and they will be here before nightfall."

"Father, this is not going to plan.," says Brus, "the Guardian armies are in front of us, now the Comyns, Douglas and Graham's have joined Wishart in the parley and they have brought with them near fifteen thousand men from their Scots Borders and Highland estates." De Clare enquires, "How many men do you think is on the field against us in total my Lord?" Brus exclaims "That's nearly thirty thousand men on three sides of us…" Brixs' steely eyes focus firmly on the parley. He barks out an order "We will wait I said…"

"Look over there lord Robert," exclaims De Clare "riders are coming our way… and they fly a flag of truce," De Brix replies, "Send them to my war tent to await me. Earl Robert, I want you to observe the Guardian army keenly, when the parley men arrive, do nothing but wait and watch, only when their army appears to advance do I want you to make haste and inform me, otherwise I do not wish to be disturbed during my meeting with those riders." As de Brix enters his pavilion, he notices the pennant flown by the lead rider and sees it's not that of parley messengers, but his old friend Lord Butler, envoy to king Edward. De Brix stands at the door of his pavilion as the riders arrive and dismount. De Brix enquires, "Ah, lord Butler... it is good news that you bring me I expect?" Butler replies tersely, "No my Lord Brix, you should already know it is not good news, it is far from it... Our lord good King Edward is much displeased that you act without consulting him in regards to the Crown estates of Scotland. King Edward will not be lending you his support for this confederation Pact, as you were precisely commanded to control all between Carlisle to Mercia, not start a bloody civil war in Scotland. What are you thinking my Lord?"

Clenching his fists, de Brix is clearly perturbed and also extremely disappointed upon hearing this news, but he replies courteously, "Pray come in to the warmth and sit down by the fire sir John, would you like something to eat and drink? Some nourishment or some wine perhaps?" Butler replies, "No my Lord, for I must travel back to London by return with your immediate response, and with your sworn word of retraction on all of these matters. I must remind you that our Lord King Edward will not countenance this uprising by you or your gathered Pact, he requires you to withdraw from the field immediately and on no account must you raise arms upon receipt of this command."

"Retraction?" exclaims de Brix.

"Yes Lord Brix," replies Butler, "our King is being magnanimous to you by this very gesture, for his love for you is great. Otherwise he would have commanded any other man to attend me on my return to London and have you replaced as warden of the marches."

De Brix is infuriated by this apparent slight from his lord King Edward, he exclaims, "King Eric, a mere boy, he intends to keep the young Margaret in Norway till he has support for his claim to the throne of Scotland, I will not be held to ransom by this Norse dog like I tarry for a morsel from his table... not when I have a legitimate claim to the throne of Scotland..." Butler glares at de Brix, "You must understand Lord Brix, our King is aware of this circumstance and understands your angst, and he is not unsympathetic that you vent your spleen, but he urges you to consider the greater scheme of things. What your unexpected call to arms may jeopardize is so much greater than the mere sovereignty of Scotland."

In a temper thinly veiled, de Brix replies, "My allies in the Pact have sworn to defend this realm against all, or perish together, save in our fealty to our Lord, King Edward Plantagenet, is this not good enough for our King?" Butler persists, "You misunderstand our lords displeasure lord Brix, should you persist and proceed with this reckless venture, he has pressed me to remind you that there are twelve other legitimate claimants to the Scots crown, including his own. Therefore your actions cannot be supported and it may unite all the claimants against you and you may also usurp his majesties claim by continuing with this folly and placing him in an uncommon predicament... and you shall be deemed treasonous."

"Edward would join my enemies and fight against me?" exclaims de Brix. "No Lord Brix," replies Butler, "he only has concern for your position as Warden of Carlisle and the duties you faithfully accepted and did pledge to him. Our liege has Scotland's best interest at heart, and of course those of his most loyal friend, being yourself," Pausing to sup some wine, Butler considers the gravity of the situation;

then he continues, "IF by the cause of your actions Lord Brix, Scotland does unfold into a civil war; who then does gain from this folly? You cannot succeed if you do not have Papal approval nor the support of the Scottish church, you have nothing except probable excommunication, surely you must understand that our lord king Edward cannot tempt this as an outcome."

"Excommunication..." Blurts de Brix "How can I be excommunicate when I have a legitimate claim pleading tanistry, proximity of blood and by degree of kinship to the deceased King. I who served this realm faithfully once before as Regent." Butler is now becoming extremely frustrated, he replies firmly, "Hear our King's message through my words Lord Brix, I am tasked to insist that you cease confrontation by whatever means necessary, and by his wise council to this effect, my lord Edward will display his clarity of vision to benefit the house of Brix very soon. I pray you heed this advice my lord and do accept that the maid of Norway will be regent of Scotland. Our king needs you to stand ready and by her throne, for he wishes her pledged to his son the prince of Caernarvon." De Brix blusters, "Would our King deny me his bond of Kinship and brotherhood? I only rise to defend my family name and honour, I seek to secure the royal succession, which is my right in accordance with the ancient customs approved in time and blood?"

Ignoring the blustering of de Brix, Butler speaks, "I see upon my arrival that you have opposing your single army, three larger forces this day, and in the worst of conditions that any would contest a strength of arms. Yet the mettle of your opposition show to me they are as determined to gain victory... more so. With you being the sole cause and instigator of this conflict lord Brix, you act out-with the rules of chivalry and also contrary to the laws of Scotland, therefore our King firmly believes that you cannot win on many counts. Our liege knows this and he advises to you against these rash but very understandable actions simply borne out of frustration regarding the throne of Scotland."

"Bah" exclaims de Brix "I know what I am doing." Butler speaks earnestly "There are thirteen claimants sir Robert, and you are third by right, but will you wage war on all including our liege who advises you thus against such a war?"

"Edward wage war against me?" retorts de Brix.

"If you force his hand Lord Brix, you will leave him no choice in the matter other than to intervene, then, as I said, you may force all claimants to unite against you as one. However, should you retire till the rise of spring next year, our liege Lord will have a more beneficial composure toward your claim, and then I believe, you will have been brought back into his confidence. And of course, when you publicly swear fealty to our Lord the King of England, he pledges to you great favour and patronage... Lord Brix, should you refrain till after the feast day of St Thomas the Apostle, then you may expect his full attention... and support."

"But that is next year," exclaims de Brix. Butler replies, "Another year may offer you a dynasty that may last a thousand years Lord Robert, this current venture you are so obviously set upon will never gain you another thousand hours and may end the house of de Brix forever." The ageing Lord of Annandale is dismayed, "I expected the full support of king Edward, after all the service I have given the English crown and the house of Plantagenet over my lifetime has been exemplary."

"My Lord..." says Butler "perhaps you have proved your point here this day, now everyone knows that the house of Brix is a force in Scotland that should be negotiated with, for the power you array on the field of battle and certainly with the support of our Lord Edward would be of such a magnitude, any future resistance to your claim will be deemed futile… What say you my lord?" De Brix has listened carefully to Butler, he knows now that he has made a terrible strategic error, especially being caught on these plains and seriously under-estimating the forces ranged against him. He is acutely aware that he can no longer hope to win against the combined forces that oppose him this day in a pitched battle. Perhaps this unexpected message from Butler may serve two purposes, bringing the throne of Scotland closer to him at another time, with the blessing of Edward and the pope.

De Brix paces a moment realising that he is in a precarious position, he knows he must do something, and do it quickly, or lose more than just a battle. Thinking fast, de Brix considers that perhaps Butlers' timely arrival may give him the opportunity he needs to retire with his forces intact, and without losing face. "Why my dear Butler…" says de Brix "I assure you that I will call for an immediate treaty with the Guardian army; then I shall withdraw to my estates, for our lord Edward is wise and I can assure you of this, his words of wisdom has not fallen on deaf ears… perhaps I was just a little impetuous." De Brix laughs, "I think living in this wet miserable bog piss country has addled my judgment. Pray tell our Liege Lord that his wise words and advice is my command and I shall faithfully withdraw forthwith, all of my forces from the plains of Dalry, and surely do turn my back on any further confrontation with the Guardian armies."

"A wise decision my Lord." says Butler. De Brix walks to the pavilion door, "Lord Butler, attend me. We shall go to the command pavilion where I shall execute orders to terminate this little misunderstanding in a way that I believe shall satisfy all, yet will not cause any unfortunate embarrassment." They both talk freely as they make their way into the command pavilion. As they enter the pavilion of his commanders, de Brix beckons all to hear the strategy he will employ when one of de Brixs' scout's arrives and rushes into the pavilion with grave news, "My Lord… the Blackfoot Gaels of MacDougal and MacDhuibh Sídhe have been seen landing a great host from a large fleet of Birlinns at the port of Baile na ha-Uige in the south. They deliver almost two thousand warriors from the inns a' gall in the west coast and are fast approaching to join the forces of the Guardians. Our scouts say they are less than a few hours march from us." The scout continues, "It appears that the Guardians and Baliol have another army of five thousand waiting at the Border marches under the command of the lords Douglas and Comyn to stop any possible support the Pact may gain from your tenant Lands in England." De Brix turns to face his loyal lords of the Pact and sees apprehensive faces.

"My lords, we are now aware of the full extent of the forces reigned against our endeavor… and that my friends is the sole purpose of this venture. We now understand the full scale of forces ranged against us should a civil war break out in Scotland." De Brix laughs aloud, "And the fools do bring these forces to do battle in mid-winter?" Brix looks at everyone as they begin to laugh nervously at his apparent humour, though a little confused by his tactical revelation. De Brix continues, "Now we have the measure of Scotland's mettle, the fools." But still Brixs' allies are confused.

"My lord," says the scout, "there is more information regarding the fleet that landed the Blackfoot MacDougal's," he hesitates nervously, de Brix enquires impatiently, "What is it man, speak up?" The Scout replies, "There were also ships that have landed many Capetian mercenaries, also a pirate force has disembarked led by a French Corsair named De Longueville." For a moment there is a stunned silence in the pavilion, then de Brix exclaims, "The bloody Capetians?" Butler suddenly tenses upon hearing of the Capetians arriving in Scotland. "My lord" says Butler "I must speak with you now… in private." De Brix could see the perilous expression on Butlers face and walks with him out of earshot of the others, where Butler speaks in earnest.

"The Capetians setting a foot on Scotland's soil changes everything Lord Brix. This is a part the price of what our King is warning you against, with the arrival of the Capetians' to protect their own blood in Yolande's claim and interests, this could bring the whole of Christendom to war and ruin if battle should commence here this day." For the first time, de Brix appears deeply concerned as Butler continues in deadly earnest, "My lord Brix, you should know that if the Capetians' fight and any English blood is spilt, then so must Edward raise the Angevin armies against them, not only here… but in France too, then it will be so King Eric of Norway and all the alliances that must rally behind the Guardians, and there can be little doubt that Philip of France will be obliged to wage a war on England. The Pope will also become involved and factions will rally in defense of each house, both here and in Europe… this is your folly alone lord Brix, you must end this madness now before the Capetians' arrive on this field of battle and all is undone."

De Brix shows no obvious reaction, but he's stunned into silence by this news. Butler demands a reply, "What is your will my lord?" De Brix spins on his heals and addresses the lords of the Pact. "Earl of Carrick, Cospatrick of Dunbar, Gilbert of Gloucester… I require you to immediately engage in a preliminary parley with the Guardians, and you lord Stewart… I want you to lead the Parley." Lord Stewart replies, "Yes my Lord." At that moment, knights enter the pavilion and approach Brix, who remains outwardly calm after quickly containing the situation. Thinking quickly, de Brix makes an introduction, "Ah My Lords Floris of Holland, Lord Richard first lord of Ulster, and good Baron de Vesci, may I introduce to you Lord Butler, personal envoy to good King Edward."

The lords begin to make acquaintance when the Lord de Brix brings all to attention. "Alas my Lords, time does press upon us and I must ask that we now grace the parley with our attendance. I want the quaking miscreants across this plain to see that this is truly an international force and that they be fully aware how diverse our Pact confederation actually is. When we return in spring with our full forces and allies, they may bend easier on their knees and support my rightful claim." Everyone nods nervously in agreement.

De Brix looks at his confederates, all have sworn and pledged allegiance in exchange for great land tracts in Scotland, saving their supreme fealty to Edward Longshanks as their collective lord Paramount. Gloucester enquires, "You mean, you never meant to do battle in the first place my Lord?" De Brix scowls, "No, of course not, I merely wanted to establish what forces may be gathered in opposition, what fool fights in the winter Gloucester? None with any wit for battle, we have gained the knowledge I required, which is the actual size of any force and its conviction that would do battle against us, and now we know." Lord Stewart enquires, "What will we then negotiate at the parley?" De Brix replies "Make them hop awhile lord Stewart, soon I shall attend the parliament… but first, I want you to make them sweat this fine cold day. Now my lords, attend the parley."

When the Lords and commanders leave the pavilion, de Brix brings Lord Richard of Ulster into his confidence. "I have underestimated the strength of feeling in regards to my rightful claim sir Richard, but I have prepared for this eventuality," Lord Richard enquires, "How so lord Robert?" De Brix replies, "In your confidence of course, I thought it probable Longshanks would support my actions retrospectively, but it seems not, he has expressed that I may have acted in haste, now King Edward has sent advice to desist through our good friend lord Butler here, though our King has left the door open for further action with his prior knowledge and approval. I do know that he wants a safe and secure Scotland at his back door, controlled by myself as paladin warden of the Northern marches of England. Should our King set to war with Philip of France, which is highly likely, then surely that must be with me at Scotland's helm and not some Capetian slut, and you my good friend at the helm of the Irish."

A concerned Lord Richard enquires, "King Edward… he has indicated to you his displeasure?" De Brix replies, "No, of course not Lord Richard, nor did he censure me or call me to his court as you plainly see. I have known Longshanks since he was a boy and I've seen him do this before, it is merely a politic way of approving without being seen to fall on the side of the one who strategically took the initiative, no, he has sent his advice which I shall now enact." Sir Richard appears to be satisfied with this answer, he is also loyal to Longshanks, but he knows that in the royal court, de Brix is his favourite, "Please attend the Parley lord Richard, for I value your attendance there more than any other."

"At once Lord Robert." Sir Richard de Burgh leaves his old friend to join the Parley. De Brix turns to Butler, who has been listening, he says, "My dear Butler, I shall send to my King a message applauding the vision of his wisdom. Forthwith, I immediately desist from this campaign. We shall all return to our castles and estates as he advises and I shall await his discreet pleasure on this subject in good faith, as I demonstrated when I joined him in his conquest of Wales." Butler smiles hearing this information, he knows de Brix is a wily old fox, and warms to the thought of returning to Edward with such good news. He is also enjoying seeing the political twists and turns this play is taking and now he wants to see how de Brix will bring this day to an end without fighting a battle or more importantly, losing face while deflecting an international crisis with the Capetians, and it appears de Brix may have succeeded. De Brix sees the signal flags waving that indicates a final parley gathering is acceptable by the Guardians.

De Brix mounts his horse to join the parley, but first he issues Gloucester an order, "Gloucester, I want you to make our army is ready and prepared to attack, set the army to make it appear so that we are even more determined than ever before, and we are well prepared to take many lives with us this day and intend to make this a very costly affair for all concerned. But on no account must you give such an order, that is for me to decide, and only by my return... is that understood?" Gloucester replies, "By your return my Lord." De Brix continues, "If any man or group of men disobeys and leaves the ranks to attack that may ignite this tinder, order your archers to bring them down, then have their throats cut and behead them for good measure in front of our army, and make it so in full view of the parley, for we cannot risk a battle at any and all cost. Do you understand my orders?"

Gloucester replies, "I do understand you my lord." The parley entourage of de Brix' raise their flags of house and Pact then canter towards the Parliament. De Brix laughs to himself, thinking his error of judgment had foolishly led him into a trap of his own making. If battle had commenced then he would most certainly have lost everything, his lands in Scotland, England... perhaps even the friendship of Edward.

Now Longshanks has provided the perfect opportunity to win the day. He could hardly contain his joy, and now, he would take these fools to the edge. Feeling extremely satisfied with himself, de Brix surveys the gathering he is approaching and thinks of how much he still enjoys the thrill of war. To de Brix, the parliamentary assembly gathered on the plains of Dalry appears magnificent in the standing Order of the Rings. The horse-guards set behind each representative in a rich cluster of colours and banners fluttering in the mid-morning breeze, the glint of steel, silver and golden armour flashing raises his heartbeat. Behind the parley he can see the gathered formations of warriors standing in their ranks by the thousands.

De Brix feels exhilarated by the sight of these warriors and is sorely tempted to enact the detail that would lead to battle. Laughing quietly to himself, de Brix knows this luxury will have to wait to satisfy his love of battle. Savouring the feeling of power surging through his body, Brix knows that he alone holds the day for thousands of lives and the future of Scotland, nay, perhaps Christendom in his hands, now he would make his enemies rue the day they faced lord de Brix.

The parley assembly are dismounted when Brix arrives, a company of one hundred men from each opposing faction are standing in the traditional parliamentary ring of warriors, an ancient order where each stands shoulder to shoulder, none being more prominent than the other, with no one hiding in the shadows. When one warrior talks, all listens and none dare interrupt the speaker, for this is the way a parley is heard in ancient Scotia by the revered Cruathnie Breitheamh Rígh of legend. De Brix and his delegation take their place within the centre ring and could see all of Scotland has representation in attendance, from the Bishopric, Magnates, Barons and Mormaers', to the wild barbaric chiefs. He glances at the hostile faces of John and Ingram de Balliol, Herbert Maxwell, Will de St Clair, and the lords Douglas and de Soulis. Bishop Wishart welcomes de Brix to the circle, after the pleasantries, he enquires, "My lord Brix, why do you strike at Baliol's lands and storm the royal castles of our late King in this time of flux?" De Brix replies tersely, "Am I not within my right to strike back in retaliation for the plunder, rape and murder of my people by Baliol's Galloway mongrel Gallóbhet on my territories and estates?"

There is a stunned silence within the parley; this is not the answer anyone expected from de Brix. "You liar..." shouts Ingram de Baliol. Immediately Brix grips his sword and prepares to fight, as does everyone at the parley following his reaction to the apparent slight from Baliol. De Brix shouts at Baliol, "I demand satisfaction at this insult from you Baliol."

Sir Ingram retaliates, "Where is your proof of such deeds Brix, I'll wager none can be provided, these are base and foul words from your shallow scheming mouth?" De Brix snarls, "All of good Christian faith know these Gallóbhet are not men or women as God intended, they are nought but brute ignorant fiáin-ainmhí (Wild animals) devoid of any spark of piety or humanity as they commit every outrage at my door. It is widely known the blood feuding of these rabid dogs such is they are bred in Galloway, are the true cause of this impending state of war." Wishart pleads, "Stay your swords my lords, if it is merely bloodshed you want, then why do we waste our time in false debate?"

Everyone slowly eases the grip on their swords and return to standing in silence. Comyn spits the words, "You do cause murder and make war in support of your false claim to the throne Brix," "My Lord Comyn..." says Brix calmly "should it come to pass, you will find my claim is indeed incontestable according to the principles of ancient Scots law. And without doubt it is in accordance with feudal practice in so far as is established. I am in receipt and ownership of such Sasine writs to the kingdom my lords, but today my cause is merely the security of my lands and estates against your heathen Gallóbhet dogs and protecting our realm for the maid against you or any others who attempt to usurp her crown... yet you dare lay the title usurper falsely upon my door?"

The parliament is stunned into silence hearing these words from Brix. John Baliol exclaims, "You make a false defense Brix. What is this secretive Pact and confederation you bring to this field? It is not I who does covet the crown of Scotland... It's you who does wage war on innocents under my protection. Your claim is but a cheap veil that all can see as we witness your attempt to steal the throne of Scotland as your own."

"NO..." replies Brix "What serpent has dared to represent me on this false claim you cast upon my good name? Perhaps it is you Baliol who does make this claim to try and eliminate my god-given right to the throne of Scotland under these guised base accusations." Lord John Baliol replies, "Everyone knows of your Pact Brix, all are aware you wish to usurp the maid and take the throne for yourself." Brix hints at a smile as the parley nervously awaits his response. "Not so my Lord Baliol. You may ask any of these good men who stand by my side, it is your treacherous Gallóbhet and filthy Ceitherne who run amok and out of control by invading my estates and causing great ruination and slaughter upon my vassals, destroying crops and then taking what is mine by theft, rape, murder..."

"You lie," shouts John Baliol. Brix immediately counters, "It is you and your kin who lie Baliol... it is you and your kind who has pushed me to this retaliation by your deceitful and cunning ways. It is you who are set upon the destruction of the house of Brix and does make false claims under this scurrilous guise of accusation that you weakly submit this day. It is also known to many who do not lick your arse Baliol, that you have long planned this misadventure, if it is the throne I seek as you say, let us set to war now and settle this matter on the field of honour, for God and saint Edward the confessor are truly on my side."

There is immediate uproar in the parliamentary circle on the plains of Saint John. Amidst the commotion, horses whinny and rear at the atmosphere emitting from the parley. Warriors tense on both sides, flag bearers, archers, slingers and spearmen, all ready anxiously for any sign of betrayal from either side that will lead them into battle. Wishart raises his hands and walks urgently into the circle centre calling for order.

"My lords, pray silence, give order…. ORDER… We must have order my lords, for none may gain from the spilling of our blood this day. More than those gathered here do depend on our wit to find a peaceful solution. My Lord Brix, my Lord Baliol, we must calm this parley." Glancing at Butler, de Brix can see instantly the grave concern etched in his face. Perhaps he has pushed them all too far, though he can hardly contain his own excitement at the thought of battle. He quickly takes the initiative by stepping forward into the great circle, holding an open hand high…

"My Lord Bishop, my Lords… as a sign of goodwill, despite these infamous slights by these lords with malice intent and deceit in their hearts, I am prepared to withdraw my men from Galloway and return home… but it is under one condition…" Bishop Wishart breaks the silence of the gathered parley, "And what is your condition my lord?" De Brix replies, "A given oath before God from each Guardian here, should further infractions be placed upon me by the heathen filth who reside in Galloway and Carrick, the Guardians shall come to my aid, for if not my lords, I swear to you all gathered here this day, there will be total war waged by my family and kinfolk upon the transgressors, and no parley or Guardians' army shall save my enemies from fire and sword."

Again there is uproar in the parley as many do not trust de Brix and see this as merely another of his tricks. Wishart raises his Mitre high till all fall silent once again. He declares "If any can provide proof of these or any indiscretions by another party, then in due course the Guardians will act as peace keepers for and on behalf of the aggrieved party, for this is what must be done till we have royal authority back on the throne of Scotland... this solemn oath must surely be acceptable to you all my Lords?"

The Comyn and Baliol factions are enraged at having suffered greatly and still seek bloody revenge for the transgressions and killing of their people. "You lie through your teeth de Brix," says Comyn, "You would make the throne of Scotland your own and claim it is just cause in retaliation for false claims of robbery and murder that plainly does not exist, other than by your own hand and those at your command. Why then would you bring Irish and English mercenaries into this parliament precinct should it be only a territorial outlaw dispute, and why do you force your will on the property of the late King?"

De Brix calmly replies, "If I wanted the crown of Scotland, I need only wait, as it is mine by birthright. And as for the standing of any foreign soldiers on Scotland's soil... look you Wishart to Comyn and the Lords Baliol if you seek the original perpetrators; it is they who have brought thousands here this day from Castle Barnard in England and elsewhere. This can be no coincidence but an actual revelation of their conspiracy in bringing about this catastrophe." Comyn is outraged, "What trickery of the tongue is this Brix..." Before anyone else can speak, de Brix hold both his hands high in the air till the parliament of the rings falls silent. For a moment it appears the outcome hangs in the balance, then de Brix speaks, "My Lords, some of you dare to say it is I who does employ a false tongue. But it is easy enough for me to demonstrate here and now, that it was not I who prepared this mischief, but some of you shameless miscreants who lurk in the shadows of the Guardianship."

Wishart is gravely concerned, My Lord de Brix, your inference that the honourable members of the Guardianship are not impartial and even involved in a treasonous conspiracy does offer offence. My lord Brix, you must clarify your accusation..." De Brix continues "I would never wish to offend you good Bishop, and I know not yet who, but some here in witness this day already knows the answer to my next question... Who is it here that does invite the Frankish Capetians' to this realm that now marches a foreign army freely to this place from southern Galloway as we speak? For that must surely show to all who has been planning this bloody coupe for many months." Again there is uproar as the Scots nobles continue their quarrels...

THE BLACK CAT OF CARLISLE

William, Bailey and Coinach follow Graham until they arrive at the Guardian Pavilions, beside them are pitched the magnificent Gallóbhet war Obhainn's. Graham points to the a group of large obhainn's, "There's your fathers camp over there Wallace, I have to meet with the patrol master and brief him. You should get some warmth into your bones and eat some vittals while you can, then I'll see you back here in a wee while."

"Ta' Graham." says William. Graham laughs, "And Wallace, It may be your last meal as condemned man if we go to war this day." William laughs, "Feck Graham, cheer a fella up would yie," Graham grins as he turns his horse, "Ah'll see you soon Wallace... in this life or the next." Waving his friend away, William dismounts and speaks to Bailey, "I like Graham's humour, though it's a shame about the subject." Bailey stands beside his horse and stretches painfully backwards, "Oh my achin' back... I'm wet, freezing, hungry, thirsty... I should have went on the fuckin' crusades instead of coming to up here to Scotland, I've heard the sun never sets over there and the only rain or snow anyone sees is when they come back here." Coinach interrupts, "There's Alain coming now..." William looks round to see Alain emerge from an obhainn in the Wallace camp with Sean Ceàrr, war-dog handler of the Wolf and wildcat Gallóglaigh. Alain sees William, it's apparent the relief he feels as a broad smile sweeps across his face while walking over to greet them. "Good to see you've made it back safely boys, you had me worried awhile." William replies, "Its good to see yie too Dá, but I need to tell you what happened at Corserine and Dunveoch." Alain spoke, "There's no time to discuss this now son, I wish there was, I need you and the boy's to get yourself some scran then find your way to our archers position at the end of our left flank." Alain begins walking towards his horse, "Dá wait…" pleads William "It's important you hear this."

Pulling on his gauntlets, Alain looks at William, he says, "Walk with me son." Alain walks with purpose and an obvious sense of urgency. William says, "Dá, I must tell you what we saw at the Corserine and Dunveoch." Alain replies, "I don't have the time William, I must get back to my command."

As they pace walk together, William continues, "Dá, there's been terrible killing o' the Ceàrdannan clans, Marchal ua Bruan's clan… Auld Torquill Fletcher and his people… they're all dead." Alain stops and looks at William, it's clear this news has shocked him. He glances across the plain at the parley, "If it has no direct effect on the situation here, then I'm sorry son, it'll have to wait. If this parley comes to an abrupt end, we will only have moments from the time our delegation gets back before a battle breaks out, and everyone must be ready to strike fast and hard, for this is a day we must win at all costs." In frustration, William exclaims "But Dá…" Alain raises his hand, "We're already aware of much rapine and murder in the Galloway hills, our duty and thoughts must now be focussed on what's before us… it's the living who now depend on us keeping our heads this day."

Alain places his hands on his sons' shoulders, "I understand what you feel and I'm not so heartless as I appear to you now, but I must take my position in the line. Aicé willing, we will talk of this later. Trust me, we'll deal with these atrocities when this disaster is over and done with. Many of the Gallóbhet already prepare for a bloodlust, no matter what happens here this day, be it battle or peace treaty, for it's the Gallóbhet and their kinfolk who've suffered most by these marauding bands of cutthroats. And though the Gallóbhet be our allies, they may also bring us to ruin, yet none here could fault their hearts seeking retribution."

Alain's eyes smile as he looks at the son he thought he had lost forever. But for this madness now befalling Scotland, they would both be home in Glen Afton, talking of great things to come. "You look feck'd son, and cold, you and the lads get some hot food in your bodies then look to our Bowyers on the left flank and join them. And listen to me carefully; should battle commence before we next meet, I want you to carry your longbow. If you do not find our Flags in the melee, then you must serve Wishart with your skills, do not for any purpose or occasion enter the battle true, for you would surely all perish... we have too much time to make up for me to lose you so soon." William replies "Aye, and don't you be doing anything daft yourself Dá, for you have more tricks to be showing me if I'm to become half the hunter you are... And how would I explain it to wee Maw and Mharaidh if anything happened to you?"

"Get some vittals in yie," says Alain "then come to me when you're ready." Mounting his horse, Alain stops momentarily and looks at William, without saying another word, he turns his horse and rides at a canter towards the centre left flank of the Guardian army to join the ranks of the fierce Gallóbhet. William walks back to the empty camp of the Glen Afton Wallace' to meet with Bailey and Coinach, now sitting comfortably on the edge of a long-wagon drinking ale, looking very fatigued and worn out from their journey over the last few days. "We found some ale." says Bailey. Coinach jumps off the wagon and hands William a large flagon of ale, then he enquires eagerly, "What did your father say?" William replies, "He said he's aware of the tragedies in the Wolf and wildcats, but the urgency of the moment means that he has to leave to take his command, he said he'll talk with us after this face-off with de Brix has been settled. He also told me that we're to get warm food and vittals then join our clan Bowyers. If the battle starts without us and we cannot find the Wolf and wildcat Gallóglaigh, we're to follow Wishart's standard and use our flights to protect him."

Coinach reluctantly accepts the reply, for the moment. He says, "I will not wait long before I hunt de Percy down Wallace, with or without you… I will have my fuckin' revenge."

The tired friends sit on the back of the wagon and drink more ale while watching the dazzling display of martial pageantry. William exclaims, "I've never seen such an amazing variety o' armour and weaponry in all my life as I've seen these last few moments." Bailey stretches his weary bones once more, "The art of war right enough." Coinach sneers "Aye, till someone sticks the sharp end o' a paintin' brush in yie." William laughs; then he too stretches his sore muscles, "Let's get our tack and packs off the horses and feed them, then we should find some hot food."

Bailey points and nods his head, William grins when he sees that Coinach has fallen asleep standing up and leaning against his horse. Bailey nudges him and a weary Coinach opens his eyes, yawns and exclaims, "Awe feck Bailey, I didn't know where I was there," He stretches' his muscles too and shudders, "Fuck, I feel a lot better for that wee wink though, was I sleeping for long?" Bailey smiles, "About the time it takes to piss." Coinach mutters, "Awe fuck, it felt like ages." The three weary friends begin to remove the horse-tack and packs from their horses and brush them down, almost falling asleep on their feet as they do so. Eventually, the bivouac packs have been stowed and horse tack removed, the exhausted friends lean over a horse and rest, when a gloriously sensual feminine voice with an English accent breaks their sleepy monotony… "Cockatrice, sawn boar, red calf heads, swan giblets, suckling sow and to follow… Jeely speugh, plucked basilisk, boiled stoat feet, Rooster pottage and or jeelytom pasties… with savoury dusted mud-salt toppings."

With raised eyebrows upon hearing this sensual sultry voice, the three friends look at each other with wry smiles. Slowly, they turn around, then much to their horror, awaiting their attention is a small fragile looking pasty-faced monk dressed in a dirty dung-brown course haired ecclesiastical cassock. His head is adorned with sparse and wispy ginger hair, reaching from the back of his head and creeping over his ears like a strange orange fungus. Protruding through this ginger mange, is a pointed baldpate, seriously infected with a rash of brown weeping moles and open sores.

The odd-looking little monk trembles as he holds three large flagons filled with Heather Ale. The companions look at each other, puzzled and amused at what the little monk has just said… and the way he had said it. Bailey, still slightly confused, scratches his head and looks at William "What the fuck did he just say?" The strange looking little monk continues, "And… eh, there's also Broken catbrawn too good sirs', with fresh Gurnard Feretories', Butterwort packets or poddynox my Lords."

For a moment there is a deathly silence…

Receiving no reply, the frail little monk begins to tremble, spilling the Heather Ale all about his cassock as he holds the ale platter up to them. Tentatively, he hands each of them a flagon. William enquires, "Is that a wee monk or a wee woman?" "I don't know?" replies Bailey. "I don't know either..." remarks Coinach "Unlike you two, I've never slept with a monk before so I wouldn't know the difference." A bemused Bailey enquires, "Does that strange little creature speak in possessed tongues?" William, appearing equally puzzled, replies, "Which one? Coinach or the wee monk?" Coinach glares as William continues, "I know what poddynox is, but that's about it." Bailey glances at William, "What the fuck is poddynox... Coinach's middle name?" Coinach replies with a sneer, "Naw Bailey... it's like you... a big greasy fat fuckin' bloody puddin.'"

The three companions are greatly amused by this bewildering distraction and banter. They scrutinise the little trembling monk as he bravely continues... "My lords, I have been ordered to offer you a selection of vittals in which you may partake, in that, you may choose suitable sustenance and inform me of your culinary desires, I will then prepare the vittals for you." Smiling at the little trembling monk, William says, "It's very cold I grant you wee man, but why are you shaking like a tender leaf in a gale?" The little monk crosses himself in religious desperation, "My lord, I have never met a Gallóglaigh before, but I fear if I displease you I would surely meet my end... *Father bless me for I have sinned.*"

Bailey growls at the little monk, "You'll meet your end sooner than you fuckin' expect if you don't fetch us something hot to eat... and be right quick about it." The little monk begins to tremble once more, much to the amusement of the three friends. William laughs, "Listen wee man, firstly, we're not lords, but your compliment goes to your credit, and of course, does not go un-noticed. And second, we don't have any idea what the fuck you're talking about? Who eats this shit anyway, and who are you?"

"Yes my Lord, eh, I mean Sir…" replies the little monk. "I am Alasdair, the food servant to the Bishops. The Lord Douglas told me to serve your needs' as you had not eaten for days. The fare is of the finest dining and chosen food reserved for the lords and bishops…" Coinach enquires, "I thought those religious fuckrs only ate fish?" No one answers Coinach as William continues, "Call me Wallace wee man, these men here are my friends, Bailey and Coinach."

"Yes Sir Wallace." replies the strange looking little monk. Coinach moans, "I think this rich food is beyond anything would satisfy our hunger."

"What's your name again?" enquires William looking down at the little fellow. "Alasdair my Lord, Alasdair of saint Martainns." Bailey enquires, "Well Alasdair of Saint Martainns, what food is being served to the common man?" Alasdair dithers and wrings his hands, "Oh, eh, there's boiled cabbage, sneeds and butterwort soups, stew, gruel, pork, ham, eggs… then there is leaven ale bread, scones, biscuits and bannocks' if that meets your preference good sirs?" Bailey enquires, "What's in your gruel?" Alasdair offers a smile as his nervousness wanes, "Barley, oats, wild garlic, boiled broken mutton or pork, with honey and whisky." Taking another large drink of fine Heather Ale, Coinach enquires, "That sounds good… what's a jeelytom pasty?" William and Bailey shrug their shoulders in bewilderment. Little Alasdair explains, "It's a special meat pastie blessed by the brothers."

"I'll try one now then," says Coinach, "I'm feckn starvin." Little Alasdair fumbles about in his hemp satchel and pulls out a small pastie, "I have but one left here good sir, if you wish to taste it." Little Alasdair hands the morsel to Coinach who ravenously bites into the pastie… immediately the pleasure of fine taste spreads delightfully across his face. Coinach is in culinary heaven as he savors' the tasty morsel, "Mmmm wee monk… this is so sma'sin. (Very good) Feck fella's, ah have to say… this is really feckn tasty." William and Bailey stand in awe, watching the delight spread across Coinach's face as he takes another bite of the tasty pastie. Coinach enquires with the half eaten pastie in his outstretched hand, "Here fella's, sorry about that… do yiez want a bite?"

Their stomachs rumble with hunger, their mouths begin to salivate; William and Bailey reach out as Bailey exclaims, "Tá Coinach… I thought you'd never ask boyo." Coinach suddenly whips his hand away, taking the morsel out of reach of his friends. "Well yer no' getting any, yiez can both fuck off… ahm eating this all to me'self." Coinach quickly stuffs the last of the pastie into his mouth, laughing and pointing at William and Bailey, both standing with open mouths with a tragic look of utter dismay on their faces. "Ha," laughs Coinach, "That was worth it just to see the look on yer faces…"

"Ya dirty wee bastard," exclaims a demoralised William. An equally dismayed Bailey moans, "That wasn't so very nice boyo…" Almost choking, Coinach rolls up with laughter while observing their expressions. The little monk rummages in his bag for more morsels when William enquires, "So tell us, what was in that pastie wee man?"

"If I may good sirs," replies little Alasdair. "It is the finest of pulverized tomcat testicles in crusty crowfoot pastry fat… with pepper herbs." Bailey immediately roars with laughter and involuntarily splutters his Heather Ale out all over Coinachs face. Coinach curses and spits out the pulverized remnants of tomcat testicles while wiping his mouth vigorously. He steps forward and shoves little Alasdair so violently, the little monk totters backwards and falls on his arse into the freezing churned up boggy ground.

"Fuckin' Tom cats Bolloks?" exclaims Coinach as he

spits more remnants of the culinary delight on the ground. "Even us Tinklers don't eat fuckin' cats… we only use their feckn pelts for leggings and jack liners." Coinach thinks a moment; he ponders, "Oh and they make nice little quarter bag sporrans too." William and Bailey roar with laughter… Coinach enquires indignantly, "What's so fuckin' funny?" William laughs, "You ya fuckin' eejit,' your as bad as that wee ginger monk sitting on his arse looking so surprised." Still laughing, William picks up the little monk and starts to brush the cold wet mud off Alasdair's cassock. "No need to scare little Alasdair Coinach, he means us no harm, I mean, look at him… don't you think he's cute?"

Shaking with fear, and by way of atonement, little Alistair offers an explanation, of sorts…"Good sirs, please forgive me but, we never ever use black cat testicles in the pastries, no, we only use fair or speckled cats for that purpose." Coinach growls and reaches out to grab the little monk. Bailey mutters. "Typical Scotchmen…" Coinach glares "And what the fuck do you mean by that Cymran?" Bailey laughs "You lot, always fighting over pussy…" William laughs aloud, "He's right Coinach, only a complete fanny would mistakenly perceive the nuances of such enlightened discourse by surreptitiously misconstruing the alternatives as being seductively vulgar, or otherwise… maybe… possibly… even…" Coinach glares at them, "What th' fuck…?"

Laughing with great gusto, Bailey and William wrap their arms around each other, pointing at the confused expression on Coinachs face… "What the fuck are you two talking about?" Exclaims Coinach, completely unaware of the humour. Suddenly he lunges menacingly at the little monk, immediately William puts his arm up and steps across the front of little Alasdair. "Whoa there Coinach, what the fuck is your problem… this frail little Alasdair thing here only offers to feed us vittals, yie cannae be chastising him for his ignorance of our own daily fare." Bailey, ignoring Coinach's aggression, steps in beside William to shield Alasdair; then he speaks urgently to the little monk. "Go and fetch three large platters of bread, pork, eggs, bannocks and bowls of gruel…" Bailey begins to laugh but contains himself, "Now hurry little monk, quickly, before lord Wallace here lets this madman loose." Bailey thinks a moment then calls after little Alasdair "And bring three large portions of Poddynox back with you." Alasdair quickly disappears into the throng of soldiers and tents to proudly pursue his duties. William enquires, "Coinach, what's wrong with you? I thought you were going to kill the wee fella."

"NO," shouts Coinach as he points toward the assembled forces of the Pact, "It's them there across this plain I have come here to kill." Coinach continues in a rage, "Any of those bastards that I meet this day will have no quarter given from me." Many of the soldiers and passing cavalry stop and look at Coinach on hearing his outburst. William puts his hand on his friends shoulder, "Coinach, you should be careful and don't start this fuckin' war all by yourself, anyone hearing you might think it's a command or an order that you're calling out, then where would we be? Fighting a feckn battle… and we've not even had our scran."

Bailey agrees, "Settle your angst Coinach, for fucks sake."

Glaring at William and Bailey with a venomous expression, Coinach shouts at them, "Have yiez forgotten Corserine, Dunveoch or Affric so soon? This place is a fuckin' madness ah tell yiez, why do we wait here while the enemy is but a hundred fletch yard's away…" William groans, "For fucks sake Coinach, go sit yourself down and drink some more Heather Ale. We've eaten nuthin' but cheugh mutton and salt eel meat for near on three days." Bailey moves to the other side of Coinach where the three friends sit on the tailgate of the wagon, heartily drinking their Heather Ale. They sit awhile in silence, looking toward the parley conference in the centre of the plains, many moments pass before anyone speaks. William, focusing intensely on the parley, utters, "Fella's… I think I'm fuckin' drunk?" His two friends say nothing for another moment, then Coinach speaks, "Me too ah reckon…"

"And me…" says Bailey. The three friends sit a long time before another word is spoken, then William speaks again after much thought, "That'll be bad news then…" Coinach readily agrees, "Aye… ah reckon so…"

"FUCK…" Exclaims Bailey "we might have to fight a battle in a little while."

"Awe naw," says William "I hope its no' this day… ma head is totally fucked." Coinach and Bailey look at William as the seriousness of their dilemma becomes apparent to them all. Suddenly the three friends fall back into the back of the wagon in fits of laughter with tears running down their faces. "Fuck me," sighs William "This is so funny." The three friends howl with laughter, while many passing by think them witless. Coinach is doubled up laughing. William is choking as tears roll down his face, he points at Coinach, "Tom Cats Bolloks…" Bailey laughs and slaps Coinach on the back, after a few moments of great mirth, they all manage to settle down.

"Here," says Bailey "Listen up you two… I'll tell you boyo's a true story about some monks and a black cat… maybe it'll sober us up by the time the battle begins." William leans back in the wagon, "Go on Bailey, hopefully the wee monk Alasdair will be back with some fine scran before the battle, for I'm feckn near starvin' to death." Bailey makes an announcement without taking his gaze from the Parley. "Hold on to your crucifix' then boyo's and I'll tell you of the strange and very frightening true story of… the evil black cat of Carlisle."

Coinach laughs, "We don't have any crucifix Bailey, we're feckn heathens, remember?" Bailey replies, "Well, hold on to your pricks, bollocks or something you can believe in then."

Looking curiously at Bailey, William enquires "What evil black cat? Have you eaten one or is this just an opportunity for a confession before we all die in battle because yiev fucked one?" Coinach sniggers, then all three laugh out loud, breaking heartily the angst of moments past.

Bailey continues in an imaginary storytellers voice, "No, do not mock me good sir… and you too Coinach, it is a true story I shall tell to you, upon this mug o' ale, I do swear. This tale is about a cat and a veritable cluster of Godly monks who dwell near an old English hamlet called… Carlisle. A damned place if the truth be told, where those proud religious and pious English men of God had visited upon them a terrible affliction and a manifestation of such ugliness, they were punished with disgusting open pus sores and weeping boil's upon their heads, faces and most distressing of all good friends… on their manhood's."

"Whoa there," says Coinach "Just hold it right feckn there Bailey, how would you know about the manhood problems of English priests?" Bailey replies nonchalantly, "A novice nun told me." William laughs, "I've got to hear this." Both William and Coinach grin, then they look at Bailey who's observing the Parley through bloodshot eyes. "Well," says Bailey, "When on my way to Scotland, I had travelled through many strange places, but it was in that fateful hamlet of Carlisle that I saw some very strange things indeed…"

"Including your own reflection." laughs Coinach. "Shhhhhhh I need to hear this," says William with a chuckle. Bailey clears his throat and begins his story. "One day, not so very long ago, I arrived in the little hamlet just outside

Carlisle castle, near to the English frontier with you lot, and on that very day there was a big commotion going on. I enquired as to what was happening and I was told it was all about an evil black cat that was possessed by demons. Well I tell you boyo's, the place was a' frantic with people running about screaming, wailing and a' crying, with much community beating of beggars, orphans, dogs and little old spinsters in the streets of that tiny little hamlet…"

"Busy wee place." laughs Coinach. Bailey pauses for a drink of his Heather Ale, then… he says nothing. Once again moments pass by till Coinach can wait no longer, slightly annoyed he demands, "Go on Bailey, tell us about this evil fuckin' black cat then…"

"Well boyos', it seems that the local priory had gotten two cats for mousers. One cat was black, the other one was fair, and it came to pass those cats wouldn't catch any mice. Well then, the monks in their faith and wisdom did agree after much debate and ecumenical discussion, that a cat who does not catch a mouse has no shame, so they drowned the fair one in a bag filled with stones, hoping that this pious example of godly encouragement would strike fear into the black cat. And miraculously, it was not long before the black cat did accept God into his heart and thereon he did mouse with such righteous vigour, whereupon the black cat did eventually catch a mouse… But to the monks' horror and consternation, the mouse did escape. Later that night, another monk swore by the holy relics that he did see that same black cat fornicating with the devil. He bravely tried to save the cat, but the black cat scratched him wretchedly about the face and body with wild abandon." Bailey stops talking and takes another sup with his two friends, still engrossed in the strange story…

"Well?" enquires William, "What happened next?" Bailey

continues, "It would appear that very soon after that, the monk in question suffered a terrible affliction of weeping pus sores over his mouth, head and manly tackle, quickly followed by the rest of the priory attracting the same 'pox' as they called it. They could only believe that it was caused by none other than the demon possessed black cat, so… the monks held a public trial of the evil black cat, they found it guilty of sorcery… then they sentenced it to death by public hanging… and hung the black cat upon the gallows outside Carlisle castle."

"What… they did what?" Exclaims Coinach. An astonished William enquires, "Are you jesting us Bailey?"

"I jest you not," replies Bailey "It was as I arrived that sad day along with the rest of the hamlet population that I witnessed the public execution of the evil black cat of Carlisle." William and Coinach look at Bailey in disbelief. Bailey confirms triumphantly, "And before you two fuckers ask me if it's true, as sure as I sit here beside you … it's true."

"Really?" enquires a curious Coinach, "Naw, I don't believe it Bailey, you're drunk."

"Lord Bailey speaks the truth." Says a familiar feminine voice from the side of the wagon. Little Alasdair and two equally strange looking little monks have returned with platters of hot food and drink for the three friends. "It is the truth lord Bailey tells to you good sirs, for I too witnessed the trial of the heretical black cat." William enquires sarcastically, "I thought it was an evil black cat?" Little Alasdair continues to explain as he delivers the platters. "The Carlisle assizes trial and revelations is the very reason we will not eat black cats, we only eat fair ones." Little Alasdair lifts all the empty flagons then he and the other monks leave without saying another word.

A puzzled William enquires, "Did he just say that?"

"Don't even try to understand." advises Bailey. William sighs, "I suppose that's one black cat that sure was unlucky." Coinach enquires, "Did anyone notice the scabby cracks all over those wee monks lips, and all the open sores and boils on their heads?" He sighs as he passes William and Bailey their much-needed hot food, then he exclaims, "Feckn religion…"

Not realising how ravenous they are, they gorge their vittals while keeping a keen eye on the parley. Bailey finishes his food first, then he stands up…

"We had better sharpen our swords after that meal, for all this strangeness that has visited us these last few days might have dulled not just our wits edges… We are here to prepare for battle after all." Dumping his platter, William jumps off the wagon, "I'm going to loosen all ma arrowheads." Coinach calls out, "Wait Wallace… I'll join you and loosen mine too." Bailey enquires, "Why do you two loosen your arrowheads?" William replies, "A couple of reasons, Wee Graham up at the Craig told us that if you ever have to pierce a man with an arrow, you should loosen the heads first, then, when you shoot at the poor bastard and maybe miss, the arrows cannot be shot back at you, but we never miss." Bailey enquires, "What's the second reason then if you never miss?" Coinach explains, "When you stick your target and someone tries to pull the arrow out, the arrowhead stays in the body and tumbles about tearing up the innards, another thing too is, if you dip the arrow heads in shit beforehand, this ensures your enemy will not forget you for the little time they may live."

Bailey sighs, "You learn something new every day…"

As they set about preparing their equipment, the Graham approaches on horseback and dismounts "Wallace, will yie accompany me over to my pavilion, there's someone there I want you to meet."

"I'll loosen yer heads." Says Coinach. William agrees and

they walk over to the Graham pavilion and enter, there they see many young knights in full armour preparing for battle, all looking proud and a' swagger in their magnificent colours of house and Clan heraldry. William and Graham stand just inside the large doors of the pavilion when a handsome young knight approaches them. "Ah, Andrew," says Graham, "I'd like to introduce you to an old friend of mine, this fella here is William Wallace, Ceannard o' the Wolf and Wildcat Ceithernach and the son of Alain Wallace, Kings hunter of Glen Afton, Black Craig, Cumno and the Wolf and wildcat forests. Nephew to Sir Malcolm Wallace, knight of ach na Feàrna, Ceannard of the Garda Ban Rígh and personal council to the late King Alexander."

"William Wallace?" enquires Andrew. William nods his head in response, Graham continues, "Wallace, may I introduce Andrew de Moray of Petty and Hallhill from the Black Isle, chieftain of the Moray clan, son of Sir Andrew de Moravia Lord of Avoch, Boharm and Botriphnie, acting as the king's chief law-officer in northern Scotland..." Graham pauses then he throws his hands in the air, "Ach fuck it... you two are both Ceil Aicé..." William and Andrew look at each other and laugh out loud then shake hands warmly. Moray exclaims, "Why didn't you say that in the first place." Graham shrugs his shoulders "Ach well, I tried to go with court formality and chivalric propriety as yie do, but you two are so alike it would be a waste o' feckn time." Moray smiles, "I've heard much about you Wallace, from my cousin Davy up at Bothwell Castle, its good to be meetin' you at long last."

"And I you Moray," replies William "aye and It's a warm welcome returned, for the Morays of Bothwell are good friends to the Wallace o' Ach na Feàrna. Your cousin Davy and I, with another wee priest called Blair, we used to get up to plenty mischief about Bothwell, Davy told me a lot about you in particular." Moray jokes, "All good I hope." William smiles "Aye, he told me many stories about you fighting abroad as a mercenary in the low-countries, is that true enough?" Suddenly they're interrupted as Bailey comes rushing into the tent, "Wallace, the signalmen from the parley have let it be known we are on a call to arms, all must make ready for battle, come, quickly, Coinach and I have already saddled the horses."

"Follow Me," shouts Moray, "I'll take you to your fathers position in the line, the Afton Bowyers stand with the Avoch and Gallóbhet archers on the left wing." Everyone rushes from the pavilion where Coinach waits with their horses already prepared, William and Bailey run and jump into their saddles as De Moray and Graham mount and ride at full gallop toward their positions in the line, quickly followed by the three companions close behind. War horns blast, signal flags wave back and forth, drums beat like a giant heartbeat murmuring beneath their feet. The call to arms appears chaotic but belies a well thought out plan and organisation of the Guardian army.

With breathtaking speed, everyone quickly falls into to their positions in the ranks, setting their hearts determination on imminent battle. William, Bailey, Coinach and Moray arrive at the rear of almost a thousand warriors, mainly archers from Afton, Cumno, Carrick, Avoch, Ayr and Galloway, all standing in disciplined ranks of good order, one hundred in each line facing their opposing force. Every bowyer has an array of arrows stuck in the filthy ground at their feet, each has their bow loaded and taught, ready for pull and loose when the order is given, noticeable is that many archers hang three arrows in their draw hand for speed loosing. The second line are men holding large shields who will raise them as a wall for roof-like protection in the event of return fire or onslaught arrow storm that will certainly be incoming. This formula alternates by each line of the Guardian army from front to rear. "Good luck Wallace," Shouts out the Moray as he rushes away to join his own clan regiment in the line. "And you too Moray." Calls out William. The three companions run to where Alain stands at the front of his men. Alain turns his head to see his son come stand by his side. "William," says Alain, "Wait a moment and I'll give you orders." Alain sees Bailey and Coinach too, "Its Good to see you boys,"

'*Fuck*' thinks William '*I don't know what I'll do if this lot goes to war.*' He feels exhilaration and excitement building up in his chest. He enquires, "What's happening Dá?" Alain replies, "William, Bailey, Coinach, come close and heed my orders." The three friends stand very close to Alain to hear his command. "I don't have much time, so it's vital you do exactly as I bid you do and nothing more, do yiez understand?." Alain continues, "I want you to take your longbows to the extreme left flank away over to those gorse fields. There you'll meet with the Gallóbhan archers led by a warrior Aicé called Faolán. She'll give you your orders… and don't give me any shite that it's a woman who's in command; Faolán and her Gallóbhan are expert, ruthless and vital to my strategy… Now tell me that yie all understand?"

"We understand." reply the three companions. Alain looks at Bailey who smiles and nods toward Alain, confirming he knows his orders would be obeyed without question… and William would be guarded well. "Go now," says Alain "And fare yie well." Acknowledging his father, William and his two companions hastily leave Alain's side and sprint over to the gorse on the sloping hill, where they come upon the virtually invisible Gallóbhan. Much to their surprise, they see hundreds of armed women spread throughout the gorse with their hablar war ponies held not far behind. As they search for Faolán, they can see that every woman they pass has a look in her eyes that shows no fear, nor any emotion regarding the forthcoming conflict. The women carry a variety of bows, crossbows, light spears and long darts, each of the warrior women also carries two long curved blades that look like butcher's skinning or fleshing knives. The scene before William confuses his senses, for these handsome women are all very attractive… yet he knows that any who looks back at him, has nothing on their mind but the impending battle… *'No fear in their eyes, no fear in their hearts'* thinks William as he looks on in amazement.

Alongside the Gallóbhan archers there are female slingers, long dart, Javelin and ring-spear throwers, all wearing dun brown plated leather armour, very similar to his own, but he had never seen it in full battle dress… especially on a woman, not until they had met Faolán and the other Gallóbhan earlier. He notices the Gallóbhan helmet is similar to their male counterparts the Gallóglaigh, with the addition of a long horsehair topknot and small visor skip above the eyes rather than a nasal guard. They also wear a long sleeved battle-jack, with many small boiled leather armour plate-squares layered and riveted into the jack, cut high above the waist and overlapping. On their lower extremities they wear individual long and broad leather armoured strips, akin to their battle-jacks, but hanging like long skirts that appear to split when the women move, offering all over protection and great ease of mobility. On their feet most are wearing sheep or pigskin boots that ride high above the knee, thickly padded and bound tightly to keep them warm and hog-greased to be waterproof. Bailey nudges William, "There's Fiónlaidh and Lihd behind Faolán; she's waving at us to come over to their position." The three friends run at speed over to where

Faolán stands at the front of her troops "Hurry up." shouts Fiónlaidh. '*Fuck*' thinks William, '*Everyone here knows what they're doing except me.*'

The adrenalin pumps furiously throughout his body. He doesn't know if it's fear or the ale, but he knows his senses are heightened as never before. Faolán turns to see the three friends arrive by her side and immediately speaks to them. "Bailey, you've fought in battle before, Wallace, Coinach, you two have not… that's correct?" Bailey nods, William and Coinach glance at each other curiously. Coinach looks at Faolán, "How would you know If I have had ever fought in a battle or not?" Faolán glares at Coinach then she walks up and towers over him. William, still in awe, looks at Faolán, so regal and commanding in her polished steel and brass war helm, with jaw guards sloping around her cheeks and a single long black horsehair hanger streaming down her back from the topknot on her helmet. All that is really visible of her beautiful features is her piercing blue eyes, now looking down intensely at Coinach.

Faolán speaks firmly, "Coinach, I see that your heart is brave, but I want you to go back and stand with Alain Wallace of Glen Afton, he needs strong men like you, the fight of the Gallóbhan is not in your heart, now go… there is no time to be wasting here." Coinach appears confused… and angry. Faolán raises her voice… "MOVE…" At that moment, a young girl in full Gallóbhan leather armour approaches with a hablar, and thrusts the reigns into Coinach's hand. He doesn't utter a word as he mounts the horse and spurs it towards the gathered ranks where Alain and the Black Craig and glen Afton archers stand patiently. Faolán turns to Fiónlaidh, "Bailey and Wallace will fight with us; bring them into our Sparr." Faolán returns to where she can oversee the plains of Dalry below. William looks at Bailey, "What just happened there with Coinach?" Fiónlaidh replies, "Faolán knows… she saw in Coinach's heart that something dark and grievous is troubling him. Add to that he has no experience in battle, then many of our Gallóbhan would die this day simply because of him. Coinach is better to be fighting with his own kind, the men."

William exclaims, "But I have no battle experience, I've never had anything but a brawl at most." Fiónlaidh looks at William "You didn't question Faolán." Bailey agrees, "Fiónlaidhs' right. Warfare and battle can only be won by obeying respected leaders without question. If your father has sent us to fight with Faolán and the Gallóbhan, that's good enough for me."

Fiónlaidh motions for William and Bailey to follow her. They walk a few short steps to a small peat fire glowing just behind where Faolán stands. William watches as young girls and boys run about, placing clutches of arrows, Bolts, Javelins and slinger stones at the feet of all the Gallóbhan spread throughout the gorse on the small hill. William's attention us brought back to the moment when he sees Fiónlaidh grabbing a handful of arrows, lay's them on the ground, then she pulls her leather skirts aside and squats over them. William watches in disbelief as Fiónlaidh begins pissing on the arrowheads. When she's finished, she sticks the heads into a pile of human excreta nearby.

Cleaning her hands with snow then sfaggy moss, Fiónlaidh turns back to William and Bailey sitting beside the small fire. "What do you require of us?" enquires Bailey as he and William warm their cold fingers in the glow of the small peat fire. Fiónlaidh replies, "When the battle commences, you stay with our Sparr, usually it's three of us who fight together, but today we are five. You look to where Faolán looks, when she looses on a target, then you loose at that same target, do you both understand me?"

"Aye," reply William and Bailey, both nodding in agreement. Satisfied her orders are understood, Fiónlaidh continues, "Look over there to the centre of our army, do you see Fergus of the Gallóglaigh, Moray of Avoch, Wallace of Glen Afton and De Graham of Dundaff?" William and Bailey nod their heads as Fiónlaidh explains, "There will be three main types of arrow flights in this battle, storm, arc and trace. There is little we can do about the first two, it is the trace archer we must concentrate on this day. We must follow Faolán's eyeline; for she will pinpoint any who looses a trace arrow directly at any of the chiefs I have pointed out for you, it means that an archer is firing a power arrow at one of our chiefs set to kill them, while the other archers simply storm or arc arrows in the hope that when the arrows drop from the sky they will kill someone. Our first work today is to take out the trace Bowyers and their captain's as quickly as possible, do you both understand me?"

Both Bailey and William reply, "We do..." At that moment Lihd appears and stands at the left side of Faolán. She turns, sees Bailey and smiles. Bailey grins and smiles back at her then she turns away to scrutinize the same outline of the plains that Faolán is keenly observing. Fiónlaidh continues, "Bailey, I want you to loose your arrows beside Lihd to the left of Faolán. Wallace, you join me and loose your arrows to my sight." Bailey smiles, he recognises that Fiónlaidh knows that by grouping people of friendship together, it makes for more passionate extremes of energy in war. Fiónlaidh says, "If our army moves forward, then we move parallel with the chiefs, the right flank of Faolán protects the chiefs, the left flank protects us from tracer or cavalry." Fiónlaidh pauses, then she enquires, "There is one gift you may now offer me now, or you must leave the Gallóbhan and join the men over in the plain." Bailey smiles when William enquires, "What is the gift we may give to you?" Fiónlaidh replies, "Your life for Faoláns." William didn't flinch as he replies stoically, "My life is my gift." Bailey repeats the same reply with sincerity, "My life is my Gift." Fiónlaidh smiles, "Then I accept your lives for the guardianship of Faolán, our Gallóbhan Aicé. And I welcome you to our Sparr, for that is all that we require of you mo charaidhean." (my friends)

Suddenly the air is filled with the noise of horns blasting and drums beating furiously, the sounds of the two drone bagpipes start playing, dogs of war bark and howl... then there's a large roar of voices from the two armies gathered on the plains of Saint John, the surrounding hills echo with this insane uproar of war. Faolán calls out, "TO ME..."

Fiónlaidh immediately picks up her horse-bow and rushes over to take her position at the right side of Faolán. Bailey stands to the left of Lihd and William takes his place beside Fiónlaidh. They keenly observe the parley as men from the inner circle begin to mount their horses. The outer circle pennant riders slowly back their horses away, all simultaneously raising their pennants high, as though a flower of nature opens its petals to the morning sun. All the horsemen continue to walk the horses backwards till the three rings dissolve to form two single lines aggressively facing each other. Tension mounts as both armies fall silent, waiting for a signal... The plains of Saint John fall into a most un-natural silence, filling the air with a palpable electrifying excitement.

Eagerly watching this unveiling of mans primeval power en masse, William feels his body tense, waiting for the unknown. His heart pounds like an inner drum beats wildly in his chest as though its about to explode. Adrenalin pumps through his veins as never before, taking his senses to an exhilarating peak. He wants to scream and run at the enemy and fight when Fiónlaidh knowingly glances at him, smiles, then turns away. Her glance seems to calm his angst. He waits impatiently as the riders' turn their horses then canter in good order toward their own encampments.

More moments of unbearable silence follow; then William sees the Guardian army raise their arms, pennants and flags high into the air, followed seconds later by an almighty roar rising from the plains of Saint John of Dalry. As though in unison from another giant bull, a similar action of arms and roaring comes from the Pact army. William feels total confusion, excitement and bewilderment as to what is about to happen; then he notices two Knights ride out of the Guardian front line on magnificent and powerfull stallions. The two horsemen gallop at top speed toward Faoláns' position. William watches as the Knight's ride furiously over slush and muddy ground. They appear to be looking very surreal as time and pace transforms their appearance to horses galloping in slow motion. The powerful hooves of the war-stallions kick up lumps of mud, dirt and splash through the slush. The skirts of the horse caparison flow in unison to the flapping of the pennant flags.

Fascinated, William stares at the heart shields and coat of arms of both horse and rider pennant's, as though he is mesmerised by the primeval majesty. As the knights gallop towards them, William sees the leading knight's shield of azure blue background with two small silver stars above one large silver star, the border edge lines of his shield mid-set with fleur de lyse inserts. The second rider William recognises as the coat of arms of his friend John de Graham, who calls out, "The Pact has relented…" Graham calls out once more as he draws close to Faolán. "De Brix withdraws his army…" The first Knight stops his horse beside Faolán then he quickly dismounts and takes off his war helm. William recognises

Andrew de Moray, who shouts out joyfully, "Faolán, Wallace…
De Brix relents and he promises to withdraw to his castles
and send his allies homeward, there will be no battle today…"
Graham dismounts near Faolán who persists on keeping a
vigil on the Pact forces. William notices Graham approach
Faolán; she takes her hand off her bow and waves him back.
"Faolán does not trust De Brix," says Fiónlaidh, "she's waiting
till they disperse their archers before she stands us down."
Graham calls out to William, "That's good news about the
uprising Wallace."

"Aye," Replies William, "It would have been madness to
fight, for darkness will fall soon."

It's not long before Faolán is satisfied that de Brix truly has
truly stood down when she sees the Pact archers disperse.
She takes her helmet off and smiles, "That's a pity, it would
have been to our vantage to finish this folly of the Pact once
and for all." William enquires, "Why do you say that?" Faolán
ignores William's question and looks towards a Ceithernach
standing nearby. She simply nods towards her… The young
Ceithernach quickly removes a large circular and ornately
embossed hunting horn from her back, puts the mouthpiece
to her lips and blows long and hard.

A shrill piercing clarion blast could be heard above all the
noise coming from the plains. William and Bailey notice
Faolán looking to the far flank of the Guardian army as both
she and her command watch and wait. A second blast from
other hunting horns echo around the hills… Suddenly from
behind the tree line on the right flank, an equal number of
Gallóbhan archers step onto the plains. William watches
in awe as these warrior women emerge, he thinks of how
Galloway had rightly held on to such a stoic fighting force
that all others had rejected in Christendom.

"Some sight," quips Graham as he points to the right

flank of the guardian army. To his surprise, William notices away on the right flank of the Guardian army, what appears to be hundreds of jet black coloured cobs and bay hablars' emerging from the woodland behind the Gallóbhan archers, with riders dressed in armour similar to Faolán. He could barely make out the detail, but they have a proud and defiant profile in their movement, Bailey exclaims, "Fuck, look behind us… look up at the ridge rise."

William turns around to see an equal number of horsewomen appear over the summit behind where they stand. He recognises the lead rider as Eochaidh, looking so majestic, so serious, her intent could not be mistaken by other than a fool. As she passes William, she looks down and smiles then leads a column of horse numbering over two hundred past them, he can now see more closely what these mystical looking horse warriors look like and what they use as weapons. Lihd stands beside Bailey and together they watch the Gallóbhan cob and hablar cavalry pass by silently on their way down to the camp.

"Who are these women?" enquires William. Lihd replies, "Gallóbhan-Sídhe. (Gallo-ban-shee) They're the women who ride with the spirit of the black horse. Eochaidh there is an Aicé of the Gallóbhan-Sídhe."

"Eochaidh Gunn?" Exclaims William, "she's an Aicé?" Lihd smiles, "She is, from the western Machars of Galloway." Watching these women warriors from this ancient Kingdom impresses William greatly, with their poise and air of genuine capabilities. "Bahn Sídhe?" enquires Bailey, "I thought that's what you called an evil spirit of death?" Lihd laughs out loud, "Aye you could say that, but only if you get on the wrong side of us. For our people the words simply means 'the good woman, an expert in healing… or killing, it's your choice." Bailey looks at Lihd with respect, for he too could see in all of these women a special something that is vacant or missing in their English counterparts, something very special indeed. Bailey thinks, '*Perhaps it's the fact the Gallóbhan have choice to stand beside their men, respected as warriors of merit. Whereas women in England and Wales are denied this choice.*' His thoughts are disturbed when Fiónlaidh calls out, "Here comes Faoláns' guard." Fiónlaidh laughs then she says, "It's lucky for de Brix a peace was declared this day, for those women would have torn the heart out of his army if darkness had fallen."

William and Bailey look round and notice the rear units of the passing cavalry is brought up by beautiful long unfettered black horses, he could see that the women warriors who mounted these beautiful steeds were different from the Gallóbhan-Sídhe, dressed in a smoke black leather armour, almost identical to that of Faolán's. The varied weaponry carried by these women is nothing like the weight or style of weapons men use. Their swords are short, slim and curved like the swords of the Saracens. Hanging on the sides of their horses are long conical wicker quivers filled with long thin javelins and ring spears. To the front of their saddles hanging on either side, are lengths of rolled hemp with what appears to be grappling hooks attached. Curiously they all wear amazing looking raven and crow feather brats.

'*The Morríaghan,*' Thinks William, then he notices something he thought was but a legend. He turns to Fiónlaidh and enquires, "Are those ring spears?"

"They are." replies Fiónlaidh proudly. William exclaims, "Fuck me Bailey, those things are rare, I have only ever heard of them in legends, but never have I seen them before." Bailey looks at Lihd and enquires, "What's a ring spear?" Lihd replies "It's five or six finely honed thin strips of metal, each shaped like a thin leaf with a tiny nick near the top, all held fast by a metal ring at the shoulder of the blades to pull each of the strips together, when the spear-head enters the body, the skin around the wound pushes the ring down the blades toward the shaft... as more of the blades enter the body, the blades separate and curl in different directions inside the body, when you spin and pull the spear back out of the body, the separate blades slice and tear your innards to pieces, no one survives that."

"Fuckin' hell..." exclaims Bailey. Lihd enquires, "Do you see those small grappling hooks hanging by their saddles?" Bailey and William nod as Lihd continues, "When the Bahn-Sídhe ride past an enemy, those hooks are thrown into the massed ranks to grip a man by the flesh of his back or legs, then he's dragged out, tumbling many men in front of him and making great gaps in the ranks for the mounted archers, javelin throwers or ring spear cavalry to ride into." Lihd smiles seeing the expression of sheer respect so obvious upon Bailey and William's faces, she continues, "They have many weapons about them that you may see with your eye, but many more that you don't see." Bailey enquires curiously, "I thought Bahn Sídhe were the screaming evil spirits heard by men before they die?"

"True," replies Lihd, "The Gallóbhan-Sídhe prefer to attack at dusk on their black horses. They scream, curse and blast their hunting horns as they charge forward. They're mostly dark women on black horses who never take a prisoner, except for amusement... or they may free one soul to tell the chiefs of our enemies that the women of the dark horse took the lives of their army." A proud Lihd continues, "Of course men will fear these women, but rather than say it was a woman who has killed the warrior men, on occasion the survivors, when there are any, do say with false pride, it was something else that defeated them, like an evil ghost or the screaming spirit of death that comes for them." Lihd and Fiónlaidh raise their eyes and laugh, "Men…" Pulling her two curved skinning blades from her belt; Lihd spins them in her hand in front of Bailey then enquires, "Do you see these short little brands Bailey?"

"Yes?" replies a slightly hesitant Bailey. Lihd continues, "We use these at close quarters where we slice at soft places, like under your arms or the tendons of your legs or maybe your eyes and throat, but our cut of the Goddess is when we reach between your legs, bury our blades deep in your arse, then rip the blades forward, separating your bonnie wee eggs." Lihd slowly draws the blades along Baileys crutch in a demonstration, of sorts. Bailey dry-swallows as do William, Graham and Moray who are all watching nervously, all three unconsciously clutch their manhood while the women smile at the men's apparent distress.

"I think Lihd likes you Bailey," jokes William. Faolán, who has been enjoying the angst shown by the young men, steps forward and says in humour, "Not this day Lihd, we must return to our camp. I want the Gallóbhan Ceannard to attend me, there is to be a gathering of the chiefs to receive all of the full detail of the peace accord from Wishart."

"There will be a lot of relieved celebrating this night." says William cheerily. Faolán glares at William, "Wallace, I do not take you for a fool, so why talk like one… Is it the stupidity of youth or merely that you are simple… Or perhaps is it just that you are inexperienced in the art of war?" William feels acutely embarrassed at Faolán's curt words.

Faolán is about the same age, but clearly he has says something stupid in her mind. Fáolin walks away and issues orders for everyone to return to camp, she also gives orders for rotational guards to be maintained and vigilance to be kept throughout the long night. Bailey comes over to William,

"I'm going to wander back with Lihd…" He looks closely at William, "Are you all right?" William stands watching the activities down on the plain as though mesmerised. Bailey put his hand on William's shoulder, "I'm going to go down to the camp with Lihd, are you coming?" William replies, "Naw Bailey, I think I'll wait here awhile longer. I'm so feckn exhausted and tired. Everything we've been through, then preparing for battle… it seems now as though all the strength I had sourced is fast draining away from me. I think I just need a few moments rest to take it all in" Bailey understands, "Don't be long then, the night chill is coming and you don't want to fall asleep up here or you'll freeze to death."

"I'll be fine Bailey," says William, "I'll see yiez all down at the camp soon." Everyone but the sentinel guard make their way towards the camp. William watches Moray ride away, then he notices Faolán, Graham, Bailey and Lihd walk down towards the camp and thinks how fucked up everything is, only a little while ago, the four people he observes now, were preparing to kill as many as they could with vengeful ferocity and without mercy. He was in little doubt they were also prepared to die for a cause that still wasn't clear to him. How bizarre it feels to see them walk together like they've been on a springtime lovers tryst.

Sitting down on a raised flat boulder beside the small peat fire, William pulls his brat hood up over his head to shelter from the icy breeze. Sitting alone, he thinks of all he has seen at Corserine and Dunveoch, it's haunting his soul. Leaning forward to heat his cold hands, he stares into the glow of the fire, thinking about Affric and her zest for life and how everything had changed for her so dramatically, now she fights for life itself. He wishes she was with him now… then he thinks of Marion, he has a love for Affric, but he feels he is missing Marion too. 'Feck,' he thought,

'*I really do love Marion.*' Laughing at the irony of his young life, he suddenly sees in his minds eye the faces of the dead women and children of the massacres, he can't comprehend the same thing happening to him or to those he loves, it's almost too much to think about. Exhausted, his tired and weakened spirit brings emotions to the surface that's been welling up inside his heart for days. As the adrenalin ebbs, a morose mood replaces the excitement. He sits alone for a long time hunched over the small peat fire, lost in a world of deep thought. Suddenly he becomes aware off gentle hands resting on his shoulders, he spins round as someone jumps back in surprise…

"Fiónlaidh…" exclaims William, "how long have you been standing there?" Fiónlaidh smiles, then without a word says between them, she sits gently on his lap and rests her head upon his shoulder, in a such a way that he knows is not a gesture of love making, but of something greater between two souls who find a moment that no words could ever express, a moment shared to sooth their aching hearts. He pulls his brat round Fiónlaidh and holds her close in his protective arms.

All sense of time is lost as they rest awhile in silence. William senses Fiónlaidhs' deep pain, then he feels her gently sobbing, this ferocious little warrior now cries softly in his arms. He could do nothing but comfort her while feeling his own emotions reach breaking point, tears well up inside of him too. The two soulmates' sit a long time till Fiónlaidh shakes her head and pops out from below his brat. William could see in her beautiful bright eyes that she's been crying. Something of her inner beauty makes him feel grateful for the trust she has placed in him, to be for her what she really needed. He too had felt the same need for this intimacy. Fiónlaidh smiles, followed by a long sigh…

"Thank yie Wallace… I really needed that." William stands

up and stretches, then he yelps in agony, his muscles are seizing in the freezing cold. He speaks as he lowers his arms, "Fiónlaidh, I'll be thanking you too, for I needed that as much as you did I reckon." She laughs while wiping a tear from her eye, "Its your fault anyway Wallace."

"ME... my fault?" exclaims William. "Aye you," retorts Fiónlaidh. "I was fine sorting out the sentinel duties, then I saw you hunched over the wee fire. As I closed in behind you, I felt a great and powerful wave of sadness. I was going to leave you alone, but I was drawn back, for I knew that I should lay my hands upon you to help release the spirit of sadness and pain you were feeling, then it somehow overwhelmed me too and I felt my own emotions breaking."

Gazing into Fiónlaidhs' eyes, William says, "I was thinking of unspeakable things I've seen Fiónlaidh... Then I thought about the love of my family and love in my heart. Sometimes I just don't know what's happening in this witless world."

"I know and I feel the same as you do Wallace," says Fiónlaidh, "but we had better get down to the gathering, for we will be missed soon and we don't want to start today's war tonight because we were both stuck up here star gazing." William agrees, "You're right, we had better go down, for the dark of night is all but complete." then he thinks of something, "Fiónlaidh... why did Faolán call me stupid earlier, I mean what did I say or do that was so wrong? Fuck, she sure wasn't happy with me." The two new friends begin walking down towards the camp as Fiónlaidh answers Williams question. "You must excuse her abrupt manner Wallace, Faolán is a beautiful, spiritual and wonderful woman, a mother and a sister to us all... but in war she is a ruthless leader who we love and trust with our lives, she is young, but she is a proven leader in battle."

William thinks about what he could have says, he just

couldn't understand why she would call him stupid. "I hope you don't gain this experience Wallace, but if it does come to pass, you must remember what I tell to you now. If two opposing forces such as was stood here this day meet on field to do battle, then they make a peace accord, the most dangerous period is not before the battle, but after the peace."

William repeats, "After the peace?"

"Aye," Replies Fiónlaidh, "Many have gathered here for the cause, but more are here for blood tax vengeance … as many different reasons as there are warriors. If we celebrate this night, then we would be at our most vulnerable to attack, and many of the Gallóbhet will still be seething because they cannot fulfill honour for the injustice brought upon their families by de Brix and the Pact." William enquires, "What will happen tonight then?"

"Guards and sentinels will be tripled on the perimeters, everyone else will make sleep wherever they can, most of the Gallóbhet will be put under watch guard for they have more right than any to attack de Brix's camp, they're confined to their own camp till the morn."

"No loud music, no dancing, drinking or bonfires?" enquires William "No celebrations at all?" Fiónlaidh looks at William and shakes her head, "No celebration, under pain of severe punishment for those that would break the martial law of the Breitheamh Rígh Wallace."

William ponders a moment then replies, "That makes sense, though I would never have thought about that. You really have to be here to understand the reality of war… and peace." William and Fiónlaidh wander along talking intensely about what they have seen and experienced on the lead-up to this day, when a voice calls out in the darkness. "Where have you two been?"

William and Fiónlaidh suddenly become aware they've

wandered all the way to the edge of the camp, they hadn't noticed they were once more lost in time. "Wallace..." says the voice. William looks to see who is calling him, then he sees the silhouette of a knight standing in front of a fire, he recognises Moray with a Gallóbhan, "Moray, I didn't recognize you... what's happening?" Moray replies, "Your friend Coinach is bedded down with his Gallóglaigh kinfolk, Lihd has taken Bailey away for an, eh, education..."Everyone laughs. Moray smirks, "I see you have been making relations of your own." Fiónlaidh and William laugh as Moray continues, "Wallace, this is Sinéad (Sheena) she's a Ceannard in the Gallóbhan horse." William and Sinéad greet by clasping each other's wrists. As they all walk toward the Obhainn lodges, William says, "I'm impressed by the women of the Gallóbhan and black horse cavalry."

Sinéad, a slender brown haired beauty, giggles as she clasps Moray by the arm. William thinks `I must be drunk or someone has slipped me herbal medicals. How can these women who could and would rip you apart on the battlefield, be so full of feminine charms in their ways when at peace.'

Moray speaks to William "There'll be a gathering the morn Wallace, Wishart and the commanders will explain everything about the parley and issue new orders to the Chiefs and Ceannards. Your father says he'll see you in the morn, for tonight he meets for deliberations with the Guardians in Wishart's pavilion." The small group chatters awhile longer. As they prepare to part, Moray says, "Please my friends, heed me, keep sharp wits not only this night, but when you return to your homelands." William enquires, "What do you mean by that?" Moray looks about to see that what he says next is for their ears alone. "This days troubles are far from over, though we may joy in the thought of peace this eve, I must tell you something of great importance, but you must keep this information close as it is but a rumour till confirmed… but, the Maid of Norway, she's dead… some say she has been murdered." There's a stunned gasp amongst the friends, then a moment of silence in disbelief. Moray continues, "It's not known yet if this is true or false information going round the plains in order to bring us to war, but it would seem that without proof, it may just that, a scurrilous rumour. But if de Brix has backed off because of the Maids imminent arrival and should she now be dead, then this battle for the throne of Scotland may yet take place at first light… so be ready."

Solemn moments pass as the small group considers the extremes of emotions that has been their experience of late… and the possible implications that a new confrontation may face them again in the morn. Moray grabs William by the hand, "Anyway Wallace, you go find yourself a warm crib, Sinéad and I must be settling ourselves if this is to be our last night on this earth." William laughs, "That's a fair point yie have there Moray, I dearly hope we have more than one last night on this earth, for I've much yet to do." Moray and Sinéad laugh as they bid William and Fiónlaidh a good night.

"Well…" sighs William "It's time that I find somewhere to sleep too for I'm dying on my feet." Moray looks back, raises his hand and calls out… "I'll see you in the morn upon Wishart's roll-call Wallace, Oidhche math mo chara."

"Oidhche math." replies William. Fiónlaidh takes a hold of William by the hand, "Come with me Wallace, for Moray may be right. The morn will bring us either peace… or war."

Stellar Matutina

Pacing the chancellery, Edward sups from a goblet of wine while enjoying the faint sounds of the distant choral choir. He turns to observe his council, who immediately stop chattering when sensing his piercing focus is upon them. Edward feels elated at the council findings, then his expression changes as he begins to analyse the last piece of the puzzle to be brought into his plans, he utters… "Scotland…"

"Sire?" Queries Burnell. Edward looks at Burnell and studies his loyal man of outstanding wit, "I wish to know more of your plans regarding Scotland Burnell. To what level does that realm truly prosper?" Burnell replies, "Scotland is fast becoming one of wealthiest realms in all of Christendom sire. And it is the last territory upon these islands to be colonised to favour the inauguration of the Great Cause…" Edward replies coldly, "Scotland is a sovereign realm, and an ally." Bek replies "That is true Sire, but Scotland will always remain a threat by varying degrees. The miserable perfidious Scotch are no better than the Irish, Welsh or Jewry… the Holy Scriptures does refer to them as such in all but name, for they do exchange God's truth for lies and deem to worship nature and creatures created rather than the revered Creator…" Edward retorts, "Bek…do you forget that I too have Scots blood coursing through my veins? Do you also forget that my good sister Margret was once the Queen of that Kingdom before her demise?" Bek blusters and tries to salvage his error of judgment. "Fear not my dear Bek," says Edward "the question of Scotland and its sovereignty is as I say, in hand. It is widely accepted and most common knowledge that my newborn prince I did intend his betrothal to King Alexander's granddaughter Margaret. But my lords, I will soon own the hereditary rights to that northern estate and Crown of the North, both shall come to me in due course… And as for young prince Edward, I have better uses for him that are more strategically vital for our kingdom." Edmund queries, "Other plans…"

"Yes Edmund," replies Edward. "I have been giving much consideration for my son's betrothal to Philip's daughter Isabella for a while now." Edward pauses to gain a reaction from his gathered council. As they murmur approvingly amongst themselves, Edward continues, "We shall discuss the Scotch question this eve in much greater detail. The elimination of Scotland is the last piece of the puzzle that shall soon begin in earnest the Great Cause. Now Edmund, what say you on the Jewish question?"

Edmund replies, "All is prepared Sire, we will immediately enact the edicts by your seal of approval and masterly guidance from the imperial laws of Constantine's Codex', Theodosianius and Justinian. Furthermore good Bek here has absolved us from all restraint regarding morals, in order that we may do God's blessed work by fire and sword against the accursed Jewry."

Edward enquires, "How soon may we strike at the Jewry?" Edmund replies "I have an army ready to strike at them by first light of the morning star sire. Messengers await to execute the edicts with extreme diligence; then a pogrom will be enacted in all your provinces and territories here in

France. Within one day the net will close and no Jew shall escape your benevolent justice Sire, not one silver Steorra nor its clippings shall pass, other than to your exchequer." Edmund Pauses as Edward consumes this information with obvious delight. "Sire," says Edmund, "I have men in Scotland who have been counselling with many dissident Norman Scotch Nobles, lords and Barons, they dearly long for the day when they may swear fealty and perform great service to you as their true King."

"Good, very good..." says Edward. He casually points at Burnell and Bek, he says, "Look at these two men Edmund... they are surely our pillars of God's justice with their wit, cunning and diligence of planning, our father King Henry's vision becomes more a reality as each day passes." Burnell replies, "Sire, it is you who is our divine inspiration, and so it is to those of our allies in pursuit of the Great Cause who do attend you now."

"The Northern brotherhood is gaining strength sire," says Edmund, "There are many emissaries gathering in St Jean d'Angely as we speak, but surely this gathering must be noted by Philips spies?"

"It will be noticed," says Edward, "have no doubts about that my lords. It is what Philip doesn't notice that is as more valuable to us. Patience, misinformation and half truths will have the Capetians running around France like scared little mice chasing their own tails..." Edward glances at a great tapestry map of Christendom, falling full drop from ceiling to floor and twice as broad. "While that upstart Philip of France struts with the weight of his new golden crown upon his shoulders listening to the sycophantic courtesans of Paris, he does not see final nightfall approaching the crown bloodline of Capet. Though his unworthy petulance demands I pay homage and fealty, it has given our alliance a unique opportunity." Edmund enquires, "How so sire?" Edward replies, "The Kings Adolph of Nassau, with Albrecht of Habsburg, Christopher the Magnus of Sweden, Wenceslaus of Bohemia and all the princes of the Low Countries... save that of Flanders, have all reached agreement in regards to the division and rule of Christendom when Roman influence is annexed. We will soon meet in the chancellery of Saintes to pledge a bonded oath as the Northern Brotherhood of Kings." Edmund enquires "And then France will be ours?"

Edward replies..."Patience dear brother... Our allies require urgent financial support to put down rebellions and small wars within their own realms, this is what we must finance with the Jewish and Flemish accounts, we must also assist our allies with men and supplies. It takes time to prepare and collect the vast amounts of monies required to execute, but all do urgently wish the speedy destruction of Philip, that we may push the influence of the Vatican back behind the Pyrenees, leaving all from Scotland to the Bospherus and everything North in our hands. By our swords and by our faith, we shall rule all."

"Sire," says Bek "I have recently gained the confidence of Bernard Saisset, the Bishop of Palmiers." An enthused Burnell speaks, "He's a very useful individual Sire, his following is vast and almost matches that of Philips army in numbers." Bek agrees, "It's true Sire, Saisset despises Philip and the house of Capet, he damns the black blood of the heretic Philip and he's a fervent supporter by oath and pledge to the house of Angevin Plantagenet." Edmund too agrees. "Saisset is a powerful and influential magnate sire, not only amongst our gathering allies in the north, he also has the ear of young Wenceslaus and the Magyar's of the Balkans with his heathen allies the Bulgars." Bek speaks, "Saisset has many followers as far south as Aragon and Catalonia, all of whom do support him fervently. He is extremely focused on his own vehement opposition to King Philip and an end to the house of Capet." Relishing this information, Edward comments, "I have heard favourably of this Saisset, apparently he is an ardent Occitan aristocrat from an old noble family and I too am aware he despises the Capetians. He would be welcome as a formidable ally my lords... I believe our cause finds another unwitting supporter."

"Sire, by your grace..." says Bek "I will nurture this mans torment. I am informed he does urgently request an audience with you upon your next trip to Paris." Edward replies, "A meeting could be possible, meanwhile Bek, do nurture his angst with Philip and keep me informed. But now my lords, to more pressing matters, we must return to the minutes in hand. To reiterate Burnell, can you confirm that the new edicts and taxes we propose will compensate our allies?" Burnell replies, "If we move immediately on the Jewry here in France and England without delay sire, then the answer is definitively yes, then..." Edmund interrupts "What of the eastern Kings' alliance brother? I have met recently with the young King Ladislas, he is impatient to bring his Cuman and Patzinak horde together with Albert of Brabant's armies to storm Paris from the north."

"Ah yes, the Cumans," says Edward "we cannot yet bring them into the alliance, for as we are aware of their warring intentions, then so to is Philip. It is another secret conspiracy to be found by Philip in order to flex his French bluster, by looking the wrong direction I fear." Everyone laughs as Edward continues "I have planned a little unrest here in France and arranged with the Duke of Rochelle, the Bergun-dians' and our loyal allies the Gascons' to press dispute with the Parisians. If we support Saisset discreetly, these thorns will keep Philip busy while we progress our Great Cause further." Edmund states proudly, "A formidable alliance is gathering with us brother." Edward smiles contentedly, then changes the subject of conversation. "Tell me of Scotland Burnell, how fairs your plans?" Before Burnell could reply, a voice is heard calling outside the great door of the exchequer, followed by a loud knocking on the door. Edwards captain of the guard enters... "Sire... Walter of Hemingbrough, master chronicler to the priory of Lanercoste, he does beg an audience." Edward nods his head in approval.

The captain of the guard opens the door and beckons in a tall thin almost skeletal individual, wearing a grey cloth habit of the Franciscan monastic brethren and small skullcap of a studious cleric. His deep-set dark sunken eyes strangely match the grey pallor of his skin. Walter of Hemingbrough enters the chancellery like an unearthly ghoul to gain his Kings pleasure. Regarded by all who know Walter is as an extremely intelligent man, despite his emaciated impoverished appearance. Walter is master chronicler of all current events, laws and statutes printed in England for consumption by the royal, Baronial and religious classes of the realm.

The Franciscan chronicler has travelled from the northern priory of Lanercoste in England, where his life is dedicated to overseeing the biased recording and publication of the vitally important Northern Counties and Lanercost chronicles, recording for posterity the history of England on behalf of the Crown. These important chronicles are a life-blood of information for the clerical hierarchy and lawmakers of England, keeping all informed of English state affairs, from the Shires, towns and cities to the most remote corners of the land. The avid readers absorb the contents of the chronicle eagerly, as if written by Gods hand himself. "Walter of Hemingbrough, how good it is to see you," exclaims Edward "your timing could not be more judged than if God himself had sent you here to me this night." Walter replies "Sire." as he grasps the kings' right hand with his long bony fingers. Walter kneels and kisses the royal signet. "It is Gods will Sire." Edward comments, "You look tired Walter, have you travelled directly from the Hemingbrough priory?" Walter replies "Lanercost Sire, though I now reside permanently in great solitude at the Grey-friar House in Carlisle with the Franciscan brothers. A place of heavenly solitude Sire, where I employ their zealous Minorite authorship upon the Chronicles, to which, the end is better served."

"Good, good… Now, pray be seated Walter," says Edward "you shall soon be enlightened in regards this nights proceedings. We are about to examine with scrupulous attention these writs you see before you laid upon this table. In this task, all will be revealed from the councils' previous discourse this eve." Walter of Hemingbrough takes his seat as all welcome him to the council table.

Many hours pass, with the privy council meticulously going over the charters and writs time and time again until they are collectively satisfied the minutia discussed and agreed could not be undone by the lawmakers of England, nor by canon edicts or papal bulls from Rome. Edward and his council continue working tirelessly until the priory bells of Saint John the Baptist ring out across the land, heralding the coming of the midnight hour. "Good sirs'…" says Edward "We should have much needed sustenance, for this scrutiny and discourse will continue and prove to be the making a long night of deliberations. Edmund, summon more food and wine from the captain of the guard?"

"Sire." replies Edmund. He turns and walks to the door and commands the captain of the guard to bring refreshment as Edward and his council settle to a more relaxed and cordial atmosphere discussing the night's work. The sustenance soon arrives and they feast while continuing to deliberate, till all are completely satisfied their work has been successfully concluded. Stretching his legs under the table for a moment, Edward rises and walks towards the windows while supping wine, pausing a few moments at the open window to savour the midnight moonlit beauty of his French province. He speaks with his gathered council… "My lords, shall we remove ourselves from these quarters and complete the deliberations in surrounds of the sanctum of the Stella Matutina, it is more befitting for the conclusion of this eves work." Edward turns again to look out the open window to absorb the wondrous beauty in the skyline, savouring the strategic brilliance of this nights work. He knows these plans confirmed with his council will change the stalemate he faces in his ambition to be the new '*Justinian*' of Christendom.

Meanwhile, his council are busily securing all the documents and charters in order for the council to proceed to the Stella Matutina and discuss the last of this night's topics.

Approaching the King, Edmund informs Edward that all has been made ready and everyone is prepared to leave the exchequer at his pleasure. Edward crosses the floor, bidding all to follow. Edmund enquires discreetly as the others chatter amongst themselves, "Why the Star Chamber brother?" Edward replies, "It has been a long eve Edmund, and the character of the chamber better suits our need for spiritual inspiration." Glancing at the expression on Edmunds face, Edward smiles, "And so it is with the spirit of the Matutina Edmund, for above the inner sanctum is nought but the heavens and our one true God… and who better to observe with utmost clarity our thoughts and to nurture our deliberations, than our blessed host." Edward crosses his chest making the sign of the cross. The atmosphere as they prepare to leave for the sacred chambers is greatly relaxed by comparison to the intensity of the last few hours; though much now depends on the decisions that have been established by the meeting of these powerful individuals coming to fruition.

As they leave the exchequer and walk towards the chamber stairwell, Walter, Bek and Burnell converse while Edward and Edmund hold their own council as they ascended the tower stairs. Speaking quietly to Bek and Burnell, Walter says, "I am concerned that Alexanders granddaughter the maid of Norway's imminent arrival in Scotland will threaten our Great Cause." Burnell replies, "I agree, should she reach Scotland alive, this will most certainly confound the sovereign ambitions of the Angevin Plantagenet's. And should she ascend the throne of Scotland…" Bek interrupts with a sense of urgency "We cannot risk any links left alive between the houses of Canmore, Llewellyn and Capet."

Burnell nods in agreement, "What also compounds this moment is the house of Capet does grievously covet all our Lord's territories… the Plantagenet Angevins' have ruled from Jerusalem through western France to the Pyrenees, Cyprus, Ireland, Wales and England for a hundred years or more, I fear lord Edward still smarts that the Angevins' were defeated so decisively by Philip's grand father Augustus Capet, and more so that now our King must pay homage to this Capetian youth Philip."

Walter says, "It was certainly a disaster when Phillips' father decimated the Plantagenet alliance of English and Teutonic armies at Bouvines, now our Lord's claim to the Scotch throne, though extremely tenuous, was severely weakened by Yolande Capet's marriage to the King of Scots. Alexander may be dead, but now, should the maid of Norway reach Scotland alive, Edwards' plan for the Great Cause may face ruination." Burnell says, "I share your concerns Walter, but our king is a brilliant tactician, he would never tilt his lance at this ambitious cause if he didn't have more than one way to skin this Scotch wildcat and the little French twat... both at the same time methinks."

"I concur," laughs Bek "our liege Lord Edward's planning and tactical skills will surely re-establish the Plantagenet Angevins' as the true and rightful royal house of Christendom, and impose proper rule of order in the world for a thousand years or more." The council make their way through the vast array of corridors and stairwells till they finally reach the top-most tower of the château, where four powerfully built guards and a sergeant-at-arms stand on a permanent duty roster, allowing none other than the King and his chosen guests to enter. The guards open the great ornate doors of the outer chamber of the Stella Matutina. Edward enters first, followed by his council; then the heavy doors are securely closed behind them. A low yellow light from the flickering wall candles casts a sinister cascade of shadows across another inner corridor filled with armour and weaponry hanging on the curved tower walls. Holding a hemp cord torch, Edmund walks along the corridor in front of Edward till they reach a pair of lavishly carved oak doors.

Edmund grasps two golden ring handles hanging from the mouths of silver embossed ram heads, beautifully encrusted with gold and jewel embossed horns. Edmund pulls the rings to open the heavy doors and the council enters the stellar Matutina sanctum, where all but Edward carry lit hemp cords to light the myriad of candles placed around a mystical room, panelled with protruding tri-shells forming a geometrically precise ten-sided alchemic Angevin Star Chamber. Edward walks into the inner sanctum as the darkness slowly makes way for a yellow tinted illumination, revealing a fantastical compartment of medieval opulence and vector symbolism, purposefully created to inspire a comprehensive vision of the godhead and universe. Each 'Visiteur' ceremoniously places their individual cords into planters then extinguishes them. The smouldering hemp incense begins to wafts into the chamber, filling it with soothing aromatic influence throughout. In the centre of the Stellar Matutina stands a large perfectly square table above a floor of polished black marble, decoratively inlaid with two white granite interlocking triangles to form an knotwork hexagram within a perfect inlaid outer circle of pure white granite, precisely encompassing the four corners of the table by degree's.

Around the table are placed six large thrones, four of which are covered with bear, bull, horse and wolf hides. Two major thrones are more opulent. The first principle throne faces east and is made from ancient bog oak, engrained with hundreds of silver starlight pearls all held in carved oak clusters, embossed in gold leaf pearl encrusted stars. The head of the throne is embedded with a beautiful mosaic of rare Persian lapis lazuli gems. This throne is cloaked in Leopard, mink and ermine pelts, with oak supporters master crafted with intricately carved images of birds, vine, broom, plant and leaves of polished bronze. Undoubtedly the throne of a Plantagenet King, with such exquisite craftsmanship it could have been built by Hiram Habiff for the court of the great King Solomon.

The second major throne faces west, also constructed of ancient polished bog oak with master-crafted Dragons intertwining with tails and back claws forming base legs. The flighted Dragons wings support the back and armrests, with the bodies establishing the back-plate. Centered within the backrest is a simple ox-blood cushion in the form of a red shield. The neck of each dragon reaches up and supports the dragonheads, both facing inwards, simulating emissions of fire breathing directed towards the centre of the headboard, from which a most inspiringly crafted two-headed Phoenix with reptilian eyes of precious blue Paraiba tourmaline emerges. About the necks are circlet rings of rose gold above a breast plumage of beaten white gold on brilliant blue translucent oyster and tortoise shell feathers. The phoenix heads are tipped with golden beaks and protruding ruby encrusted tongues.

Each throne is positioned precisely inside the outer parabola of the base hexagram to ingratiate the seated individuals as the living embodiment of the Holy Spirit within the earthstar. The heavily polished French oak walls panels of the Stellar sanctum are adorned with thirty-two ram, bear, mastiff, bull and stag skulls, aligned with thirty-two human skulls, all affixed on plinths encircling the chamber. Each individual skull is gilded with silver, gold and precious jewels. A myriad of gemstones sparkle in the flickering candlelight, representing all the twinkling stars of the universe.

Candle-flame reflections are cast from larger gems in the eye sockets of these primeval skull trophies, creating an illusion the eyes are alive, watching and constantly observing, as though in judgement of all that would be enacted by those who sit within the hexagram. All around the chamber, outer walls and stained glass windows, are moulded or painted images of demons, dragons and Christian martyrs. Stout beams of English oak wall panel and border supporters are carved with bi-lingual ambigrams, recording the ancient lineage of the Angevin Plantagenet dynasty.

Edward sits upon the throne of the leopard while bidding his council be seated at the square table of antiquity, reputedly supported with wood from the sacred cross of Calvary and lain with planks of wood removed from the Ark of Noah, demonstrating the almost supernatural strength of grain needed to support the original manuscript laden upon the face of the table. The *Vulgate of the Morning Star*, a codex containing the religious history of man, written in rare Latin Cyrillic and Glagolitic script. This ancient bound manuscript was especially created by Herman the Recluse in the Benedictine monastery of Podlažice, and weighs as much as two full-grown men. Its inner velum leaves and exterior covers are allegedly made from the flayed skins of one hundred and sixty heathen children. Each Visiteur in turn touches the holy book with reverence and utters a prayer before taking their seat at the table.

Edmund walks over to a set of heavy gold chains hanging from the ceiling of the star-chamber and pulls on them. As the flow of endless chains gain speed, a noisy mechanism creaks and groans, causing the roof to slowly open up in five leaf panel sections, mimicking the midnight orchid emerging for its rare seven-year bloom. Each panel is gilded in azure blue and polished silver with a triangulated golden outer casement enclosing each petal, on each edge-face are more engraved hereditary symbiotagrams in a bejewelled font, impressed by the polished precious metal panels radiating a brilliance from the light of a full moon.

Finally, the roof opens completely as one all-seeing eye, revealing the infinite heavens above for the gratification of the gathered defenders of England's Plantagenet Kingdoms.

Edward studies the men sitting before him and is pleased with what he sees, for these are the men who will be the catalyst of a new European Christian kingdom, '*The Great Cause*' of the Plantagenet Northern Brotherhood of Kings. He looks to his younger brother Edmund and can visualise him wielding the blessed sword of God at the helm of his armies. He looks to Burnell who has made legal all his actions in law, then Bishop Bek who has absolved him of any and all actions religious, sanctifying the law of God and his will into palatable writs for England's restless barons. Edward glances at Walter, the most influential source of independent literate religious propaganda in all of medieval Europe outside the Vatican. Edward has good reason to feel a rush of power flowing through his veins, for the near future will soon bring this Norman Anglo King total power, as overlord supreme of Christendom. All sit in silence, waiting on Edward's introduction in this hallowed chamber. He knows he's correct in his judgement to bring them to this special place, for there are no others who could affect the future and millions of lives than these men now gathered before him.

Edward eventually speaks "We have deliberated long on the subject of taxations my Lords… now we must account for a pressing issue much closer to home, and perhaps unlock the last obstacle in the destiny of England's future glory." Edward utters once more…

"Scotland…" There is muted silence in the chamber as all hang on the very word, "Scotland."

Each in attendance search Edwards face for any nuance that would divulge more of his thoughts, but in vain. His steely character gives nothing away. Edward enquires of his sanctum brothers, "Scotland my Lords, pray tell me about this rebellious Kingdom who refuses my gracious offer of allowing them submission and fealty, they appear to have been much misguided by the influence their late King Alexander Canmore…?"

"May I?" enquires Edmund… Waving his hand in approval, Edward makes a gesture that permits Edmund to speak "Sire… My Lords… at this very moment, we have Berwick surrounded by loyal spies who await the signal that Yolande is leaving that place with little or no guard. Whichever group of men does receive such a signal, they are to vantage the opportune moment to witness another grievous but most unfortunate accident." Bek says, "Sire, we also have loyal men and women placed in Yolande's household, and given the opportunity, they will administer the Devils broth to this Queen of Heathens as we have done so before by two of Alexander's sons and youngest daughter." Listening thoughtfully, Edward says, "Since the death of my sister, who brought that heathen King to the guidance of the Lord, Alexander had since became a salacious fornicating blasphemer and rebellious sinner, that our God in is wisdom, has now ordained to be slewn. The house of Canmore is all but finished, it is only a matter of time till the detail of the Maid is acquitted, then this ancient line of pagan Kings' will be at an end."

Edward pauses as his council stare at him, almost in wonderment. He continues, "I will have no truck with this former union of Alexander and Yolande, that Capetian whore who now plies to return to France, I will not let the Scotch through the proposed coronation of Alexander's granddaughter, thwart my God given right to be Magnate supreme and overlord of Christendom. Let none here forget, Alexander's father led a heathen Scotch army in support of Montfort, Yolande's granduncle, against my Father Henry in the first Barons insurrection. It was then that the Scotch forces invaded our realm, bringing with them death, pestilence and they did reach the south coast of England to the port of Dover, such was their vigor. And it was also there that Alexander's treacherous father paid homage as an ally to the despot pretender, Prince Louis of France, and by doing this evil in exchange for lands in England. When Alexander married my sister Margret, he then failed miserably to pay homage to me as my rightful and lawful King and liege lord, for these besmirches alone I shall never forgive house

of Canmores' blood line, nor their supporters." Placing
his hand on the great Codex resting upon an onyx tablet,
Edward pauses; then he looks up and speaks to his faithful...
"We should not forget that Louis of France, Philips father,
was chosen by the Scotch King and our own rebel barons
to replace my father King Henry. Had not my father gained
the Popes blessing and support from loyal English barons,
including a mercenary army of Scots who fought for us
under sir Robert le Brix, we would not be here today. It was
only the fear of God and excommunication that the Scotch
armies did return to whence they had came. Take heed my
lords, it was not their fear of war that the Scotch returned
to Scotland, it was their fear of God... and that is the fibre
of men that I need for my armies. I will have the Scotch by
my side my lords and in my armies ranks, or any record
of their wretched existence will be entirely wiped from the
face of history."

Instantly Edward changes his demeanor, in a light hearted
voice he continues, "I suppose in some mysterious way
known only to God, the Scotch actually enabled the House
of Plantagenet to regain the throne of England, and this is
now why I, as Gods chosen envoy, see that the Scotch must
now come to my fold in base servitude." Edward looks
menacingly around the table, then he enquires, "Dear Walter,
you are my personal chaplain, confidante and you exonerate
and bless all actions I require to enact as the living emissary
of God on earth. Do tell us your thoughts in regards to the
Scotch question?"

Walter clasps his hands together, "The French whore
Yolande and her recent threat of a Royal half breed Canmore
bastard on the throne of Scotland Sire... we cannot make
the same mistakes King John or your late father King Henry
made, we must strike at the heathen Scots at their very heart

before they have even thought to resist you. The subjugation or elimination of the Scotch marks the very beginning of the Great Cause that we have planned and waited so long and so patiently for. My Liege, this I do set my path to God upon. We must make all the native Scotch pay dearly for their fathers soiling of our holy land of England. The Scotch are worse than the heathen Irish, Jews or Welsh, for they freely fornicate, blaspheme and are most certainly the ruination of Gods good order on earth."

"Sire," says Burnell "You are and have always been blessed with foresight, and we all agree the Scotch must now be brought to submission. If the trade resources and manpower of Scotland is brought to our fold, for it will overwhelmingly turn the tide of fiscal woe and ruination that does face us now. If we delay much longer in bringing them to heel, I fear that many English Barons led once more by the De Montforte and Mortimer families, may once again lead to further dissention and rebellion. With the Scotch army supporting such an uprising, we could be facing a civil war in England that we simply cannot afford. And should it come to pass, we may lose… Also, if Scotland's ports are allowed to join the Hanseatic Varjag, then upon such twin calamities, exile may not be an option for us."

Edward retorts in a fury, "Lose… Is not God on our side, is God not an Englishman? Have I not brought the feeble-minded Welsh to heel and thick Irish neck under my boot? Do the Jews not worship me for succour for shelter like dogs of the feasting table? The Scotch I think you will find my lords, have grown fat and feeble. After all others we have subdued, they will be our simplest of conquests. Already plans are set in motion that will eliminate the Scotch question once and for all, bringing the devoted Norman Barons of that shit realm to my side and sending all native dissenters to their heathen hell." Edward continues in a darker vein "When Alexander married my sister Margret, he was expected to swear fealty and submit to my superiority, but he reneged on his oath, and whilst my good sister lived, Scotland and her assets would eventually be mine. But now that she and Alexanders children have passed from this life and then his subsequent marriage to Yolande Capet of Dreux, a bloody Capetian whore of all things, my God? No... I have set my lance to end of this corrupt dynasty of Scotch savages, we shall now chain their Scotch unicorn to our crown."

Burnell spoke, "With Alexander now dead Sire, the Scotch may yet still resist us in force, can we afford a war with them? They are a small tenacious nation, yet they have thwarted the mighty armies of Romans, Saxons, Norse... they even defeated the jutes and Angles who previously drove our ancestors to ground?" Glaring at Burnell with cold eyes, Edward retorts, "Who has mentioned war? Have I not already bought most of the Norman nobles of that shit place to my cause, and the ones who are loyal to Yolande or indeed the maid, they will soon wither and fall under my boot. I cannot foresee any problem with the Scotch. Many of the Scotch nobility are already bought and sold for silver or gold. Others come running to kneel before me to sort out their petty squabbles. The ignominious Scotch grow faint of heart my lords and will not have the stomach to resist me."

Gazing at the Codex, Edward continues, "The house of Canmore and its bastard spawn shall be removed from this earth in their entirety. If only but one survives to resist, then it will be a war of annihilation on all Scotch my lords... make no mistake on my countenance." Edwards' stern attitude fades as he continues; "There are more subtle methods we may employ upon them first before war. Burnell speaks, "But Sire, if the maid of Norway ascends the throne of Scotland, we will have sitting at our back door the potential of a deadly foe allied to our enemies in France, with the Capetian and Flemmard royal dynasties in particular, including claims by Yolande's family to Scotland's throne. She may yet call upon the support of her De Montfort family in England, we must be rid of this source of pestilence, and if the Scotch are allowed to join the Varjag and Hanseatic federation, we are doubly undone. Sire, we cannot be caught in a vice by this unholy matching of sovereigns." Burnell pauses, waiting to gain tacit approval from Edward; then he continues, "Alexander's grand-daughter Sire, if she is allowed to take to the Scotch throne, this will allow King Eric of Norway to make a claim too and add an even greater threat to our realm. Should none of Alexander's spawn survive, then the throne of Scotland falls to our crown by right of first marriage, which is by far the best and only option that I can see."

Edward says, "I know the Maid of Scotland and my son prince Edward could still be betrothed as the favoured option for the Scotch, but her demise would be more advantageous to us. Isabella, Philip's daughter is available, as I have said before, she could be betrothed to my young prince. This particular union will eliminate all of these threats at once, ending forever both Norse and Capet claims to the Scotch throne. My son's betrothal to Isabella would ally England to Philip of France and will leave the Scotch isolated and ripe for the plucking, but as you say Burnell, we must move soon before the Scotch join the Varjag and Hanseatica Federation..." Edmund agrees, "We must invade Scotland now Sire, while they are at their weakest..." Walter enquires, "What legitimacy would we call upon to stave censure from his holiness and also stay an attack from France should we invade Scotland?" Burnell looks to Edward, "May I?" Edward nods in approval.

Burnell continues, "It is this simple my lords, we trick the Scotch army into crossing the border into England in retaliation to some slight, then we may attack the Scotch realm with impunity in defence of the realm."

"Masterful in its simplicity..." exclaims Bek "All the Baronage of England must then support you free gratis sire, as our blessed realm will have appeared to have been invaded by another sovereign realm, the Barons will have no other choice by previous oath but to come to arms in support, or be deemed treasonous by their very own *Charter of the Forest*."

"Ah my lords," says Edward "I fear all this fine food and wine has you flexing martial thoughts to exercise the mind, but as I say, there are other methods already in play of far greater subtlety to bring the Scotch to submission. The Scotch army would be best served at my disposal for future campaigns as battle fodder rather than us losing a few good and stout English yeoman during the process of their elimination, is that not so Walter?"

"Sire," says Walter, "all is prepared to set in motion. Soon the threat in regard to Scotland's sovereignty will be at an end and the final elimination of Canmore's house will be completed. We have already had application from the Scotch for you Sire to arbitrate in their effort to avoid a civil war." Burnell says, "We must not forget about Elen ferch Llywelyn, she is the bastard daughter of Llywelyn the Welsh prince Sire, she married Duncan MacDuff the earl of Fife and they begat sons, they must also be elemenated, for they pose a resurgent threat to both the crowns of Scotland and Wales, and we know by experience that by leaving any offspring alive in a dominion that believes itself soveriegn, can be a problem."

"Eliminate the potential and you eliminate the problem," says Edward. "The Scotch and their appeal for me to arbitrate is idiocy beyond beleif, but it plays into my plans, and as far as the MacDuff and Llewelyn problem is concerend, in due course Burnell. We shall deal with their nobility first, then their army and fleet, then we must look to their heathen faith leaders..." Edward pauses then enquires, "What say you Bek, you have many close associates in the Scotch church, are there any who we may trust to aid our cause with vigour?" Bek replies. "Sire, all Norman lords and Scotch with lands and vested interests in England do promise fealty. I also have the Bishop of Saint Andrews William Lamberton with his hand in my purse; he's a very gullible fellow. He sees in the pontiff a future where no elevation of status or recognition may be worthy of his ambition while he resides in that small Scotch backwater. I also glean from him that the sole threats of any ecclesiastical resistance may come from The Bishop of Glasgow, Robert Wishart, Bernard of Kilwinning and from Duns Scottus... an imminent theologian who resides here in France."

"How so?" Enquires Edward. Bek replies "Both Wishart and Bernard are renowned for their zeal in the continued independence of the Scots church sire. Resistance will also come from the armies of the Guardians, the Garda Rígh and so-called Garda Céile Aicé; they are the hereditary Guardians of the Queen of Scotch. Together they control Scotch religion, army and their small fleet. No approach has been made to them for fear of revealing your plans."

Waving his hand aside like he's swatting a fly, Edward replies, "Old men and boys, with old fashioned ideas of Chivalry and honour. Bah... these are modern times my Lords, when we cut off the heads of those bodies, they too shall wither and succumb. If not, we will send them all to join their beloved King... a small matter in the scheme of things." Edmund enquires, "Sire, how do entice the Scotch that they would send and armed body across our border that we may invade Scotland? For our Barons are exempt from service in any expansionist war." Edward replies, "When this comes to pass dear brother, I have plans to rattle the nests of both the Scotch houses of Comyn and Douglas on the western border marches of Scotland. With the help of Robert de Brix and Sir Brian le Jay, we shall set rat bait to tempt Scotch rats when the time is right. Lord de Brix has already shown the Scotch his hand and made many enemies because of his lust for power, unwittingly and by my guidance, he shall entice the Scotch across the border to attack his residence in Carlisle Castle, and of course we will be waiting with our armies at Norham, prepared to attack Berwick in response to an *invasion* by another sovereign realm... is that not so Bek, does this not compel our Barons to arms?"

Smiling at the strategy, Bek replies "It is so Sire, a Scotch invasion means the Barons must attend our Crown army in person with their entire retinues in defence of our realm, or die on the block for treason." Everyone laughs at this simple but effective ploy to trick both the Scots and Edwards testy rebellious Barons and justify an imperious attack on Scotland. The merriment is interrupted by the sound of a bell-ringing coming from the towers of the château lofts, home for the messenger pigeons so vital for efficient communications.

Edward immediately barks a command... "Edmund, go to the keeper of the Lofts, for the ringing of that particular bell may herald the deliverance we so urgently require on this subject." Edmund replies, "At once Sire." Rising from the table, Edmund quickly exits the chamber to acquit his mission, while Bek, Walter, Burnell and Edward remain seated in silence, for none wishes to speculate upon the Kings urgency. Time passes like an eternity before Edmund returns. Eventually he burst open the doors of the chamber, breathing heavily from his exertions. The tension amongst all save the King is excruciating, "SIRE…" Exclaims Edmund breathlessly; Edward demands coldly, "Well Edmund, you have something to tell us?"

"I do Sire…" replies Edmund, almost choking in his haste to deliver the news. "Then speak good sir" commands an irked Edward. "Sire… It's Robert de Brix Sire, it would appear he has heeded your advice and backed away from causing a civil war in Scotland. The messages also confirm that he was attacking Baliol from the east with his levies and some of our northern English Knights in attendance. His son Robert de Brus the earl of Carrick and Richard the earl of Ulster were pressing Baliol from the north and west. Baliol was trapped with the sea at his back and was nigh finished, but Lord Butler now confirms de Brix has pulled away from the brink of war." A delighted Edward exclaims, "Ha, the Scotch already do our work for us. The rats now nibble at my bait, and soon too our little Norwegian fly will be caught in a web that shall see her demise, yet the deed must not be executed in England, nor in Scotland…"

Suddenly Edward's countenance changes, "Does anyone know where this Guardian army is now, that was spoken of earlier?" Edmund replies "Sire, there are two main Guardian armies, the Northern and Southern, they are mostly a royal guard, when the heir to the throne is chosen, they will be stood down… There was also news Sire that Capetian mercenaries had landed on Scotch shores set on protecting the Crown for Yolande… but they were turned back and sailed for France upon news of the peace accord struck between the Pact and the Guardians."

"Capetians afoot in Scotland…" exclaims Edward. "My lords, we must keep a tight reign on our God-given work. Allowing Brix too free a hand almost caused us all we have worked so diligently to achieve… Our commands must be adhered too at all times and at all costs. Make sure the penalty for disobedience is much worse than any temptations' my lords." Edmund says, "Sire, the actions of de Brix were reckless in the extreme, he may even have acted treasonous towards you and the Crown. I know and I am well aware the orders that you gave to him, he could have caused us to war with France, Norway and Scotland at the same time my lord had you been forced by circumstance to intervene on his behalf. This action and his ambitions do show that the house of de Brix too cannot be trusted."

"I grant you Edmund, de Brix has been impetuous, even reckless, but never treasonous. I shall bestow upon him public leniency for the greater good my Lords. I must be seen to be impartial and above any local or territorial disputes. But de Brix has also demonstrated that perhaps the Scotch may not be so fat and feeble as I first thought, a mistake I will not make again. We will make use of de Brixs' ambitions for the moment, he may even secure for us the crown of Scotland by other means, and when we have used him as he believes he uses my good nature, we will dispose of the old fool and his brood of usurpers like so much shithouse garbage in good time. Edward stands erect; then he lays his right hand upon the great Codex. He grasps the Holy Cross from its plinth and holds the crucifix to his chest; then he looks up to the heavens above... "For God, Christ and England... we will now prepare bring that Scotch land of pagans, heathens and sinners wholly to the Christian faith... and to the bosom of our protection."

Robert Burnell stands behind his king while Bek and Walter both kneel and pray, all are busily making the sign of the cross and lowering their heads in respect of the Holy book before them. Edmund, ever the warrior, kneels with sword in hand and kisses the cross quillons. Edward turns to see his loyal compatriots in holy prostate. He looks once more to the heavens above and sees the morning star fall over the horizon of France. He watches the diminishing brilliance of the star against the radiance of the rising sun.

Walter gazes at the morning star too, points and utters, "Ah, lucem ferre, helel Ben-Shachar my lord." Bek whispers… "Phosphoro, Archangel of the illuminati…" Smiling as though transfixed, Edward whispers, "O' morning Star the son of dawn, now has gone to another place Alexander Canmore, the little king of Babylon." He turns to face his council; then he continues, "The Scotch minions now fall in upon themselves, eagerly ridding us of that vermin race. Soon we shall tread our boots upon their Scotch carcasses. My lords, the emergence of a new Christian Angevin dynasty is being born under Gods glorious illumination… it is time, the Great Cause now begins in earnest with the final subjugation, Scotland…"

To be continued
in
Book 3 - Outlaw